CAPOTE'S WOMEN

ALSO BY LAURENCE LEAMER

CAPOTE'S
WOMEN

A TRUE STORY OF LOVE, BETRAYAL, AND A SWAN SONG FOR AN ERA

LAURENCE LEAMER

G. P. Putnam's Sons

New York

PUTNAM
— EST. 1838 —

G. P. Putnam's Sons
Publishers Since 1838
An imprint of Penguin Random House LLC
penguinrandomhouse.com

Library of Congress Cataloging-in-Publication Data

Names: Leamer, Laurence, author.
Title: Capote's women : a true story of love, betrayal, and a
swan song for an era / Laurence Leamer.
Description: New York : G. P. Putnam's Sons, [2021] |
Includes bibliographical references and index. |
Identifiers: LCCN 2021023471 (print) | LCCN 2021023472 (ebook) |
ISBN 9780593328088 (hardcover) | ISBN 9780593328095 (ebook)
Subjects: LCSH: Capote, Truman, 1924–1984—Friends and associates. |
Capote, Truman, 1924–1984. Answered prayers. |
New York (N.Y.)—Social life and customs—20th century. |
Authors, American—20th century—Biography.
Classification: LCC PS3505.A59 Z6843 2021 (print) |
LCC PS3505.A59 (ebook) | DDC 813/.54 [B]—dc23
LC record available at https://lccn.loc.gov/2021023471
LC ebook record available at https://lccn.loc.gov/2021023472
p.   cm.

Printed in the United States of America
5th Printing

Book design by Katy Riegel

To Raleigh Robinson
No Better Friend

Contents

CAPOTE'S WOMEN

1

===

Answered Prayers

For years, Truman Capote had been proudly telling anyone within hearing that he was writing the "greatest novel of the age." The book was about a group of the richest, most elegant women in the world. They were fictional, of course . . . but everyone knew these characters were based on his closest friends, the coterie of gorgeous, witty, and fabulously rich women he called his "swans."

Truman understood what these women had achieved and how they had done it. They did not come from grand money but had married into it, most of them multiple times. Their charms were carefully cultivated, and to the outside eye, they seemed to have everything . . . but for most of them happiness was an elusive bird, always flying just out of sight. This was something the fifty-year-old Truman knew about. He was calling his novel-in-progress about the swans *Answered Prayers*, following the saying attributed to Saint Teresa of Ávila: "There are more tears shed over answered prayers than over unanswered prayers."

In 1975, Truman was one of the most famous authors in the world. Even those who had not read a word of Truman's writing knew about the diminutive, flamboyantly gay author. His 1958 novella, *Breakfast at Tiffany's*, had been widely celebrated, and the movie starring Audrey Hepburn was a sensation when it premiered in 1961. Millions of Americans had devoured his masterful 1966 true crime book, *In Cold Blood*, and countless more saw the 1967 film adaptation. The "Tiny Terror," as Truman was called, was a fixture on late-night television, mesmerizing audiences with his outrageous tales.

Truman's richly evocative style and the astonishing global success of *In Cold Blood* several years before had created an audience that waited impatiently for his latest work. *Answered Prayers* would be a daring literary feat, an exposé of upper-class society that blended the fictional flourishes of *Breakfast at Tiffany's* with the closely observed narrative nonfiction of *In Cold Blood*. No one had ever gotten that close to these women and their elusive, secretive world. Marcel Proust and Edith Wharton had written classic novels focused on the elite of their ages, of course, but they were children of privilege, raised in that world and of it.

Truman, on the other hand, was an interloper. Since coming from a small town in Alabama decades earlier, he'd carved out a unique spot in New York society: a scathingly sharp, always entertaining guest whose charm opened the doors to the most exclusive circles . . . and whose eyes and ears were always open and observing what he saw there.

As much as Truman was drawn to the beauty, taste, and manners in that world of privilege, he was repulsed by its arrogant sense of superiority and ignorance of life as most people lived it. Life had a way of intruding and teaching hard lessons. The tension between those two beliefs would create his immortal book.

Crucial to Truman's masterpiece would be evoking the world of the swans. And that world could be summed up in one word: sumptuous. These women knew the power of money (what it could buy, what it could compensate for). But despite what their spiteful detractors might have suggested, their allure wasn't due to money alone. "It may be that the enduring swan glides upon waters of liquefied lucre; but that cannot account for the creature herself," Truman wrote in an essay in *Harper's Bazaar* in October 1959. His swans were wealthy, yes. But that wasn't all.

To Truman each swan was the personification of upscale glamour in the postwar world. She was the confluence of a number of unique factors. Her good looks and elegant demeanor made both men and women turn and look at her. A woman could not simply buy her way into this. "If expenditure were all, a sizable population of sparrows would swiftly be swans," he wrote. He would reach beyond the gold, the silver, and the jewels and see his swans as they truly were. Each woman had an extraordinary story to tell, and Truman was the only one who could tell them.

The swans were all famously beautiful as well—was it their looks that defined them?

Not so, Truman maintained. The swan was lovely, yes, but it was not just her beauty that created the attention—rather, it was her extraordinary presentation. Many of these women had been celebrated for years, even decades, not just for their looks but for their unique style. A swan had not only the money to buy her clothes from the finest couturiers but the style to wear them at their best. Other women imitated her fashion sense, and men eyed her with appreciative (and often covetous) eyes.

But a swan's beauty wasn't just skin-deep—she was clever, cunning even. Her wit and patter intrigued even such a merciless critic as Truman. She knew that while looks could capture a man's attention, it took intelligence and wiles to keep it. And keep it she would, at all costs. It took discipline and focus, Truman knew, to create such a persona and maintain it decade after decade, long after other women gave up the illusions of youth.

There were probably no more than a dozen women who Truman could have deemed true swans. They were all on the International Best-Dressed Lists, they were each celebrated in the fashion press and beyond, and they all knew one another. These women had no idea—and neither did Truman—that they were a vanishing breed, a species that would live and die in one generation.

Truman chose his swans as if collecting precious paintings that he wanted to hang in his home for the rest of his life.

Barbara "Babe" Paley was first in Truman's mind. She was often called the most beautiful woman in the world, and Truman just liked looking at her, admiring her incredible panache.

Nancy "Slim" Keith was a stunning California girl with a far more causal style than Babe. Droll and supercharged, she could match Truman bon mot for bon mot.

In the Renaissance, Pamela Hayward would have been renowned as one of the great courtesans of the age. In the modern era, there were other terms for such conduct. Truman was first taken aback by Pamela's shameless behavior to get and keep the attention of the rich men upon whose good graces she depended. But in the end, he was seduced by her talents and charm, as so many had been before.

The Mexican-born Gloria Guinness was the only other swan who compared to Babe in her beauty. Married to Loel Guinness, one of the richest men in the world, Gloria lived a life of splendor in homes across the world. Fiercely intelligent and perceptive, there was nothing Truman could not discuss with her.

Truman saw Lucy Douglas "C. Z." Guest standing tall and elegant at a bar between acts on opening night of *My Fair Lady* on Broadway in March 1956, and he knew he had to make her his friend. Born a Boston Brahmin, C.Z. had an inbred self-confidence rare in Americans. An elitist of the first order, she was roundly dismissive of people she thought unworthy. But if she liked you (and she liked Truman), she was a wonderful friend.

Of all the swans, none came from such an exalted background as Marella Agnelli, who was born an Italian princess. Married to Gianni Agnelli, the head of Fiat and Italy's leading businessman, this highly literate, creative woman was in some senses Italy's First Lady.

Lee Radziwill had more than a casual familiarity with First Ladies since her older sister, Jacqueline Kennedy Onassis, had actually been one. Truman thought Lee far more beautiful and a far better (and more interesting) person than her famous sister, and he devoted himself to her more than he did to any of the other swans.

Truman sailed on their yachts, flew on their planes, stayed at their estates, supped at their tables, and heard their most intimate tales. Heterosexual men loved to sleep with these women, yes, but they often were not deeply interested in them as human beings. Truman was. He appreciated what they did with their lives and the various, complex ways they made themselves such creatures of elegance. What some dismissed as trivial and self-indulgent, Truman saw as a kind of living art.

A brilliant observer of the human condition, Truman had spent as much as two decades with some of these women, two decades to explore the deepest recesses of their lives, two decades to understand them. He appreciated the challenges of their star-crossed lives, what they faced, and how they survived. He had everything he needed to write about them with depth and nuance, exploring both the good and the bad, the light and the darkness. *Answered Prayers* would be his masterpiece, he knew—the book that would give him a place in the literary pantheon alongside the greatest writers of all time.

Although Truman had hinted at the novel's genius for years, celebrity is a cacophony of distractions, and it was taking him longer to write it than he'd promised it would. Far, far longer. His publishers were growing anxious, the advance payment they'd given him had long since run out, and the literary elite were starting to whisper that maybe this book wasn't all it was cracked up to be. Maybe Truman wasn't even writing at all.

This maddened him. These feckless critics just didn't understand his *process*. To show them, he published a chapter of *Answered Prayers* in the June 1975 issue of *Esquire*. When "Mojave" had less of an impact than he thought it would, Truman decided to publish a second chapter, a "proof of life" missive that would reveal just how explosive and revolutionary his new book was. One that would return him to the glory days of his literary stardom, when he was celebrated beyond measure.

During the summer of 1975, Truman showed his authorized biographer, Gerald Clarke, the excerpt, "La Côte Basque 1965," he planned to run in the November issue of *Esquire*. Truman had said he was writing a tome worthy of sitting between Proust and Wharton— one that would offer an intimate, wise, and perceptive look at the follies and foibles of mid-century, high-society life. Clarke was . . . underwhelmed. Although the story that Truman handed to Clarke was written in the author's exquisite style, it was little more than a string of gossipy vignettes, repeating the kinds of ugly stories that were whispered at elite dinner parties.

Stories, Clarke easily realized, that were mainly drawn directly from the lives of Truman's beloved swans and their friends. Clarke could tell immediately who most of these subjects were—the swans, after all, were some of the most famous and feted women of the day—and those he could not decipher Truman told him. Clarke had a largely candid relationship with his subject, and he told Truman that those written about in this way would recognize themselves immediately . . . and they would *not* be happy.

"Naaaah, they're too dumb," Truman said. "They won't know who they are."

2

===

Babe in the Woods

When William S. "Bill" Paley flew down to his estate in Jamaica in January 1955, the television mogul invited his closest friend, David O. Selznick, the producer of *Gone with the Wind*, to join him. Selznick said he and his wife, the actress Jennifer Jones, would be delighted . . . but wouldn't it be even more interesting if their friend Truman came along?

The multimillionaire businessman knew only one Truman. It wasn't the diminutive author but the former president of the United States. Sure, bring him along, Bill assented. He'd never met Harry Truman, but the CBS founder was not surprised that the politician would want to fly off on his plane—after all, Bill was one of the richest and most influential men in America. What former president wouldn't want to spend time with him?

So Bill did not find it amusing when this little man who fancied scarfs so long that he almost tripped over them came traipsing onto the plane and introduced himself as Truman.

"You know, when you said Truman, I assumed you meant *Harry* Truman," an irritated Bill told Selznick once the plane took off. *"Who is this?"*

"This is Truman Capote, our great American writer," replied Selznick. The Selznicks had gotten close to Truman in early 1953, when he spent two months writing the screenplay for the John Huston film *Beat the Devil*, in which Jones costarred alongside Humphrey Bogart and Gina Lollobrigida. The film was shot over ten weeks in the Italian Amalfi Coast town of Ravello. For most of that time, Truman stayed only a scene or two ahead of the actors, writing dialogue charged with mordent wit.

Truman's creativity was not just for the screen. He was at his irrepressible best when he was off somewhere like this, in an isolated hotel with a group of intriguing people, not unlike the setup for *Beat the Devil*. Selznick found Truman a "wonderful but bad little boy." An irreverent impresario, Truman created unforgettable dramas each evening as intriguing as the story they were filming.

Nobody interested Truman more in Ravello than Jennifer. Wanting to make the actress his friend, he rushed forward with intimacy, pushing himself into the inner recesses of her life. By the time the shoot was over, Jennifer embraced Truman as her closest friend.

When Truman walked down the aisle that winter morning, he sat down not beside Jennifer but next to Bill's wife, Babe. As Jennifer looked across the aisle, she saw this incredible bonding going on. It was like a mating dance, as Truman and the statuesque, five-feet-eight-inch-tall Babe whispered excitedly off in their separate sphere. By the time the plane reached Jamaica, Jennifer knew that she had been supplanted by what was as much love as friendship. Jennifer had what she called "a few jealous pangs because up until that time I had been his best friend," but for something of this magnitude, there was nothing to do but look at it with awe.

As subtle a writer as he was, Truman often spoke with drum-beating hyperbole. Thus, Babe was not only the most beautiful woman he had ever seen but "the most beautiful woman of the twentieth century." He had spent two months in the same Palermo hotel as Gina Lollobrigida, a gorgeous young actress of overwhelming sensuality. She was by most standards stunningly beautiful, but the voluptuous Italian did not qualify for Truman's definition of beauty. As he saw it, you could not have beauty without class, and Babe was the epitome of class.

"When I first saw her, I thought that I had never seen anyone more perfect: her posture, the way she held her head, the way she moved," Truman reported, breathlessly. Everything about Babe was exquisite, from her porcelain skin to her aristocratic demeanor. There was not a hint of excess, a nose a bit too large, eyebrows a bit too small, on her long oval face.

Truman knew that this sort of beauty and perfection did not just happen. He saw Babe as an artist who had created herself as an inspired work of living sculpture. In an era when soup cans and scribbles on a canvas were high art, why couldn't Babe be seen as the ultimate piece of performance art?

The Paleys posed an extraordinary image to the world, and during those few days in Jamaica, Truman saw them at their best. Bill was one of the most powerful executives in America, but what set him apart from many of his peers was his fierce interest in his social life, a concern he shared with his wife. There were several guest cottages on the property, and the invitees enjoyed a sojourn that could not have been matched in a first-class resort hotel.

Truman would never have gotten so close to Babe if he had not gotten along with Bill. In fact, the CBS chairman embraced him and reveled in his company. Truman was a circus of endless delights. Gluttonous in all things, Bill could not get enough of him. When Truman spent the weekend at the Paley estate on Long Island or traveled the western world in Bill's plane, Truman, Bill, and Babe were the three musketeers, all for one and one for all. It didn't hurt that the madly jealous Bill did not have to worry that Truman might try to seduce his wife.

For the most part, Truman did not feel comfortable around many men, because they were often, frankly, uncomfortable around him. At grand parties—when after dinner the gentlemen went into the drawing room for cigars and cognac and often tedious talk of politics, sports, business, and sex—Truman much preferred to stay with the ladies, whose conversations he found far more interesting. When he talked about his first orgasm with graphic detail, the men listening to this gay tale were likely to be embarrassed or threatened. The women egged him on. As much as Truman enjoyed kibitzing with Bill, the real talk began when he was alone with Babe.

"Mrs. P. had only one fault," Truman wrote in his notebook. "She was perfect; otherwise she was perfect." Sometimes Truman's most epigrammatic utterances had to be turned inside out and shaken to grasp what he meant. Being perfect was not being perfect. One had to work with ceaseless diligence to maintain it. Babe slept in a separate bedroom from her husband. She was up before him, applying her makeup before she even saw her husband. She could never have a strand of hair blow out of place, even in a November wind, or allow a look of displeasure to pass across her unperturbable countenance. Bill was as much a perfectionist as Babe was, and he berated her in an instant if things were not as they were supposed to be.

Babe prepared dinner parties with what to anyone else appeared perfection, finishing her work with place settings perfectly attuned to the invitees. Bill could come home, look at the table, and change everything with no concern for his wife's efforts. As generous as he could be to others, Bill was penny-pinching to Babe, doling out money to his wife like a child's allowance. "You know, he liked keeping the budget low because it made her more dependent and more supplicant to him," Truman reflected. That was probably true, but he also wasn't about to squander money on a person he did not have to impress.

The saying "You cannot be too rich or too thin" was sometimes attributed to Babe. It was an absurd adage. Babe had seen how wealth could consume a life. And she knew how in her desire to stay impossibly thin, a woman could become anorexic, her life becoming one narrow obsession.

Truman took in each human experience, storing it away to be paraded out and used one day in his artistic expression. It was here, early on in this friendship and several years before he came up with the idea for *Answered Prayers*, that he first saw in full display that money did not buy happiness. It was one of the great themes of human existence. That it was a truism did not mean it was untrue.

As much as Truman projected an image of sophisticated worldliness, he was still in some measures that little boy from the Deep South come to the big city. Babe was his guru, teaching him how he must behave if he was going to get easy entrance into the homes of the anointed. She taught him how the elite decorated their homes. Appreciation of art was another marker of acceptance, and she educated him about art that the rich and worldly hung in their living rooms. Truman could not afford a Picasso or a Matisse, but he could comment knowingly about the art, another measure of his supposed journey into the inner circle.

In their endless conversations, Truman was a teacher too, introducing Babe to some of the great writers of the age. There was Proust's encyclopedic-sized *À la recherche du temps perdu*, which she said she read from beginning to end. Then there was Henry James, Gustave Flaubert, and, of particular relevance to Babe's life, Edith Wharton.

Wharton chronicled the elite late-nineteenth-century high-society New York world in which she had been raised, writing with special acumen and deep poignancy about the upper-class woman of her day. A woman of the Gilded Age, she lived in a veritable gilded cage. Her whole life was about marrying a proper rich man and then having her daughters do the same. Education was not to be squandered on her. Best to "finish" her lightly with a proper veneer of charm and no dangerous knowledge that might offend her husband. She was skilled in the decorative arts, the most important work of art being herself. For the most part, she had no idea she was living a hothouse existence, in thrall of the patriarchal society that defined her. "There was no use in trying to emancipate a wife who had not the dimmest notion that she was not free," Wharton wrote in her Pulitzer Prize–winning novel, *The Age of Innocence*.

Babe had what Wharton called a "craving for the external finish of life." This was not just smooth lacquer painted onto the surface of life but the very essence. Strip those externals, and what was there? Dare to move outside this world and risk ending up with nothing, debased, disowned, and shunned. *The Age of Innocence* was published in 1920, but all these decades later, the social ambience for elite women in New York City high society had not radically changed.

As far as professional possibilities, women had few choices. They were welcome as teachers, nurses, and secretaries, but that was largely it. Women like Babe would never have considered doing such plebian things as teaching in an elementary school or nursing in a hospital somewhere—let alone bursting beyond the professional barriers to try something totally new. Their lives had broadened little since Wharton so vividly described their social world. As smart and energetic as they might be, well-born women knew they must never reach beyond the walls of their world.

Babe's neurosurgeon father was a far more rightfully esteemed character than the scions of privilege who floated past the reader in Wharton's novels. Dr. Harvey Cushing was one of the greatest doctors of the first half of the twentieth century. Associated first with Johns Hopkins University, then the leading research institution in America, and later Harvard University and Yale University, he understood the prime value of education. But that was for his two sons, not his three daughters, who were largely brought up by their mother, Katharine Stone Cushing.

To the doctor, his firstborn son, William, was everything, and when he sent him off to college at Yale, it was surely to spread the Cushing name to new triumphs. It was there in 1926 that William died in a car crash, a shock from which his father in some measure never recovered.

Katharine had what was any mother's dream—that her daughters marry well—only her dream was a little different. Not content with mere wealth (and certainly not concerned about love as a prerequisite for marriage), she was after European nobles with castles and grand estates for her daughters—that, or marrying them off to the richest men in America. Matrimony was a serious game—one her daughters were raised to play astonishingly well.

As Babe's mother laid out her grand scheme, it did not seem outlandish. Her daughters had been trained to please men, and when they reached young adulthood, they appeared to be ready. These splendidly finished young women were a marvel to behold as they walked by arm in arm.

In 1930, the middle daughter, twenty-two-year-old Betsey, was the first to go, marrying James Roosevelt, whose father, Governor Franklin D. Roosevelt, was part of the old landed gentry. Most would have considered young James the most enviable of matches, but he did not have his hands on any of the family fortune, and the other Cushing daughters would surely want to do better.

Two years later, when Roosevelt won the presidency, Betsey's marriage looked a fortuitous choice. The inaugural ball in March 1933 was a white-tie affair, though many of the aging politicians looked as if they were in formal dress for the first time in their lives. It was a typical Washington dance, the six thousand invitees milling around the dance floor looking at who was there and who wasn't. Through the congestion walked the president's namesake, Franklin D. Roosevelt Jr., on the arm of the most stunning young woman at the ball. Babe was only seventeen years old, possibly the youngest person in attendance, but as she held tightly onto Franklin's arm, the most beautiful of the Cushing sisters was a sophisticated presence.

That Christmas Babe attended a holiday party for young people at the White House. By New Year's Eve most of the college students had already taken the train back north. That left the president and First

Lady to greet the new year at a small party that included James and Betsey Roosevelt and Babe.

The youngest of the Cushing sisters was Babe, having a dream of a life. Then, early in 1934, disaster struck: a severe auto accident knocked out Babe's teeth and left her a mass of bruises, blemishes, and scars. Plastic surgery was in its infancy, but by the time the surgeons finished with their operations, her beauty was back, unblemished and perhaps even heightened. Surgery couldn't fix her teeth, though, so every morning for the rest of her life the first thing Babe did when she woke up was put in her teeth. This was a routine common among the elderly but certainly not in a young woman with her life ahead of her. It took a certain courage not to become withdrawn and to instead go out in the world as if nothing had happened. (Of course, if that accident had taken place in the modern era, the assumption would be that there might be unseen psychological scars as well as the physical ones—but back then, no one, especially not well-bred young ladies, concerned themselves with the emotional side of things. If a lady looked good, she *was* good . . . and Babe definitely looked good.)

With her sister recovered by 1935, Betsey threw a tea dance for Babe in the White House, an occasion that even her wealthiest and most socially ambitious contemporaries could hardly equal. No one seeing her dance around the room that afternoon could have imagined that just a year earlier her broken body had been pulled out of the wreckage of a car. This dance was a serious business not just to introduce the youngest Cushing sister to the elite social world of the Washington Cave Dwellers but to place her into the milieu where she might find a proper husband.

Betsey did the same thing for her older sister, Minnie, and there the marriage game had taken on special urgency. Minnie was in her mid-thirties, close to meriting the hated appellation "Old Maid." At a White House party, Betsey introduced her sister to Vincent Astor, whose family fortunes went back to the fur trade in the eighteenth century. One of the richest men in the world, Vincent had been married for two and a half decades to Helen Huntington Astor, a cultured and sophisticated woman who had survived by giving her quirky husband a wide berth. The Astors had no children, and it was whispered that Vincent had as much interest in sex as he had in poverty.

Most women looking for a husband would never have considered Vincent, but the Cushings saw the world and its opportunities differently. The melancholy fact was that there was only a paltry supply of the immensely rich men the Cushings considered worthy husbands. One could not cavalierly toss away a prospect simply because he was married.

Prey is easier to take down if it does not know it is being hunted, and chasing married men had certain advantages. Minnie began spending so much time with the fifteen-years-older Vincent that she appeared less a friend than a mistress. Most unmarried women would not have gotten themselves in such an ambiguous position, but the Cushings played a long-term game, with their eyes focused on the trophy at the finish line.

As Minnie chased after her golden prize, Betsey's marriage ended in divorce. Leaving his ex-wife with their two children, James Roosevelt headed west to start what he hoped would be a career in Hollywood. That added a new marital quest for Mrs. Cushing, who, after the death of her husband in 1939, moved to New York to be near her daughters.

Babe's sisters' lives were both an aspirational and a cautionary example. Babe had her own life to make. She was not dressing simply to appeal to men or to display her style to the world. Fashion was her skin, her real skin, and she adored the whole process. It made sense for her to join her mother in New York and become an editorial assistant and later an editor at *Vogue*.

The upscale fashion magazine was a stunning publication, with writing as intriguing and elegant as its fashion photos. Just before World War II, *Vogue* and its sister publication, *Harper's Bazaar*, were not only as good in their ways as any magazines in America, but they were overwhelmingly female worlds where an upscale woman like Babe felt comfortable making her way.

Photographed frequently for *Vogue*, at first Babe was timid, afraid to confront the camera and its possibilities. But slowly she learned and made the camera hers. The *Vogue* offices were like a fashion runway, with well-dressed young women sashaying back and forth through the halls. No one was more stunning than the model-thin Babe. Designers vied with one another either to give her their clothes or to sell them to her at large discounts so that she would walk through the corridors and the elite parties of Manhattan advertising their wares. Beyond outfits from such names as Molyneux and Balenciaga, she became her own designer, creating outfits of stunning originality.

Women like Babe came in and out of the office at will, while middle-class editors did the heavy lifting. To the upper-class women who flitted down the corridors, hard work was tedious and boring. It was left to lesser lights. Babe was a talented, creative person and probably could have become a leading fashion editor. But she was not about to test herself that way. She was her mother's daughter. To be a

Cushing meant marrying well. She was in her mid-twenties, and time was fleeting.

When Truman and Babe talked, they often mused about their childhoods and the mothers who dominated their lives. Babe's mother had inculcated in her three daughters not just the aspiration but the necessity that they marry rich, socially prominent men. It wasn't happiness or children that mattered. It was a rich husband. Babe had taken on that ideal as her own and was as obsessed with it as her mother.

As a middle-class, small-town Alabaman, Truman's mother, Lillie Mae Faulk, would seem to have had little in common with Babe's mother, but they had similar ambitions to reach social heights that were above the station into which they were born. Lillie Mae's dreams were not about her only son, Truman, but about herself—she was determined to take her rightful place among what she considered the "best people." Her dreams of reaching that world consumed her, however, and eventually led her to tragedy.

Truman's greatest trove of literary treasure by far was his childhood in the South. No matter how far he wandered, how widely he roamed, the stories always came back to his mother.

Lillie Mae was from Monroeville, Alabama, a town of a little over a thousand that merited only gravel streets. Lillie Mae's widowed mother had died when she was thirteen, leaving her enough of an estate to fuel those grandiose dreams of life far beyond Monroeville. A petite woman scarcely five feet tall, she was definitely a looker.

There's no telling what Lillie Mae could have done had she kept her eyes on the prize like Babe had, but she made the mistake of attaching her dreams to a young man named Arch Persons, a hustler with a golden voice who came floating through town in a fancy car, making all kinds of promises never to be kept. Lillie Mae was only seventeen years old, in the midst of training to become a teacher, when on August 23, 1923, she married twenty-five-year-old Arch in a ceremony in the family house in Monroeville.

Lillie Mae Persons gave birth to Truman Streckfus Persons, the son she wanted to abort, on September 30, 1924, in New Orleans. Truman thought his mother was one of the most beautiful women in the South, and it is from Lillie Mae that he developed his obsession with beautiful women, finding their loveliness a transcendent blessing. Lillie Mae was married and a mother, but Arch was often off somewhere, and when he was, she picked up men and brought them back to her room.

It was sometimes a curse to be pretty. That was all men wanted from you, and that was all that you gave. It wasn't just hotel rooms either. Truman and his mother were traveling by train in coach from Memphis to St. Louis one day when the former heavyweight champ Jack Dempsey came strolling by. Gentleman that he was, the champ asked them to come visit him in his compartment. After a while, he had his associate take little Truman up to the observation car to drink a Coke and sit there for several hours while Jack and his mother occupied themselves below.

The stories were countless, a never-ending parade of men, men, men. The worst of it was when Truman was around four and Lillie Mae started locking him in hotel rooms and leaving for the evening. "I pounded and pounded on the door to get out, pounding and yelling and screaming," he later said. "That did something to me. I have a terror of being locked in a room—of being abandoned; I have a great fear of being abandoned by some particular friend or lover." Some people thought Truman was exploiting lurid false tales to make himself more interesting. People usually lie in generalities, and truth tellers speak out with all the specificity of their remembrances, and that was the way Truman talked. He told these stories for decades, and unusually for him, he told them almost precisely the same way, with the same detail and the same pain.

During the summer of 1930, Lillie Mae dumped Truman on her cousins in Monroeville and set off for parts largely unknown. It was there, living in a house with three unmarried sisters and their bachelor brother, that Truman discovered a world that he would chronicle in his fiction. His mother and father came back sometimes, always separately, bright spirits representing a world far beyond Monroeville, leaving as quickly as they arrived.

In a life dominated by an ever-changing array of powerful women, it was appropriate that the all-powerful person in that house was not the taciturn, asthmatic Bud Faulk, who did a desultory job managing his farm, but his sister Jennie Faulk, who ran a successful hat shop on Main Street. Their youngest sister, Callie, managed the books and was in all ways dominated by Jennie.

People said the oldest of the sisters, Sook, was "simple." Sook had almost no education and never traveled more than a few miles outside Monroeville. When she had a mastectomy, the doctor prescribed morphine. It was the most tempting of drugs, and Sook used it to smooth out her days and nights. Maybe she was simple, but in a gentler age, there was much that a person of her goodness could do. She cooked enormous meals beside Aunt Liza, the elderly Black servant, and knew all kinds of useful things. Sook became Truman's closest friend.

"Perhaps it was strange for a young boy to have as his best friend an aging spinster, but neither of us had an ordinary outlook or background, and so it was inevitable, in our separate loneliness, that we should come to share a friendship apart," Truman wrote in his short story "The Thanksgiving Visitor." "We hunted herbs in the woods, went fishing on remote creeks (with dried sugarcane stalks for fishing poles) and gathered curious ferns and greeneries that we transplanted and grew with trailing flourish in tin pails and chamber pots." Sook showed Truman that people society deemed almost worthless may have lives full of blessings; listening to them closely, a person could learn much.

In Monroeville, Truman made his first friend his own age. She was Nelle Harper Lee, a tomboy who was almost as much on the outs as Truman. Nelle's father was a lawyer, and she was in and out of the Faulk house like family. She and Truman had a tree house where they went to share their dreams and secrets. When Truman decided he wanted to be a writer and started pecking away diligently on his typewriter, he inveighed Nelle to write too.

As he always would be, Truman was an outsider, mocked as a sissy in the fancy linen shorts his mother sent him, a white-faced petite doll drudging down the dusty roads. That wispy, ingratiating voice that became so famous decades later was the voice he already had. By the time he was eight, he was writing scenes in his little notebook that took him far from the circumscribed world of Monroeville and that defined him already as a writer.

"He was a happy child until he was seven or eight," said his aunt Marie Rudisill. "Then it began to dawn on him that he was rejected by his father and his mother. He was hell-bent at that point not to be rejected again—*he* was going to do the rejecting. And he did."

Truman wasn't "normal." He didn't know or care what normal was. He probably was no more than ten or so when he began luring older boys into his bed. "I was always right out there," he said. "The other kids liked me for that. I was really quite popular. I was amusing and I was pretty. . . . People start out by being put off by something that's different, but very easily disarmed them. Seduction—that's what I do!" Truman did not care if a boy fancied himself a heterosexual; he would soon disabuse him of that limited notion.

Truman had a love-hate relationship with his mother, often with an emphasis on the latter. Despite his feelings, Lillie Mae was in her world an intrepid woman displaying characteristics that her only son inherited in a royal flush. It took daring at the age of twenty-six and without much of a formal education to make her way to New York City to start over in what to her was the ultimate place.

Lillie Mae got a job working in a restaurant in lower Manhattan. Before long, she hooked up with Joseph Garcia Capote, whom she had met five years before in New Orleans. Joe was hardly taller than Lillie Mae, and when they walked down the broad Manhattan avenues, they looked like a couple of porcelain dolls.

Capote came from a substantive Cuban family with Spanish roots. Like Arch, Joe had his hustler's dreams, but unlike Lillie Mae's estranged husband, Joe worked substantively to make them real. Starting out in the city as a lowly shipping clerk, in the evenings he studied accounting and business at New York University and rose to be the office manager of a textile-brokerage business. He wasn't running General Motors, but he had done impressively well in a short time, and the future glistened ahead.

Lillie Mae and Joe fell in love, each one immensely proud to have such a partner. She divorced Arch in November 1931 and four months later married Joe. At that point, Lillie Mae had custody of Truman nine months of the year, but she made no move to bring him up long-term to New York. He stayed in Monroeville, feeling as abandoned as ever.

If the Cushing sisters had constructed a perfect husband for Babe, they could not have done better than Stanley Grafton Mortimer Jr. His lineage went back to John Jay, the first chief justice of the United States Supreme Court. The economic lineage was just as stellar. Mortimer's maternal grandfather was a founder of Standard Oil. As for Stanley, he was a Harvard graduate and an executive in the advertising industry. He put in a few hours each weekday, but he appeared far more excited about his afternoons at the Tennis and Racquet Club, where there were competitions that truly mattered. Stanley was stunningly handsome, and when he and Babe walked together, people stopped and looked at them.

But the foundations of the family's wealth weren't as solid as they may have appeared from the outside. Stanley's paternal grandfather had inherited a fortune that he slowly lost in "investments" over many years—a genteel way of referring to the crazed gambling and endlessly profligate spending that had dissipated much of the money the family had once had. His son followed dutifully in his father's footsteps, squandering millions more and doing nothing productive.

These men were pure inheritors, disdainful toward the entrepreneurial energy and excitement of America. As long as they stayed within their enclaves, they were revered gentlemen, not the worthless wastrels they might have been considered if they stood boldly in the broader world. "No one held it against them that they were incompetent, and they seem to have been not at all embarrassed by their failure," wrote Eve Pell of her grandfather and great-grandfather. "But actually earning money—now, there was something to embarrass a gentleman."

Still, there was enough fortune (and importantly, social standing) left in the family to make Stanley Mortimer a strong match for the stunning and vivacious Cushing daughter. Twenty-five-year-old Babe wed twenty-seven-year-old Stanley on September 21, 1940, at St. Luke's Episcopal Church in East Hampton. Babe's sister Minnie grabbed the wedding bouquet, spearing it over the heads of far younger women. The fix may have been in, for Minnie married the newly divorced Astor a week later.

When Stanley was out on the town with Babe, there was not a more amusing and socially ingratiating gentleman; but that was only half of the equation. "Uncle Stanley was a manic depressive," said Pell in 2020. "When he was up, he was the most charming man in the world, charming beyond measure. When he was down, he disappeared and stayed by himself."

One time he came into his club after a long absence. A staff member said to him, "Mr. Mortimer, we haven't seen you for a long while."

"I've been depressed," Stanley said. "It's very expensive. I wouldn't try it if I were you."

Stanley was only at the beginning of a long, painful decline that would come to a head in 1969, when he shot himself in what police concluded was an unsuccessful suicide attempt. But that was decades in the future. For all his self-indulgent qualities, when the Japanese attacked Pearl Harbor on December 7, 1941, Stanley went the next day to enlist in the Navy Air Corps. Babe was pregnant. She joined her husband as he took the train south for naval cadet training in Pensacola.

The long train trip was full of abiding ironies. Babe had just been named as the second-best-dressed woman in the world, right behind the Duchess of Windsor. This new list by the Fashion Institute was a public relations gambit, a way to promote the industry, but it was widely circulated. The other women on the list were all far better known than Babe, whose fame reached no farther than the East Side of Manhattan, but with the honor she was soon being written about in newspapers across America. And there she was at this special moment, traveling south to become part of a world where khaki and blue were the only colors of note and a military cut the one that mattered.

The northwestern Florida seaport town was full of a bewildering array of Quonset huts, jerry-built buildings, bars, hookers, dust, and heat. Babe was not the only well-born wife of a cadet suffering through the conditions, but she could not take it, even if it meant leaving Stanley alone. It was not what was expected of a wife in wartime, but she did not appear to care. She had seen enough of how the lower classes lived in Pensacola, and she had no intention of spending further time in that world.

The war opened up a new world to millions of American women. Before it was over, around 350,000 women served in the military. Women went into the factories to build guns and tanks. They flew planes across the country. They learned to repair cars and got as greasy as any male mechanic. There were many women from upper-class backgrounds out there marching with their sisters, exploring a far broader world than they ever could have as children of privilege.

But Babe had been brought up to believe there was only one place for her, and it was not among such plebian efforts.

Taking the train back to New York, Babe found her editor's job at *Vogue* waiting for her. As she faced the war alone, her sister Betsey scored again, marrying the polo-playing, art-loving, debonair John Hay "Jock" Whitney, a man almost as fabulously wealthy as Vincent Astor.

Stanley took further training in Quonset Point, Rhode Island, as an aviation administration specialist before being shipped out to the Pacific. Babe gave birth to a son, Stanley, in 1942 and a daughter, Amanda, two years later. She had a mother, nannies, and maids close by, and she smoothly handed the child-rearing burden to others. This was the way many upper-class women—and it wasn't just Babe—raised their children (or did not raise them, as the case might have been). A woman of profound emotional disengagement, Babe had no problem relieving herself of the irksome parts of motherhood.

In the evenings, Babe often headed out into the inviting world of New York's café society. In the era Edith Wharton wrote about, no respectable married woman and mother would have gone out alone to clubs and restaurants, and those deemed part of Society ate at home. But the war years opened up the strictures of American life, and women of all sorts went practically anywhere. Americans were dying in Europe and Asia, but the nighttime venues of Manhattan were frivolous places far from the sounds of battle. Only the most socially privileged escorted Babe to these venues. One of her most devoted admirers was Serge Obolensky, a Russian prince.

No one engaged this world with such intense devotion as a group of rich Europeans, beginning with the Duke and Duchess of Windsor. Nobility-deprived Americans fawned over the former British king and his twice-divorced American wife and considered them the height of elegance. If you hosted them at your ringside table at El Morocco, you had everything that mattered.

Manhattan's nightlife might go on as exuberantly as ever, but the Best-Dressed List took a hiatus. At a time when the clothiers on Seventh Avenue were making the most utilitarian of clothes and the haute couturiers of Paris were dressing the mistresses of Nazi officers, it seemed a trivial indulgence to continue the annual list. But as the war news turned better and victory appeared in sight, the fifty voters at the New York Fashion Institute cast their ballots for a new list announced in January 1945. Babe headed the list, as she did the following year. For the rest of her life, one way or another, Babe never left the Best-Dressed List.

The doyennes of the Old Society considered the list an offensively public display of matters that should be decidedly private. That Babe felt otherwise and valued the cache the honor gave her showed that she no longer aspired to be part of the rituals of the world of her childhood. She was part of a new kind of Society, in which publicity of the right kind was a decided blessing.

In some other quarters there was a measure of irritation at a best-dressed list in a time when people around the world were dying. Asked the columnist Henry McLemore: "Would the outfits with which Mrs. Stanley Mortimer got the institute's blue ribbon, have been the best for her to wear had she suddenly found herself alongside those Russian women snipers who helped turn the tide at the Battle of Stalingrad?"

Babe dealt with the criticism by trying to create an image of herself as the populist's choice, saying she had won "with a navy wife's wardrobe pared to a packable minimum—mostly three plain suits and lots of hats." Modest to a fault, she refused to estimate her number of hats.

By the time Stanley arrived back in the States at the end of the war, their marriage was near an end. Those years apart would have stressed any relationship, but there had hardly been a foundation to sustain it. As the couple worked out their divorce, they were like two strangers divvying up the assets in a long-dormant account. When she accused him of being "habitually intemperate from the voluntary use of alcoholic liquors," that was the kind of statement required to get a divorce in Florida in May 1946, but it was also the truth. Stanley gave up custody of a son and daughter he hardly knew and settled a $40,000 trust fund on his ex-wife. It was time for Babe to go husband hunting again . . . but that process had already begun while she was still married.

3

══

Lilies of the Valley

WHILE BABE WANTED her husband and the father of her two children to come home safely, she was already thinking about a future that did not include Stanley Mortimer. By the time Stanley returned at the end of the war, Babe had likely already begun a relationship with Bill Paley.

Babe and her mother were realists when they looked at her future. In much of middle-class America, divorcées were outcasts, scarlet women whose days were not complete unless they stole a husband or two. In Babe's New York world, however, divorce was no worse than a bad cold. Her sister Betsey had done far better with her second husband than her first, and that showed what could be accomplished for a shrewd, marriage-minded woman. In his way, the founder of CBS was as impressive a person as Jock Whitney, except for one major problem: Bill was Jewish, and Babe's world—though not Babe personally—was anti-Semitic.

If Babe married Bill, she and her new husband would be forbidden entry to the private clubs and establishments that were the natural habitats of her sisters and their husbands and many of her friends. That was the indisputable reality.

Then there was the question of the man himself. Babe found him terribly attractive. She thought he looked like Jean Gabin, though the French actor exuded an aura of sensitivity that was not part of Bill's persona. The six-feet-one-inch-tall television executive was more a bigger version of Humphrey Bogart. A man of forceful masculinity, Bill projected a take-charge, endlessly solicitous manner toward women that many found irresistible. That was another problem. Babe and her mother presumably did enough due diligence to know something of her beau's past.

As a young man in Philadelphia working for his father (who was the biggest cigar manufacturer in the United States), Bill spent his free hours with "showgirls," a generic term for the kind of women one didn't take home to Mother. After college at the Wharton School of the University of Pennsylvania, Bill moved to New York, where he founded the wildly successful CBS network.

In 1931, Bill met Dorothy Hart Hearst, who had a model's looks and a cultured patina. Attracted to Bill's sheer animal magnetism, Dorothy divorced her troubled husband, John Randolph Hearst, the alcoholic son of the newspaper tycoon William Randolph Hearst, to marry Bill.

Dorothy was seven years younger than thirty-year-old Bill, but in many ways she became his sensei, guiding him on the nuances and unspoken rules of higher society. When she met him, he dressed like a funeral director, but soon she had him visiting a Savile Row tailor for his suits. When he walked into a room with his new wardrobe, he stood transformed. She had a similar effect on his living quarters; his bachelor apartment (with its utilitarian furniture and sports prints) displayed little but an appalling lack of taste. It was soon overhauled with her exacting eye. Under Dorothy's tutelage, Bill learned that taste was not something external. It was there every moment of one's day.

In the first years of their marriage, Bill listened to Dorothy like a schoolboy in the front row of the class. Slowly he was transformed, from a rough-edged salesman into a sophisticated New Yorker. Eventually, after all those years of following Dorothy's endless suggestions, he woke up one day and realized he had nothing more to learn from her. Her instructions on décor and decorum—once so valued—had become nothing more than endless hectoring.

The Paleys could not have children, so they adopted a son and daughter, but fatherhood did not end Bill's compulsive affairs. One of these was Geraldine Kenyon Bourque of Battle Creek, Michigan, a woman who could have been Myrtle Wilson, the tragic working-class lover in *The Great Gatsby*. Married to a Pontiac auto worker and saddled with a baby daughter she did not want, Geraldine deserted them to make her way in New York. She apparently had dreams of becoming an actress, but her ambitions in that regard went nowhere. After about seven years, the twenty-eight-year-old woman returned to Michigan with at least $1,500 in her purse and took a seventeenth-floor suite at Detroit's Book Cadillac Hotel. Taking out artist's paint and a brush, she wrote a number of names on the mirror—including William S. Paley's. At the bottom she wrote, "EXIT SMILING." Then she jumped out the window to her death.

Among Geraldine's belongings was an unsent love letter to Paley. The police also found a number of passionately felt, personal letters that had no addressee but were clearly intended for Paley. "You are everything in this world," Geraldine wrote. "I worship you, and even though you are sometimes a little cruel to me, I have no choice but to go on loving you. There is only one alternative to that."

During the Second World War, Colonel Paley left his lucrative and thriving business in New York to serve in the Office of War Information (OWI) in Allied headquarters in London. As CBS reporters like Edward R. Murrow and his team were making legendary names for themselves broadcasting from London, Bill's star rose in England, and he was soon embraced by the British elite to an extent the Jewish businessman had not been by New York high society. His position allowed him plenty of opportunity for socializing (and more) as well. Although eclectic in his pursuit of the opposite sex, he appeared to take special delight in sleeping with married women. One of them was Pamela Churchill, the stunning wife of Randolph Churchill, the son of the British prime minister—and a woman who had as many conquests as Paley.

The war was a time of casual dalliances, and no one looked askance at Bill's behavior. Only his wife understood that her husband's ravenous infidelity was driven by something deeper. "I knew this was his illness," Dorothy said. "He never stopped. It was absolutely pathological. . . . There was not going to be a cure for him."

At his meetings at the OWI, Bill sat doodling. The images he sketched were often perversely disturbing, a large penis on a camel, the backsides of pigs and monkeys, a defecating camel.

After her divorce, Babe and her two children were living with her mother in Mrs. Cushing's apartment on Eighty-Sixth Street. She was still going into *Vogue*, but it was not easy starting a new life. It was made even more difficult when Babe came down with a serious enough case of phlebitis that she ended up in the hospital.

As Babe lay in bed nursing her illness, Bill arrived with a warming container carrying two dinners from one of Manhattan's best restaurants. Babe maintained her wispy figure by eating like a sparrow, and food was not the way to her heart, but it was the way to his. Night after night for the whole month Babe was in the hospital, Bill arrived with meals from grand chefs. Bill loved not only eating but also discussing food, and he talked about the courses like a curator at the Museum of Modern Art dissecting a Manet or Chagall.

If Bill had chowed down blintzes and burgers with the same ferocity that he devoured boeuf bourguignon and confit de canard, he would have been considered a glutton. But these were splendid repasts, and as he lapped up the last drop of sauce, he had the right to consider himself a gentleman gourmand.

Bill spent those weeks studiously observing Babe. This remarkable woman was Dorothy without the mouth. That was her great allure. She was as cultured and beautiful as his soon-to-be ex-wife, but she was not about to lecture him on his supposed failings. Her mother had trained her too well for that. After the month, Bill decided that he wanted to make Babe his second wife.

The CBS executive wrote about the unique way he wooed Babe in his autobiography, *As It Happened*. In the 418-page volume, Bill devotes only seven pages to the woman who was his wife for thirty-one years. In the book, Bill tells the tale of his bringing superb meals each evening to Babe's hospital room as a mark of his generosity and thoughtfulness toward Babe—when it was more accurately a mark of his generosity and thoughtfulness toward himself. Nowhere is there the least interest in what Babe may have felt.

Bill appears to have been too egotistical to realize he was as much the hunted as the hunter. As much as this conquest mattered to him, to her it was a game she had to win. To Babe, her mother, and her sisters, you had everything or you had nothing, and Bill was everything.

Babe played her game not with grand gestures like Bill but in nuanced little moves, drawing him nearer and nearer. As she did so, she was as much a prisoner of this world as any of Wharton's heroines. When Bill asked her to marry him, there was a final set in the match: he insisted on a prenuptial agreement. Married to Bill, Babe would be a guest in his life that he could dismiss at modest costs to his treasures. She was akin to a splendid piece of art that he laboriously acquired and set out on his drawing room wall, a vivid symbol of his good taste, to be admired but rarely discussed.

When the couple married in a small ceremony on July 28, 1947, Babe was a month pregnant with William Cushing Paley, a minor glitch in the scenario. As they set out as a married couple, there was affection, respect, and physical attraction, but ultimately theirs was a business deal. Babe gave Bill entry to a measure of *haute société* and elevated taste, and Bill gave Babe money so she could live the way she and her mother believed she was born to live. His largesse toward her was not generosity but a shrewd investment so she would play the role he married her to play.

As Truman looked on at the relationship, he saw that Bill's immense wealth was crucial in Babe's becoming the notable character that he believed was her destiny. "Being a great beauty, and *remaining* one, is, at the altitude flown here, expensive: a fairly accurate estimate on the annual upkeep could be made—but really, why spark a revolution?" Capote wrote.

Babe's role as Mrs. Paley began with her dress. She wore clothes as well as if not better than any model. That was why for years designers had given her free or wildly discounted clothes. Babe no longer required such largesse. In the postwar world, upscale women were becoming obsessed with designer clothes, wearing them as advertisements for their taste and affluence. Babe not only wore the latest fashion, but she transformed the clothes into her image. When she walked into Le Pavillon for lunch with Truman, wearing a Chanel or Givenchy, the designer disappeared—it was the inimitable *Babe* arriving, dressed in her own unique style.

Occasionally Babe created her own fashion. It was so hot on her way to La Grenouille for lunch one day that she took off her scarf. Having nowhere to put it, she tied the scarf on her handbag. A photographer captured Babe as she walked into the restaurant. Within days, women in New York and later across America began displaying their scarfs in a whole new fashion.

Babe was expected not only to dress marvelously but to create a splendid, enveloping world. Beyond her personal adornment—which Bill considered a tribute to him—Babe had a primary responsibility to see to it that the Paley homes were exquisitely decorated, further testimony to her husband's taste.

Bill had purchased his eighty-five-acre country estate on Long Island in 1938. He did not buy his home in a socially undesirable town like the fictional West Egg, where Gatsby acquired his place, but in the much-vaunted Manhasset on the island's North Shore. Set in a countryside full of summer mansions inhabited by some of the most prominent members of the WASP elite, Kiluna Farm was Bill's forceful statement that he belonged as a member of the American establishment.

The sprawling twenty-room structure had given Dorothy Paley plenty of room to display her refined taste. To exorcise Bill's ex-wife's memory, Babe completely transformed the interior. One decorator would not do. Better a contingent of the best, everyone from Billy Baldwin to Sister Parish, Albert Hadley to Stéphane Boudin, each one competing to make their own stellar impression. The result was a far more formal house than it had been, elegant, surely, but with a heavier feeling than was usually found in country homes.

The walls of the dining room were covered in red lacquer. Around the room was a menagerie of porcelain lions, horses, and swans. Even the table itself was not free of decorator touches. Separating diners from one another rose two four-feet-tall Louis XIV candelabras. It was a setting to make one socialize with the same decorum that the dining room evoked.

Bill liked to show off, and with his new wife and stunning homes, he had found the proper way to do it. When he arrived to spend the weekend at his country estate, it was like the arrival of a grand potentate. Babe had everything ready for him. During the week she sometimes traveled as far as Idlewild Airport or Lexington Avenue in search of the delicacies her husband desired.

The staff of twelve at Kiluna Farm were ready for the weekend guests, who received solicitous concern rarely equaled in the grand estates of England. Invitees did not have to pack or unpack or draw their baths, and if they dropped clothes on a chair, the items mysteriously disappeared to be returned washed and ironed. There were all kinds of special soaps and oils stocked in the (many) baths throughout the house, which were adorned with flower displays, magazines, and books.

And when the guests dressed and went down to the dining room, they were presented with meals equal to those served in the world's grand restaurants, and conversation was as varied and sophisticated as the food. If the guests hoped to be invited back, they did their share in filling the evening with gossipy tales and witty repartee as light and fluffy as the soufflés set before them.

When Bill was growing up, his father dominated dinner conversations with stories of the cigar business. Bill would have none of that at his table. As a Jew, he would never be able to enter the portals of the old money clubs where business was discussed, but he would create his own club at his own table, where the word "CBS" was almost never heard.

Bill was able to re-create every aspect of the old WASP elite—except its essence. Seymour St. John, Choate's revered headmaster, talked about "the sheer restfulness of good breeding." It took no more than a decade or so of close observation to effect all the external behavior of a lady or a gentleman, but it was that restfulness that occurred only over generations. As much as Bill pretended, he did not have that quality—and neither did Babe, standing so close to her husband that she became in some ways his emotional clone.

When Truman was at the table, he banished dullness from the earth. His gossip sometimes tiptoed up against the edge of bad taste, but it rarely reached beyond it, and he kept his auditors in his firm grasp. On occasion he would talk about a childhood that was as exotic to most of the other guests as an upbringing among the Buddhist monks in Lhasa.

Truman could take any part of his life and turn it into an

irresistible tale that mesmerized the other guests. One of his set pieces was to talk about the devastating role his mother had played in his life. Even those sons with ambivalent attitudes toward their mothers are usually reluctant to speak harshly of the woman who brought them into this world. Truman had no such reticence to speak about his mother, who he called "the single worse person in my life."

When Truman moved to New York full-time and entered the third grade at Trinity School, an elite Episcopalian boys' school on the West Side of Manhattan, in the fall of 1933, everything seemed bright and new. His new stepfather, Joe, was making lots of money, and he and his bride were pushing to become part of New York's fluid café society. Joe loved his bride immensely and was trying to be a good stepfather, moving to adopt Truman and change his last name to Capote.

Lillie Mae changed her name to Nina, dropping the moniker that she felt branded her as a southern hayseed. Nina evolved into a New Yorker with a veneer of sophistication. When she went out with her new husband, to Truman's admiring eyes she could have been Miss America. She was that stunning. And when she embraced him and spoke fond words, all was well. But then she would turn on him, or ignore him, or berate him, or accuse him of terrible things. She knew what hurt, and she struck at him to the core.

Truman seemed to be in a secure home, but he still had that omnipresent fear of abandonment. That made him almost pathologically jealous. It infuriated him that he had to share his mother's love with Joe, and he soon turned on his stepfather. A natural actor and mimic, Truman affected Joe's rich Cuban accent, treating it as an affront to English.

Nina now had the perfect life with the perfect husband. That perfect life did not include a precociously gay son fathered by a man she hated. She took Truman to a couple of psychiatrists to see if they could rid him of what she considered a cursed affliction. When they could not, she kept looking for someone with a miracle cure.

In those years, it was generally assumed that if a boy displayed effete characteristics, he could not be an athlete and should stay away from the playing fields where "real boys" played real games. Truman, in fact, was a fine athlete. He had strong, firm legs and a hard stomach and likely would have been devastating as a wrestler in his weight class. As it was, he was excellent in gymnastics, especially floor exercise, and a splendid ice-skater, making artful loops on the frozen surface.

Truman found it impossible to focus in school and was a mediocre student during his fourth, fifth, and six grades at Trinity. His most significant experience at the school may have been with one of the teachers who occasionally walked him home. They stopped on Broadway and 107th Street and entered one of the back rows of the darkened Olympia movie theater. There the teacher fondled Truman while he had the boy masturbate him. Some men when they tell such tales have tremors of horror in their voices. Truman told it matter-of-factly.

To a ten-year-old boy who they feared might become gay, Nina and Joe did the worst possible thing. They sent this tiny, beautiful, sensitive child to St. John's Military Academy in upstate New York. It was like feeding him to wolves, but wolves would have made only one meal of him, rather than feasting upon him night after night.

When the senior students ordered Truman into their beds, he says it was innocent sexual games, little more than "kissing, fondling, and 'belly rubbing.'" To anyone who knows anything about these schools, it went well beyond that. And the sex wasn't the worst part of it. It was that it was devoid of human emotions, a rude cleansing of certain valves. One could wash away most of the stains, but the dehumanizing essence of it could not be scrubbed away.

In June 1939, the Capotes moved to Greenwich, Connecticut, an upscale commuter community a half hour out of the city. Nina loved the hyperactive society life, but she was becoming a bad drunk, spewing out words she should not have spoken.

The Truman who entered tenth grade at Greenwich High School that fall looked far younger than his classmates, but in his life experience, he was far older than most of them. Loud and demonstrative, he was small in size and great in unpopularity.

The list of those who could not stand Truman grew dramatically after his behavior during a school play, *If I Were King*. The choicest role was François Villon, the great French hero. One of the worst roles, hardly a role at all, was the executioner who has his moment at the end of the play. That was the role foisted upon Truman. When his modest time came, he improvised a soliloquy that was Shakespearean in length if not in quality. The drama teacher found it an intolerable intrusion. Even before the curtain went down, the livid teacher chased the hangman around the stage.

Truman did not care about being popular. He cared about having a select group of friends who admired his wit and daring, and he had them at Greenwich High. They fancied themselves the smart set. As the writer in the group constantly producing stories, Truman had a special place among his friends. Years later, he would say mournfully that he was little but a court jester with everything but bells on his cap, a loquacious fool who was invited to entertain. But that is the role Truman set out for himself as a teenager, gathering his friends around him and mesmerizing them with his stories.

The group was obsessed with *The New Yorker*, which in those years was not yet the storied, substantial publication about current affairs and culture it would one day become but rather one that celebrated a particular mindset and a place: the forbidden paradise of Manhattan, to which they all aspired.

The queen of the smart set and Truman's first love was Phoebe Pierce. A stunning brunette who had a woman's body when she was twelve, Phoebe was sophisticated beyond her years, with probing perceptions of the world. She was the emblematic woman of Truman's life. Even though Truman had no desire to possess her sexually, at one point the teenager asked her to marry him.

Truman loved to be around women. Men often put him down and talked about things that did not interest him. Women were more intimate, more self-aware, more observant, more concerned with the details of life in the same way he was.

In those years, Phoebe knew Truman better than anyone. "Always from the time I knew him when he was twelve or thirteen, he was fascinated by society," Phoebe said. "When he was in Greenwich he knew people who were terribly boring, but he was interested in their houses and the way they lived. He was always fascinated by the intricacies of that society."

Phoebe added, "It wasn't just social climbing. I mean that's ridiculous for someone of the subtlety of Truman's personality and mind. There was something that he wanted in that group, that world, and exactly what it was frightened me so much."

Truman looked out on that world and thought he saw beauty and grace that was not in his life. And he thought he could get them without paying much of a price.

Babe had two children with Bill, William and Kate, and two children with Mortimer, Stanley and Amanda, while Bill had two other children, Jeffrey and Hilary, with his ex-wife. But there were rarely the joyous, raucous sounds of children running through the rooms at Kiluna Farm, interrupting dinner parties with their interjections. The Paleys copied Old Society in everything, including child-rearing, and so they shuttled the children into the arms of nannies and private schools, out of sight and, often, out of mind.

"I once said if I write a book about a classic WASP upbringing, I am going to call it *Orphans with Parents*," said the novelist Michael Donald, reflecting on his upbringing in a traditional upper-class home. With the Paleys, as with so many families of that class in that time, children were simply not a central focus of their lives.

In some measure, Truman took the place of the children in the lively Kiluna Farm scene, and he was delighted to do so. As impish as the most irreverent teenager, as unpredictable as a two-year-old, he was the most intriguing and daring of the Paleys' guests. Babe did not have friends, per se, though she used the term promiscuously. She had acquaintances with whom she shared mutual interests. It was too big a risk to trust people, disclosing confidences that might one day be used against her or her husband.

Truman was the exception. Theirs was the kind of friendship rare among adults, and almost never between a man and a woman.

Truman was the sort of friend a teenager might have, a kindred soul who seemed to understand without a word spoken, a kind of intimacy that usually disappeared when confronted with the complexities of the world.

But Babe and Truman had that sort of kinship, and they maintained it for decades. "We had an understanding," Truman said. "If I suspected she was feeling bad about something, no matter what time of the year it was, I would send her lilies of the valley, without any note. And she would do the same for me." They needed no note. They understood. They spoke their own secret language.

As Babe and Truman talked, he realized that nothing in his closest friend's life was as it seemed. She spent her life creating this image that she had everything, but it was simply not true. Here was this woman envied beyond measure for her perfect life, when Truman was the only one who saw that her existence was a tragedy.

Babe was afraid of her husband, and that was the most frightening thing of all. Bill's equanimity was destroyed by the tiniest glitch or imperfection. From the time in the morning when Babe put in her teeth and donned her eyelashes to the time in the evening when she bade Bill goodnight, she looked to prevent matters that might set her husband off. It could be anything: a veal chop that was too salty, a painting that was hung askew, a limousine that had not been properly washed. She never knew what would provoke him or how angry he would get, but whatever it was, it was Babe's fault. While the weekend guests reveled in the luxury and social pleasures, Babe fluttered around like a butterfly, nervously trying to make everything perfect.

Truman spent so much time with the Paleys that he saw Bill in ways that only Babe had seen him. He told a story (that Bill denied) of traveling to Venice with the Paleys and having dinner with a gay count, who danced much of the evening with Babe. Afterward, in their hotel room, Bill was convinced the count was trying to seduce his wife. Nothing Truman could say would dissuade him. When he started flinging furniture around the room, Babe and Truman locked themselves in one of the bedrooms and pushed furniture against the door as further protection. As hard as he tried, Bill could not break down the door. Babe and Truman waited for him to calm down before they finally came out.

In being endlessly solicitous to her husband's every want, Babe helped to create a monster of self-regard. It was difficult enough when he was there, but when he was away, she had another kind of worry. Bill had long before concluded that sex was not necessarily better on fine Porthault sheets. When he was not working or at home, he was usually off with one woman or another. And when he was not engaged in the sack, he was looking.

One evening in the mid-fifties, Truman invited Carol Saroyan to his basement apartment in a Brooklyn town house for dinner. Carol had known Truman since they were teenagers, and she was delighted to attend one of the author's sparkling dinner parties. She had gone through two divorces from the playwright William Saroyan. With two young children at home, she was looking for a new husband. Carol was startled to see that she was the only guest.

Over dinner Truman rolled out his charm like yard goods. When he had displayed what he thought was enough, he came to the subject for which he had clearly asked Carol to make the trek from Manhattan. The most direct of men, there were times for even Truman when gentle euphemisms came into play. He began by segueing into a discussion of the greatness of William S. Paley in the business world. Then after describing Bill as her fan, he said he would be willing to make the introduction to the television mogul so she could begin a relationship.

"But he's married, of course," Carol said, not about to be caught in the mistress trap. She was stunned that Truman was blithely betraying Babe, the woman who was his closest friend.

"Oh yes, but he'd take good care of you, honey," Truman said at his most beguiling. "That's one thing you wouldn't have to worry about."

"No, thanks."

"A lot of people would say you're crazy, honey."

Bill would have thought nothing of taking as his mistress a woman who was in his wife's circle. He did such things not to shame Babe but because he did not care. He simply did whatever he wanted to do.

Even though Babe saw herself described as the most beautiful woman in the world, she knew that she was so undesirable to her husband that he spurned her. Bill devoured everything from gourmet meals to masterpieces of art to young women. To her husband, Babe was just another acquisition, a priceless mechanical bird that when he waved his hand near to it, it fluttered its wings and broke out in song. He hadn't had sex with his aging wife for years. Did she hate him? Perhaps. Did she disdain him? Yes.

But Bill was useful. Despite all the indignities she had to endure, Babe was undeniably at the very top of New York social circles. Babe pretended that she was above caring about her position, but it was one of the few unabashedly positive things she had in her life. This was the one place in the world where Babe could display her ambitions, and she ascended the social heights with a full measure of calculation and cunning.

Babe's life was a magnificent performance. When Truman had lunch with her at La Côte Basque or Le Pavillon, her entrance was the grand moment. Although flawlessly polite, her manner was slightly imperious, and she looked neither right nor left. Truman believed that if a woman like Babe faltered by showing some sign that she was aware of the excitement her presence created, it would be "as though, attending a banquet, one had the misfortune to glimpse the kitchen."

Babe occasionally sought other men, not out of revenge but to have someone warm and caring beside her once in a while. One such companion was an American ambassador, a gentleman with professional manners. Her lover mattered enough to her that one day she introduced him to Truman at a lunch at a restaurant on the West Side where they were not likely to be seen. Soon after that, she ended the relationship, telling Truman "she was afraid Bill would find out." It was better to be alone.

Bill was still a serial betrayer. Babe was ashamed of it, not for him but for her. It challenged her own ideals of femininity and her values as a woman. She told only Truman about Bill's myriad lovers, holding little back. And afterward, Truman ran out, clutching her secrets and telling them to another friend, half whispering these tales that he said were "only for her alone" . . . until he reached the next friend, and then the next. As dear as Babe was to Truman, her confidences were not as precious.

Babe and her friends shared a manicurist, who took an intense dislike to Truman. Sometimes when the woman was doing Babe's nails, Truman would be lying on the bed telling savage tales about the other friends. When the manicurist went to the home of one of the other women, Truman would often be there too, sprawling out royally on the bed, telling the same mean-spirited tales, only this time Babe was in the mix. Wherever the manicurist went and Truman turned up, it was the same.

Babe may not have known consciously that Truman was betraying her in his fashion as brutally as her husband was in his, but she had some sense of her terrible aloneness. Truman said that Babe tried to kill herself twice, taking pills and slashing her wrists, and that he saved her. Did she take as many pills as she could and cut her arms deeply because this was the only way she had left to speak?

There came a point when Babe could not take Bill any longer, and she decided to leave. Despite all Truman knew about the daily indignations of life with Bill, he urged Babe to stay. "Bill bought you," Truman told her. "It's as if he went down to Central Casting. You're a perfect type for him. Look upon being Mrs. William S. Paley as a job, the best job in the world. Accept it and be happy with it."

Truman had a far deeper understanding of women than most men of his generation, but in this crucial moment, his advice was staggeringly conventional. Like her sisters, Babe had sought wealth and position, not happiness, and she had achieved precisely what she wanted. She must, Truman advised, buck up and live the life she had so successfully sought.

And so, Babe did.

4

Slim Pickings

Truman loved to go to dinner parties at Diana Vreeland's apartment. He was always comparing women to birds, and he thought Diana looked like "some extraordinary parrot—a wild thing that's flung itself out of the jungle." She had a beaked nose, prominent lips splashed with red, cheeks rouged in red circles, and pitch-black hair. Her looks were provocative and over-the-top, and with her stunning sense of style, the fashion editor of *Harper's Bazaar* made herself a focal point of attention wherever she went.

Diana wanted the Fifth Avenue apartment she shared with Reed Vreeland, her devoted husband, to look like "a garden in hell." Most of the small two-bedroom apartment was covered in scarlet cloth, and a red carpet covered the floor. Everything was so compressed, so minutely calibrated, that the place seemed like a suite on a ship sailing on uncharted seas.

In the L-shaped central room, the couple gave memorable dinner parties for no more than a dozen people. Diana was a connoisseur of humanity, and nobody in New York had such eclectic guests. For

Truman, one evening was especially notable, for he anticipated he would be meeting a woman who might well become another of his swans. Like Diana, Truman saw in a woman's projection of beauty an assertion of a life force, a mystical, magical thing that transformed all who touched it. He liked to be near such women, and he collected his swans the way others did Fabergé eggs.

The woman Truman had come to meet that evening was Nancy "Slim" Hayward. Her dearest friend was Babe, and Truman would have known all about Slim. Her husband was Leland Hayward, a leading Hollywood agent who had become a powerful film and Broadway producer. Many ambitious authors would have cultivated his wife to get a connection with Hayward. But that was not at all what Truman was doing.

Like almost all of Truman's swans, Slim was tall—five feet eight and a half inches tall, to be precise. She had legs that went on forever and seemed like an anomaly, something beyond nature. Although the Haywards spent lots of time on the East Coast, Slim was the quintessential California girl. There was a casualness to her, no matter what she wore or where she went, and an athletic ease that seemed a statement about freedom and openness.

Slim was as fascinated by Truman as he was by her. "I was enchanted by him," Slim recalled. "He wasn't just bright, he was riveting—and so shrewd a conversationalist that, when he led with his vulnerabilities and quirks, you couldn't help but take an instant liking to him." Truman seemed to be exposing his most private secrets, but he was playing one of his most astute psychological games. These intimacies were valuable commodities that he used to then draw out the secrets of his listener. Once he had their confidences, he had the beginnings of what he called friendship.

It took more than one evening. Truman invited Slim to lunch and then to tea, each time further ingratiating himself. From then on, when Slim's phone rang in the morning, often it was Truman. He did not have to say hello but just started in, the words spilling over one another as he told the latest tales too sizzling for the sanitized gossip columns of Cholly Knickerbocker.

Most well-brought-up young women would have had no interest in attending a boxing match, but Nancy Raye Gross, or Slim as her friends called her, was different. When Bruce Cabot, a predictably handsome movie actor whose most notable role was saving Fay Wray from the menacing gorilla in *King Kong*, invited Slim to attend the boxing match at Los Angeles's Grand Olympic Auditorium on an August evening in 1938, she was game. It wasn't much of a main event, as Frank Androff, billed as "the roughest lumberjack ever to escape from the backwoods of Minnesota," spent ten rounds backpedaling from Big Boy Bray. Afterward, Cabot took Slim to the Clover Club on Sunset Boulevard to finish the evening on a better note.

The concrete building with tiny slots for windows looked like a mausoleum, but it was in fact an illegal casino run by the mob. Hollywood was a town of gamblers. A player could drive down to Long Beach and take one of the water taxis out to the two gambling ships, the *Caliente* and the *Tango*, just outside the three-mile limit, or drive 130 miles to Palm Springs to the Dunes. But the Clover Club was the place to play if you were in the industry. There were craps tables, poker games, and roulette wheels where the lords and ladies of Hollywood gambled, decked out in their formal finest.

All kinds of stars took their chances at the Clover Club tables, including Spencer Tracy, Marlene Dietrich, and David Selznick, who one evening won $5,700 on two spins of the roulette wheel. Director Howard Hawks was not so fortunate. A compulsive gambler, he never knew quite when to stop, and he was often in debt to bookies. It was a bewildering obsession, since Hawks held the golden key to Hollywood firmly in his hands.

Whether it was the crime drama *Scarface* or the comedy *Bringing Up Baby*, Hawks made the films that brought Americans into the theaters in droves. With all his successful credits, Hawks was still only forty-two years old. His prematurely gray hair (which earned him his nickname, "the Silver Fox") did not make him look old so much as distinguished. He dressed impeccably and conservatively, another reason he stood out in the brash, no-holds-barred world of Hollywood. Hawks had an emotionally distressed wife and three young children, a reality that circumscribed his life very little.

Hawks's other obsession was women, and there he generally held a winning hand. His interest was both professional and personal. Women played iconic roles in his films, and he chose the actresses he featured in his movies with immense care. A connoisseur of the female form, he had a precise understanding of the image actresses projected on the screen. He did not show that same concern for his many lovers.

Young women arrived in Hollywood every day, many of them carrying nothing but a cardboard suitcase. If they were pretty, they often got enough entry so they thought they were getting somewhere . . . but for the most part they were soon discarded like a Good Humor stick. The married Hawks considered women one of the natural perks of his position. He spotted his prospects, bedded them, and quickly moved on. It was just no big deal.

That evening at the Clover Club, when Hawks came out of the gambling rooms, he saw Slim dancing to the live band. There were other pretty women in the club that night, but Hawks saw something unique in the leggy, beautiful woman. Cadging an introduction, he led Slim to the dance floor.

Hawks's techniques worked so well and so easily that he had gotten predictable in his approach. "Do you want to be in movies?" he asked.

"No," Slim said. She hadn't been in LA that long, but she had seen the melancholy lives of most actresses. She wanted to live well and to be someone, but it wouldn't be through hustling her way to the film studio.

"You don't?" Hawks asked incredulously.

"No, I don't," said Slim with a tone of finality in her voice.

"Well, then, would you like to come to my house tomorrow for a swim?"

Slim acted like an innocent dropped into Hollywood from a foreign planet, but she knew all about the Silver Fox. She couldn't run off to a phone and ask a friend for her advice. She had to decide in an instant. In the past few years, she had made her way largely by judging the character of men—and doing so with impeccable discernment. She sized up this director in an instant. Looking him up and down, she said yes, and the next day Slim headed out to Hawks's home in Benedict Canyon.

The large fieldstone house and furnishings and staff were Hollywood's idea of an English country house. Slim was duly impressed that Hawks had a sense of taste sorely missing in many of his contemporaries. When she came dripping wet out of the pool, she was clearly tempting to the oft-philandering Hawks, but in this instance he remained a perfect gentleman. Not his favorite role, but one he played with aplomb.

In his films, Hawks had created a type of female character so unique for those times that she became known as the Hawksian woman. The audience paid attention to her on the screen not just because she was gorgeous but because she was something new. Bold and uncompromising, she stood up for herself. Her dialogue sizzled with wit as she challenged the male lead to act as he should.

"Listen to me, you great big bumble-headed baboon," Hildy (Rosalind Russell) admonishes Walter (Cary Grant) in the 1940 manically paced comedy *His Girl Friday*.

"Hawks liked it when they'd hold their ground and fire back," said Todd McCarthy, the author of *Howard Hawks: The Grey Fox of Hollywood*. "His women had a distinctiveness and a keen desire to give as well as they got."

Slim was the Hawksian ideal come to life. That surely was what drew him so profoundly to Slim. While Hawks didn't pounce on her at that first swim date, within a few days, the couple was having a full-blown affair. That Hawks was twice as old as twenty-one-year-old Slim was a technicality that did not bother either one of them.

Slim had not had many lovers, but she'd had enough to know what a good lover was. From their first nights together, Hawks exhibited no interest in or understanding of a woman's pleasure. "Sex was simply a physical need that had no relation to the person he was with," she said. It was already obvious this was a man who had nothing deep and true to give a woman, but that did not turn her away.

There are all kinds of ambitions, some easily cataloged and some not, and Slim had an immensity of uncharted aspirations. She was interested in living a life with a certain splendor, and she saw that Hawks had a full measure of this. Hawks represented "exactly the package I wanted," she later admitted. He had "the career, the house, the four cars, the yacht—this was the life for me." No bromides for Slim about love being more important than money and status.

Slim was born three hundred miles north of Los Angeles, in Salinas, California, in July 1917, and she was brought up nearby in Pacific Grove, next door to Monterey, the working-class fishing community immortalized in John Steinbeck's *Cannery Row*. Slim's businessman father, Edward Gross, owned several sardine canneries in the coastal town. Her father was the first and most important man in her life, defining what a man was to the little girl. To him, fear was a stronger and more powerful virtue than love, and he ruled the home like a cruel martinet. Consumed by hate, he lashed out against Jews, Catholics, Democrats, and anyone who challenged him.

Slim's mother, Raye Nell Boyer Gross, managed to stake out a tiny preserve of peace and love away from her husband, who largely ignored his children. It was that little sanctuary that brought Slim whatever happiness she managed within the troubled household.

It would have been enough for Slim to overcome such a tumultuous childhood, but then there was the terrible winter night in 1928 that changed everything. Her eight-year-old younger brother, Buddy, was standing in front of the fireplace in his long nightshirt when the garment touched the flames and caught on fire. In his panic, he tried to outrun the flames. Eleven-year-old Slim, her older sister Theodora, and their mother tried to catch the terrified child, but by the time Mrs. Gross grabbed him and threw him to the ground, Buddy was so terribly burned that he soon died.

Slim's father blamed his wife for the death—and never stopped blaming her. Thus, there were two deaths that evening, innocent little Buddy and whatever family life was still left in the house on Monterey Bay.

Slim's father placed a marble mausoleum on the family burial plot and brought Buddy's casket there. Slim went out to the cemetery to remember and honor her brother. She noticed that there were four other places in the mausoleum for other family members. It took her a while to realize that the remains of Slim, her two sisters, and her father were to be placed there. Her mother was to be buried elsewhere.

In the aftermath of Buddy's death, the family fractured further. Slim's sister mocked her as a bed wetter, and the two sisters would never be close. For Slim it was an immense blessing when she was sent to the Dominican convent school in San Rafael. The town was 140 miles north of Monterey, a good day's drive each way in those years. Yet Slim's mother never failed to show up for visitor's day each week.

One day Slim was pulled out of class and found her father sitting in the visitors' reception room for the first time. He had left Slim's mother. Slim's sister had left too, siding with her father and even taking the furniture in her room. Now it was to be Slim's turn. Her father was a man of abrupt words that sounded less like declarative sentences than firm commands.

"If you also leave your mother's house, it will prove to the court that she's an unfit parent—and I won't have to provide any support for her," he said. It was a pitiless thing to ask a daughter to do, but he sweetened the deal to make it almost irresistible: "I'll give you a horse, a little boat, a car when you are ready."

Slim was being brought up in what most Americans would have considered a life of privilege, but she still had a desperate desire for what her father was offering her. A horse, a boat, and a car weren't just things—they were freedom. Mr. Gross fancied he knew his daughter, and he would leave that day with his deal done.

For Slim, this decision would define her. "I love my mother," she said. "I'm staying with her." Her father turned and walked away. She did not see him again until he was close to his deathbed.

Slim was looking for what was indisputably her own life, one far away from the turmoil and heartache of Monterey. Several months shy of her high school graduation, her mother helped her buy a yellow Packard convertible, and in early 1935, she cruised south to the Furnace Creek Inn in Death Valley—the car's top down and Slim's brown-blond hair blowing in the wind.

The resort was an expensive oasis in the desert, with a well-off clientele who mostly drove down from LA for the weekend or a few days. It was not a place where guests typically spent two months, but Slim did. Her devoted mother did not come down once.

It was most peculiar. One of her editors later speculated that Slim may have had an abortion and driven to the desert to recuperate physically and emotionally. But Slim always turned her gaze upward and away from the negative, and the last thing she wanted to talk about was anything unpleasant that might have brought her to Death Valley.

After all, the Furnace Creek Inn was a lively place. True, most of the guests at the resort were middle-aged, decidedly not the age group with whom the teenage Slim would have necessarily chosen to spend her days. But she became energized around people no matter who they were, and with her charm and beseeching manner, others were irresistibly drawn to her.

Among those who found Slim irresistible were Warner Baxter and William Powell. Top stars at that time, they were there for a week's vacation away from the Hollywood scene. Most teenagers would have been hopelessly intimidated. But being around these intriguing, famous men energized Slim.

The actors were used to fans soliciting them for autographs and a moment's attention. That wasn't Slim. She knew who they were, but she had the uncanny ability to be herself no matter the company. When they asked her why she wasn't in school, she replied with a quick retort: "Why are you here and not working?" The two actors took an almost paternal interest in the teenager. Powell named her his "slim princess," the source for the nickname she carried the rest of her life.

After her lengthy stay, Slim left the desert and returned to Northern California to live with her mother in Carmel. She had no interest in completing her high school education, getting a job, or doing anything much beyond taking some singing lessons and having a wildly successful social life.

Truman could identify with Slim not wanting to sit in school when just outside the classroom window life was going on in all its excitement and variety. He could not wait to rush out into life, and he had about as difficult and limited a formal education as Slim. His record was so bad at Greenwich High School and his absences so many that he did not graduate with his class in 1942.

That was when his parents moved back into New York City. That at least saved him the embarrassment of repeating his senior year at the same school. Instead, his family enrolled him in Manhattan's mediocre Franklin School.

Truman thought the rituals and routines of the classroom were absurd, and he did not abide by them any more at Franklin than he had at his previous schools. All he cared about was writing, and he contributed poetry to the *Red & Blue*, the Franklin literary magazine. But as for math and what he considered other boring subjects, he wanted nothing to do with them.

However tedious his classes were, Truman found it marvelous to be living in Manhattan, to him the city of dreams and dreamers. When he was not at school, he was out there somewhere in the bright new world. With his obsession with Society, there were few things better than being around the rich.

Truman was living well in his parents' two-bedroom apartment on Park Avenue and Eighty-Seventh Street, but that was nothing compared to his friend Elinor Marcus's massive suite at the luxurious Park Lane Hotel a few blocks down Park Avenue. Her stepfather had made his fortune in the aviation industry, and his presence was felt all through the residence.

One weekday afternoon, Truman accompanied Elinor to her home. He may never have been in such a splendid Manhattan home, but it was as if he belonged wherever he chose to set himself and owned whatever he cast his eye upon. When Elinor mentioned that her younger sister, Carol, was in her bedroom, Truman took a stepladder, pushed it against her bedroom door, and looked down at the naked Carol lying in her bed.

Carol had white-blond hair and albino-like skin so white it was as if she had never been in the sun. As Carol ran into the bathroom for her robe, Truman jumped down off the stepladder and ran into her room and through to the bathroom. "No, you don't ever need to cover up," he said. "You're beautiful! I've never seen such white skin in my life. Sweetie, you must have been made on the moon."

Truman was soon one of Carol's closest friends. She introduced him to her two dearest female friends, Oona O'Neill, the daughter of the playwright Eugene O'Neill, and Gloria Vanderbilt, an heiress. The four of them hung out at 21 and the Stork Club, perhaps not so surprising a backdrop for three wealthy and worldly teenagers, but it was still a bit startling that Truman would be there with them, comfortable in their world. These teenagers were Truman's swans before he had even thought of the term, and they remained his friends for most of his life.

These three supremely privileged teenagers were emotional waifs. They did not have nurturing fathers; they barely had fathers at all. Oona had rarely seen her playwright father after he left her mother when she was two years old. Gloria had been the subject of the most notorious custody battle of the century—one that had less to do with love for her than with the competing egos of her mother and paternal aunt. Carol had literally been living in foster homes until she was eight, when her mother married the wealthy head of the Bendix Aviation Corporation.

These well-off young women had the world before them. Yet they had such desperate needs for security that they fancied only marriage to older men would bring them what they needed. Truman would never have tethered himself to a lover who throttled his freedom, but that was what these women were planning on doing—and gleefully so. It was a theme that Truman would see played out time and time again among the high-society ladies he called his friends.

Gloria was the first to go. The seventeen-year-old married Pat DiCicco, a movie producer who was fifteen years her senior. Then eighteen-year-old Oona married the actor Charlie Chaplin, who was a month shy of thirty-six years her senior—while nineteen-year-old Carol married sixteen-years-older novelist and playwright William Saroyan.

Truman hadn't even graduated from Franklin when he took on a position as a copyboy at *The New Yorker*. If that sounds like the most romantic of jobs (and it probably did to Truman, who'd been devouring the publication for years), reality set in with brutal force immediately. The copyboys were not talented young writers waiting for their chance to move up but semi-derelicts, aged relics, and various forms of youthful flotsam suited to run around the grungy corridors carrying manuscripts and packages, never saying a word or making their presence felt. It was scarcely the ideal job for the petite boy-man who wore a cape as if he thought he could fly around the office.

Truman could make friends with anyone, but not there. His one real friend was Daise Terry, the curmudgeonly office manager, a woman of such vile temperament that people did almost anything not to have contact with the miserable woman. But Truman could calm the savage seas and make Daise almost human.

Nothing was going to alter Truman's laser focus on becoming a professional writer. In the fall of 1943, he quit *The New Yorker* to go down to Monroeville and start writing seriously. But the old house that had been his home had burned down, and nothing was quite the same. It was not long before he was back in his parents' place in Manhattan and his tedious chores at *The New Yorker*.

As young as he was, Truman understood that his chances of succeeding at writing, that most solitary of professions, were increased if he built a network of connections and contacts. That was one of the reasons he decided in August 1944 to attend the Bread Loaf Writers' Conference in Vermont. Truman may not have openly lied that he was an editor or critic at *The New Yorker*, but he certainly did not go around advertising that he was a nineteen-year-old copyboy. Truman talked in such an authoritative manner that people assumed he had an important position at the magazine.

That was what the poet Robert Frost thought when he began his reading at the conference. Frost's vanity was as great as his talent, and when he looked out on the audience, he saw the *New Yorker* representative where he belonged in the first row. Wherever Truman sat, he would have stood out. He had an enormous head, far outsizing his body. It was as if God had decided enough was enough and skimped on the rest of his five-feet-three-inch frame.

Truman had no other intention but to show Frost the respectful attention he deserved, and then something wild happened. A recent bout of the flu had left Truman with a stiff neck, and for some reason only explicable to Truman, he decided he wanted to reach down to his foot. "I bent down to rub my ankle and found I couldn't straighten up again because of my neck," he said. "There I was, bent away over, with my hand on my ankle.... Being unable to straighten up, I worked my way out of my seat and began to hobble as quietly as I could up the aisle—still bent away over."

Frost was in the midst of reading one of his wonderfully accessible poems when he saw the *New Yorker* representative get up dramatically and walk up the aisle with his buttocks pointed at the poet. In his whole professional life had anyone treated the poet with such disrespect? Frost stopped the reading, slammed his book shut, and reamed out the *New Yorker* editor who thought so little of his poetry.

An outraged Frost contacted Harold Ross, the *New Yorker* editor, and Truman had spent his last day as a copyboy.

Slim's life was one party and tennis date after another, but she had gotten a taste of LA life and she couldn't get rid of it. Every month she drove down from Northern California in her convertible to spend a few days among the Hollywood set. One of her regular dates in Carmel was Winston Frost, who had dropped out of Harvard and come west.

Winston knew all kinds of people Slim only dreamed of meeting, and he invited her in August 1937 to press magnate William Randolph Hearst's belated seventy-fourth birthday party at the Santa Monica beachfront residence he shared with his mistress, Marion Davies. The beach was a favorite place for the Hollywood elite to have second homes, but Hearst's humongous estate made the mansions of Sam Goldwyn, Harold Lloyd, and Louis B. Mayer seem like modest cottages in comparison.

Nobody gave parties like Hearst. Every year there was a special theme, and that year it was "The Greatest Show on Earth." A tent large enough for a circus had been brought onto the property, as well as a carousel that Hearst borrowed from the movie mogul Jack

Warner. Hearst came dressed as the ringmaster. The five hundred guests included many stars, among them Cary Grant, Clark Gable, Carole Lombard, Tyrone Power, and Sonja Henie.

The host and hostess were inundated by people thanking them and wanting a few words, and Slim could not have spent more than a few minutes talking to Hearst and Davies. But she apparently made such an impression that afterward Hearst's majordomo, Joe Willicombe, invited Slim to Hearst's estate at San Simeon for a weekend.

The Hearst beach house had been grand, but San Simeon was something else entirely. Located 240 miles north of Los Angeles, San Simeon was arguably the most grandiose residence in America, an amalgam of styles that created a unique vision. As awed as Slim was by the unparalleled luxury of her surroundings, she had powers of observation that would not be amiss in a working journalist, and her well-honed charm was on full display. She joked with other guests, luminaries and Hollywood elite such as Cary Grant and David Niven, like old friends. Dinner was served at 10:00 p.m. in the dining room, where choir stalls from a cathedral in Catalonia adorned the walls and silk flags from Siena draped from the ceiling. It was a setting the king of England would not have found wanting—except for the ketchup bottles and paper napkins on the massive table.

Slim had no idea that Hearst's massive empire was about to come crashing down on him—crushed by Depression-era debt—but she sensed there was more sorrow than joy at San Simeon that weekend. Davies was bonded to Hearst's arm, at times almost physically supporting him, making her unable to join the guests and their playful pursuits. Although the visitors' time with Hearst and Davies was limited, Slim had that vigor and sense of life about her that made even the Hearsts want to be around her. She was a different kind of distraction, and they invited her back. She flew with them in their private plane to their ranch in Northern California and to their home in Mexico.

Slim's mother was devoted to her daughter, so much so that in the spring of 1938, Mrs. Gross and Slim moved to LA. Slim had no other obvious role in life but as a single woman with a frenetic social schedule, one that took her to events and places that almost no one who was not wired into the Hollywood world entered.

Every night Slim headed out of the charming house on Sunset Boulevard above UCLA to one coveted occasion or another. Although it all may have seemed trivial, she had a high purpose in mind: finding a rich and proper husband. She dated, but she was as careful in that as she was in everything else. She avoided the men in Hollywood who were considered "dangerous" for—among other things—treating "no" as a polite way of saying "yes."

From the night Slim showed up at the Clover Club and met Hawks, she wanted nothing more than to be with him. Hawks's wife, Athole, fell in and out of coherence—she had long struggled with mental health, and they'd been estranged for years. He wasn't living with her any longer and simply wanted out. Hawks and Slim saw Athole not so much as a tragic figure than as the sole impediment to their happiness. It was difficult to get a divorce from a spouse suffering as Athole was, and while Hawks's lawyers attempted to work their magic, Slim shared as much of Hawks's life as she could: going to his movie sets, sailing on his yacht, and traveling with him around America and Mexico. She always returned to the house she shared with her mother, and as much as she saw her lover, Slim never fully moved in with the director.

In December 1939, Slim and Hawks drove down from New York to Ernest Hemingway's home in Key West, where the director wanted to purchase the film rights to the illustrious author's 1937 novel, *To Have and Have Not*. With Hawks on her arm, Slim hung out among stars who were the personification of charisma, but they were nothing compared to the Hemingway she met in Florida. To a generation, the author was the symbol of American manliness. Like Slim, he could not abide pomposity and pretense, neither in his prose nor in his life, and they bonded in a way that lasted the rest of their lives. Hemingway was attracted to her, but he was just getting rid of one wife and moving on to the next (the journalist Martha Gellhorn), and he wasn't about to make an obvious pass at this beautiful young woman from California.

To Hemingway, physical and moral courage were linked together, and he preferred to be around people who challenged themselves in the outdoors. Hawks was a sportif type too, and Hemingway put him to the test. They shot their full share of birds down from the sky. They went deep-sea fishing, a theme Hemingway would one day use in *The Old Man and the Sea*. They went barreling through the swamp water in a boat. And everywhere they went, Slim went with them. That was the way it was meant to be. A Hemingway woman stood next to her man and supported his most intrepid adventures, much like a Hawksian woman in the director's films.

Two years later, when Slim and Hawks saw Hemingway again in Sun Valley, Idaho, for two weeks of shooting and hunting, the novelist was newly married to Gellhorn. That didn't prevent Hemingway from staying close to Slim, always proper, never indiscreet, but always there.

In those days, stars did not always set themselves off in a firmament by themselves but often went off to play together—and Sun Valley was a favored playground. Gary Cooper, who was about to star in Hemingway's *For Whom the Bell Tolls*, had made the flight to Idaho. Other stars in attendance there included Barbara Stanwyck and her husband, Robert Taylor. The Hungarian photographer Robert Capa had flown up too for this impromptu gathering, and he spent much of his time shooting pictures of the group.

The agent Leland Hayward was there in Sun Valley as well. Most Hollywood agents were brash and aggressive. Hayward was cool and reserved, aristocratic in demeanor. It shouldn't have worked, but it did, and Hayward was the number one agent in town. He was there with his actress wife, Margaret Sullavan.

Slim sought no dispensations as a woman, and when she went out hunting pheasants with Hemingway, she was one of the boys. But she was decidedly not one of the boys when she returned from a day of shooting and, after showering, sat in front of the fireplace in her dressing gown brushing her hair. "Can I do that?" asked Hemingway. When he finished, he tossed the brush on the floor and said, "You don't know what that was like. You're a very provocative woman. I can't be around you too much."

"Of course, you can be around me," Slim said in a manner that was half-mocking, half-challenging. She was as good at cooling a man off as she was at heating him up.

Not every bride had an internationally renowned film star like Gary Cooper to give her away, as Slim did when she married Hawks on December 10, 1941, three days after Pearl Harbor. She had been practically living with the director for two years, as he dealt with his sick wife whose advisors had her file for divorce. For Slim it might have been expected that it would be a neat little skip and jump into matrimony, but she was petrified at taking the leap.

"I really don't want to do this," she told Cooper, desperation in her voice. The actor, who had just played the character of Sergeant York in the film by the same name, about a military man who killed a dozen Germans in World War I before taking the surrender of 150 more, was not about to let Slim be frightened by a little thing like wedding vows.

"Well, you have to do it now," Cooper said in that famously gravelly voice. "The music is playing, the people are waiting, and the train has left the station. So, let's go."

In the first months of their marriage, both Slim and Hawks got what they wanted and more from the relationship. Hawks finally possessed the woman who had so bewitched him, the embodiment of his ideal in so many ways. And Slim got the life of luxury she'd been chasing, starting with a brand-new house tailor-made to her specifications. She could not abide the prospect of living in the same house Hawks had shared with his first wife, so Hawks had agreed that Slim could take over the design and building of their dream house. She had a natural and sophisticated sense of style that translated perfectly into building what was truly one of the most beautiful homes in Los Angeles.

The house was a perfect measure of how dreams and reality mixed together in Hollywood. It was based on the ranch-style house Katharine Hepburn inhabited in Hawks's film *Bringing Up Baby,* and Slim and Hawks lifted it off the screen and set it down in the midst of 105 acres in the foothills of the Santa Monica Mountains. There was plenty of room for Hawks's children when they were there; plenty of staff to take care of them; ample grounds for a grand pool, stables, and a croquet court; and a splendid setting for the parties that Slim gave with such panache.

But as Hawks's fortunes continued to rise in Hollywood, so too did his gambling addiction. What he didn't wager away, he spent with desperate urgency, as if guilty he was making enormous sums of money. It was a disease that anyone close to him risked catching, and Slim spent humongous sums in what—if she were married to almost anyone else—would have seemed wildly profligate ways. But being married to Hawks, she had an exemption, and she spent for the sheer fun of it on anything she wanted. Her bedroom was a suite of rooms, including the bedroom itself, a bed-sitting room, a grandiose bath, and a dressing room that had more shoes, dresses, and sweaters than most stores. When *Life* tabulated the bounty in 1946, it totaled forty-seven dresses, twenty-four suits, thirty-five evening gowns, nine fur coats, and 120 pairs of shoes.

If a new arrival wanted to be fully accepted into Hawks's creative set of stars and writers, she better have a fast-paced repartee at the ready. When it came to verbal shootouts, as young as she was, Slim was no timid ingenue but a full-fledged player. There was no wittier or inviting person to come to your party, no more charming a guest at your dinner table. She wasn't a star in the films, but she was a star in the upscale social world she and Hawks inhabited. Slim lived on the surface, and she lived there brilliantly. She wanted to amuse and to be amused.

Slim was excited with everything her new husband was doing, and she shared in his work as much as she could. Not only did she go out to the studios to see him at work, she read scripts and passed on her thoughts.

Even when Slim was doing things that had nothing to do with

Hawks, she was thinking about his work. One day she saw a picture of a model in *Harper's Bazaar* who she thought might be perfect for the female lead in the director's new film, *To Have and Have Not*. Hawks had enough faith in his wife's judgment that he flew the eighteen-year-old woman to Los Angeles and gave Lauren Bacall a screen test. Bacall had an androgynous quality that Hawks liked in a woman, and he signed her to play opposite Humphrey Bogart in the film.

The director was putting an idealized version of his wife on the screen, even naming her Slim and calling the Bogart character Steve, his own nickname. As he worked on the script, he noted his wife's witticisms and asked her what the Bacall character would say in a given situation. In the most famous scene in the movie, Bacall stands in the doorway to Bogart's bedroom and speaks in a voice as deep as a man's, "You know how to whistle, don't you, Steve? You just put your lips together and blow." It could have been Slim standing there speaking those words.

But Hawks's Slim stand-in, Lauren Bacall, was distinct from her namesake in one key way: rather than fall for the director, to whom she "owed" the role, the husky-voiced teen began an affair with the decades-older Bogart. Hawks wasn't used to settling for second-best in anything, but this time he doubled down. Not only did he have an affair with the second female lead in the film, Dolores Moran, but he also spent some time with an extra, Dorothy Davenport, who even looked a little like Slim.

Slim knew about these affairs and many others. Hawks had hardly gotten back from their honeymoon when he started up his trysts. He would come home at three in the morning smelling of another woman. It was all predictable. But that wasn't what began to gnaw at her—it was the man himself. Everything that was real about Hawks was on the screen, and that wasn't real at all.

Hawks's heroes were truth tellers, but Hawks was a serial liar who exaggerated everything about himself. He posed as the great captain of his boat, *The Sea Hawk*... but in truth he got seasick as soon as he left the dock. He acted as if he were an intrepid pilot ready to set off on adventures anywhere... but he couldn't actually fly a plane by himself. He told tales of flying planes in World War I in the legendary Lafayette Escadrille until his lungs were scarred by poisonous mustard gas... while in fact he had never served in combat.

It wasn't the lying and the philandering that got to Slim but how her husband wasn't there for her emotionally. He wasn't the Silver Fox—he was the Silver Ghost, walking through life and leaving nothing. She seemed to have everything, including the handsome, wildly successful husband, but in truth she had nothing that really mattered to her, and she was sure that no one would understand. She entered Good Samaritan Hospital a number of times for what were called "rests," a mark of the emotional exhaustion her empty marriage was causing her.

As a young woman of a certain class and time, Slim had looked out on the world and concluded the best thing for her was to marry a rich man. Most people wouldn't have considered that a career, but she had pursued the life she sought with calculation and savvy. She had gotten what she wanted, and this was where it had led her. Hawks's former wife had gone crazy, and now Slim herself appeared to be heading in that same direction.

5

The Marital Game

THERE WAS ONLY one way out: to marry another rich man. Finding him while still married to Hawks was going to be a challenge of great proportions. But Slim was up to the task.

Who was a better candidate as a lover (if not a husband) than Clark Gable, the number one movie star in the world? When his wife, Carole Lombard, died in a 1942 plane crash, Gable went to war. Major Gable flew five bombing missions over Germany, winning the Distinguished Flying Cross while still finding time to make a rousing recruiting film that stirred the hearts of many on the home front.

One Sunday in 1944, Major Gable came zooming up the driveway at Hawks's Bel Air home on a motorcycle. He was still wearing his Air Force uniform, and he cut such a striking figure that he could have been playing a flyer in a Hollywood war movie. Gable had shown up because he was interested in joining Hawks's informal club of motorcycle riders who roamed the LA hills each Sunday, before returning to Hawks's home for a buffet lunch.

Slim had other ideas to interest the star, and she soon began seeing Clark. It turned out the matinee idol was as dim as he was dashing; he needed a screenwriter to give him good lines, but he was as irresistibly handsome in person as he was playing Rhett Butler in *Gone with the Wind*. He treated Slim as if she truly mattered and was beyond attractive. That was just the tonic Slim needed. Angry at her husband and deeply competitive, what could be sweeter revenge than an affair with Clark Gable?

Slim had other good things happening that had to do with the world around her. In 1944, the United States was still in the midst of a life-and-death struggle, but there was already a bright optimism about a new postwar world. Part of that vision had to do with California, an American metaphor for freedom and lives of endless promise. No one exemplified that promise better than the archetypal California girl, roaming free from the beaches of Santa Monica to the mountains of the High Sierra. Half a world away from the formal, couturier salons of Paris, the young California woman represented a new, casual, uniquely American style.

When Carmel Snow, the savvy editor of *Harper's Bazaar*, came west, she met Slim and immediately saw in her the perfect exemplar of the California girl. Slim had a breezy beauty that felt thoroughly modern, paired with an elegance that was fitting for the magazine's upscale audience and the fantasy its pages projected to its readers. Snow asked Slim to pose for *Harper's Bazaar*. She did, and she was such a hit that her image graced the covers of four other magazines that year.

Slim was such a fashion phenomenon that Snow asked her to become the official West Coast editor of *Harper's Bazaar*. A "real" job would probably have done wonders for Slim's self-confidence and maybe even offered her a new career trajectory. But she soon discovered she was pregnant, and that decided the matter.

A new child might have gone some way in saving Slim's marriage, but Hawks had no interest in his new daughter. He was rarely around for more than the initial photo op, memorializing the birth of Kitty Stephen Hawks on February 11, 1946, before heading back to set.

When the baby was only two months old, Slim took off for the East Coast on the Super Chief, "The Train of the Stars," leaving the child in the hands of her nanny. It was party time. That was Slim's way out of depression and despair—not drugs and booze, but a non-stop social life. New York nightlife was wild in the postwar years, and Slim jumped into it like she was diving into a swimming pool.

After weeks in New York, dancing at the El Morocco nightclub and soaking up the attention she relished, Slim was bored. She determined that she would fly to Cuba and link up with Hemingway, her longtime admirer, who would deliver just the shot of appreciation she hungered for. The fact that Ernest was there at Finca Vigía with his third wife, Martha Gellhorn, did not deter her. The well-known war correspondent Gellhorn was less than elated at Slim showing up.

The atmosphere was lightened when a yacht unexpectedly appeared, bearing a group of Americans that included David Selznick and Jennifer Jones, a couple Slim adored; Leland Hayward and Margaret Sullavan, another prominent Hollywood couple Slim knew; and the CBS founder William S. Paley. Bill was single and by himself and would not marry Babe until the following year. Slim found him wildly attractive. "He was funny. He laughed a lot. He was very agreeable. And he was a full-blown sexy man," she said. "He made me feel divine. He wanted me to come on the boat with them." If Slim had accepted the invitation to sail off on the yacht with the group, she likely would have had an affair with Bill that could have led to marriage. But she decided no, and after a month soaking up the sun in Cuba, she returned to California.

But now things were different. Slim knew her marriage was going to end, and she was sizing up the various men in her orbit with a different eye. Her mind turned back to Leland Hayward, the Hollywood agent she'd bumped into in Cuba with his wife. She realized there had been a chemistry between them, a frisson that had not been there before. Who was this dashing man?

A son of the Midwest, Hayward had dropped out of Princeton, but that had given him enough of an Ivy League sheen to set himself apart in the rude Hollywood world. Leland wasn't as handsome as Clark Gable—nobody was—or even as good-looking as Howard Hawks, but his chiseled features and debonair manners had brought him all kinds of lovers, from Katharine Hepburn to Greta Garbo. His close-cropped gray hair should have made him look like an aging marine recruit, but it worked on him. Most movie agents talked quickly, but Hayward spoke machine fast, a blistering assault of words that overwhelmed his listener. Unlike Hawks, Hayward was a *real* pilot, and one of the founders of Southwest, the most innovative airline of the age.

Hayward had risen to the top of the agenting ranks, in part because he was such a good judge of human character. Not just a dealmaker, he played a seminal role in the evolution of Hollywood, breaking the grasp the studios had on their stars. When negotiating with a studio, he would be endlessly polite and then boom out with a string of profanity that would wilt flowers. His 150 clients paid him 10 percent of their considerable salaries, making him wealthier than even the most successful star.

Hayward had been married to the actress Margaret Sullavan for years, and the couple had three children. In a Hollywood world where promiscuity was rampant, Hayward was proud to call himself a one-woman man. But in truth, their partnership had been distressed for years, and his marriage was over in every way but a formal legal document.

Hawks left the party early that evening, and Hayward drove Slim home. The unspoken tension between them was palpable. When Hayward stopped in the long driveway, he turned to her and said, "Why don't you quit? Why don't you leave?" They had never spoken an intimate word and were nothing more than acquaintances. Both of them were married, and it was a wildly inappropriate thing to say. But somehow it sounded *right*, as much as Slim disavowed the idea. "Because he's my husband," she said. "He's the father of my child. What are you talking about?" Then she got out of the car and hurried into the house. But an irresistible drama had begun.

Slim had never had a clandestine affair with a married man—her early relationship with the still-married Hawks had been out in the open. But as she soon discovered, there is nothing sweeter than forbidden fruit. Slim and Hayward would sneak off to love nests Hayward rented in La Jolla and Palm Springs and arrange occasions when they had seemingly legitimate reasons to see each other. When Hawks went off to shoot *Red River* in Arizona, it made it even easier for them to continue their affair.

Hayward was as obsessed as Slim with dressing well. He had three hundred pairs of shoes, drawers full of handkerchiefs neatly set out by size and color, and innumerable shirts. Hayward thought the outdoor games and sports Hawks liked were silly, boyish things. He was masculine without having to assert it by riding with a pack of celebrities on his motorcycle through the Hollywood Hills. As manly as Hayward was, conversing with him was like talking with one of Slim's girlfriends. It was that intimate, something Slim had never experienced with a man. There was something deep and true to love in this man, and Slim loved him in a way she had never loved Hawks.

Hawks soon discovered his wife was having an affair with Hayward, a man with whom he had done many deals. Given the way Hawks had lived since the early days of their marriage, it was hard for him to play the aggrieved husband, though in some measure he did. He reacted the way he always did when something troubled him deeply. He walked away from it and pretended it did not exist. He ignored Slim in their house and looked right through her.

The stress was wreaking havoc on Leland Hayward. One morning Leland's secretary called Slim. "Mr. Hayward was taken to Cedars of Lebanon Hospital last night," she said. "He's hemorrhaging very badly, and they don't seem to know what to do." Slim immediately brought in her own personal doctor, who operated on Hayward and most likely saved him. The doctor said tension had caused the hemorrhaging. Unlike Hawks, Leland's emotions were painfully up-front. As much as he loved Slim, he had a wife and three children, and he could not forget them. The drama was overwhelming, the emotional cost enormous. From Leland's bedside, Slim called her husband and told him what had happened and where she was.

"Is he going to be all right?" Hawks asked.

"Yes, I think so," Slim said.

"Good. I know how much you care for him. I'm glad he's going to be all right."

Slim took her husband's understated words as him telling her their marriage was over. It ended with what she considered "the most impeccable ease and grace." There were no tears, no sad reminiscences of all they had shared, no anger, and no profound sense of the history together they were losing. It was as if nothing had ever been there.

Things moved quickly after that. Slim and Leland were both soon divorced, and shortly after that they moved from Los Angeles to New York, where he was embarking on a new phase of his career: Broadway producer. His drama, *Mister Roberts*, starring Henry Fonda, was an enormous success and ended up playing 1,157 performances. He then turned to work on his first musical, *South Pacific*. In June 1949, Slim and Leland had a small wedding at Kiluna Farm on Long Island, the North Shore estate owned by Leland's friend Bill Paley and his lovely new wife, Babe.

Truman's story of his early adult life was as intriguing as any of the plays Leland was producing. After being fired by *The New Yorker*, Truman left New York in the fall of 1944 to go off to write, back to what he thought would be the loving embrace of Sook and the others in Monroeville. He had largely written his first novel, *Summer Crossing*, a comedy about an East Side debutante who frolics while her parents are off in Europe. The pages had seemed witty and sophisticated when he was in that New York world, but sitting far from it, he realized the work was self-consciously clever and thinly developed and not the work to introduce him to the broader literary world. Truman was barely twenty years old, and he was already completing one novel. Even if *Summer Crossing* was nothing more than a five-finger exercise, the novel was a major accomplishment for a self-educated young man without a literary mentor.

It was a mark of Truman's growing professionalism as a writer that he could be so self-critical. At the same time, as he pushed away from what then seemed a silly attempt at a novel, he began serious work on another novel, about the Southern world all around him. He would call it *Other Voices, Other Rooms*. Obsessed with this new idea, he started writing at night and sleeping during the day, a regimen that upset the household. Truman got a Greyhound bus ticket to spend time in New Orleans before returning to Manhattan.

Truman arrived from his southern sojourn with a trove of new writing in his suitcase, and he rushed into the embrace of a new set of women: editors at *Mademoiselle, Harper's Bazaar,* and *Vogue.* These magazines were publishing the most exciting new short fiction in America, and that was where Truman wanted to be. He did not seem to care or even notice that much of mainstream media looked down upon these magazines as serving a decidedly secondary audience: women.

Truman made his debut in the June 1945 issue of *Mademoiselle* with "Miriam," a short story about an evil little girl, followed up in October by "A Tree of Night" in *Harper's Bazaar,* another nightmarish tale. It was hard to believe that this sweet little boy-man had written such menacing tales, and from then on, he was treated as someone of literary seriousness.

Most young writers would have been overawed by the heady scene at these magazines, but Truman was not most writers. He started hanging out at *Harper's Bazaar* with two of the editors, Barbara Lawrence and Mary Louise Aswell, who adored him and treated him as their personal boyish protégé. They introduced him to the formidable editor in chief Carmel Snow, as well as to others in the fashion and media worlds.

Of the many women friends Truman made early in his career, the most important was his fellow author, Georgia-bred Carson McCullers. In 1940, the twenty-three-year-old Carson published *The Heart Is a Lonely Hunter*. The bestselling novel about quirky lives in a Southern town not unlike Monroeville established Carson as *the* Southern writer of her generation. A sickly, demanding woman who squeezed her friends half to death, Carson was either going to embrace this little man who came walking uninvited into her territory or seek to destroy him. At first, she chose to help Truman, and got him an agent, who promptly sold his new novel, *Other Voices, Other Rooms*, to Random House for an advance of $1,200.

Carson's help did not stop there. Truman was still on his crazy schedule of writing all night and sleeping during the day. He was also back living with his parents. That would have worked out fine if Nina had not still been such a rousing, obnoxious alcoholic. He had to get out of there, but he had no money. Carson suggested that Truman join her at Yaddo, the famous artistic colony in Saratoga Springs.

Truman had less than fond memories of writerly gatherings. Two years before, at the Bread Loaf Writers' Conference in Vermont, he had managed to insult Robert Frost so profoundly that the famous poet got him fired from his copyboy job at *The New Yorker*. Carson insisted that this time things would be different. It was hard to be accepted, but the revered novelist took care of that, and so in May 1946, Truman joined his mentor in upstate New York.

Yaddo was Truman's idea of paradise, a group of eclectic people off together for an extended stay. Everything was free. Housed in a creepy Gothic mansion built by a Gilded Age mogul, it would have been the perfect setting for a murder mystery. As always, Truman was at the center of the social scene. He had only a small portion of the credentials held by most of the others, and he was half the age of many of the intellectuals present, but he was the impresario, ruthlessly deciding who was worthy of his dazzling company and who was not.

Truman flounced around the estate in a long, trailing scarf as if playing Isadora Duncan in her famous death scene. As Truman did everything but carry a neon sign emblazoned with the word "GAY," many people thought he had no choice but to act that way. But he was an actor and mimic and, if he chose to, he could have played the part of Mickey Rooney. Truman wanted the world to know what he was, and he was a proud, young homosexual man.

In his youthfulness, Truman was probably not aware of just how brave he was, but that did not diminish the daring, groundbreaking role he played. Sex between members of the same sex was illegal all across the United States. Even in sophisticated New York, gay men risked being accosted on the street and beaten up. In the war in the Pacific, there were navy units tasked with ferreting out homosexual "rings" and taking the perpetrators to the brig, where the military believed they could not infect other sailors.

More typical of gay men in 1940s America was another guest at Yaddo, Newton Arvin, a literature professor at Smith College. A timid, frightened man, Newton had stolen away to the women's college in the woods of Massachusetts. His gay life in Northampton was limited largely to several other professors who were in the closet with him and in later years a collection of physical culture magazines featuring male nudes. Periodically, he would take the train to New York City for the weekend. The highlight of his visit was his trip to the Everard Baths, the most famous homosexual hangout in the city. The steam and the half darkness could not hide what a grungy place of momentary assignations it was, but Newton loved it and left feeling renewed.

At Yaddo, the ebullient, gorgeous young Truman fell in love with the middle-aged, depressive Newton. Truman gave his passionate, all-consuming love to Newton and took in return not just Newton's love but aspects of his mind. Newton was a superb literary scholar who in 1951 would win the National Book Award for his Melville biography. The professor introduced his protégé to the writings of Melville, Proust, Hawthorne, and many others. For the first time, Truman saw the excitement of the life of the mind. Every weekend he could that fall, he went up to Northampton to be with Newton and to attend his classes.

Truman did not believe in closets. "Truman behaved in the most outrageous way," said Daniel Aaron, Newton's colleague at Smith. "I think he did it partly out of a sense of mischievousness, but it was a kind of camp I'd never seen before. Absolutely extraordinary. Mincing and fluttering and all these kinds of things."

Now in her early thirties, Slim had the rich, successful, creative, passionate husband she had always wanted and who was the center of her life. But the jealousy did not go away—for either of them. Leland was jealous of what Slim might be doing now or in the future. Slim was jealous even of her husband's past. Anytime Leland mentioned one of his lovers from years earlier, she bridled with anger. On their honeymoon, Leland made the mistake of talking about Greta Garbo. Slim greeted that remembrance by throwing a glass of champagne in his face. On another occasion at the 21 Club, Leland started talking about Katharine Hepburn, with whom he had been involved for several years in the 1930s. He had hardly mentioned her name when Slim hit him with a dish of marron glacé.

The Haywards purchased a large house in Manhasset in 1951. They had a grand apartment in New York, but it was the Long Island residence that Slim truly called home. Almost nobody knew more prominent creative people in America than Leland, and on the weekends, they trooped out to Manhasset for dinner.

There was one problem that Slim had not realized. She was close friends with her nearby neighbor Babe Paley, and Babe had weekend dinner parties too. Soon the two hostesses were stepping over each other, with events often overlapping and guests torn between two invitations. The two women came to an agreement: Babe would have her events Saturday evenings, and Slim would do hers Sundays.

Babe's dinners had a degree of formality unusual in weekend dinner parties on Long Island, where for the most part people came to relax. The guests acted with decorum and proper reserve, arriving and leaving on time. They were proud to have been there, appreciative of the Paleys' taste and efforts, but it was not a dinner party most people would have wanted to attend every evening.

As for Slim's events, those one could come back to evening after evening. There was no telling who one would meet and what might happen. Along the lengthy dinner table were an array of wine bottles, most of which would be empty by the time the guests left well into the morning hours. The talk was boisterous and free, Slim and Leland stimulating their guests to be at their most intriguing.

Slim was not in awe of anyone, but she was in awe of Babe Paley. No matter how formally Slim dressed, there was this spur-of-the-moment, windblown quality to her beauty, as if it was a blessing nature had given her. With Babe it was as if she existed out of time and place; her beauty was overwhelming, faultless.

Babe became the closest woman friend Slim had ever had. They went off with their husbands for long trips, and they talked endlessly. Slim saw that Babe was not only shy but had an insecurity that made no sense.

One of the things the two women shared was Truman. He always went for the most luxurious surroundings. No wonder, then, that when he came out to Manhasset for the weekend, he always stayed with Babe. Despite all that Truman told Slim, she had the wise understanding that indiscretion was not the same thing as intimacy, though Truman tried to make it so. "You never confide in me, Big Mama," Truman said, using his nickname for Slim. "That's right, honey, I don't," she said. "Because I don't trust you." It was not just that Truman was an inveterate gossip, but she thought he made things up and much of what he said was not true.

Babe told Truman *everything.* That startled Slim, who told her friend that she was making a mistake. "It's bad news," Slim said. "He's going to rat you out."

"Oh, he wouldn't do that to me," Babe insisted. "Our friendship is deep and binding. We love one another; we *trust* one another."

Slim had begun speaking out with boldness and confidence beyond what she had before. She had always had a ready wit, but now it had an acerbic edge to it, and she lashed out at Leland in savage riffs to which he rarely replied.

Leland, after all, had a lot on his plate. His health was an ongoing concern; in the summer of 1954, he suffered another mysterious episode, crumpling to the floor in the lobby of the Hotel Bel-Air. This time his hospitalization served to divide rather than unite the couple, as Slim was impatient with his illness and eager for his quick recovery.

The producer was also facing a crisis at home. His three children from his first marriage were increasingly troubled—the next year, Leland was suddenly saddled with the care of sixteen-year-old Bridget and fourteen-year-old William when their mother threw them out of the house. Leland was a man who delegated everything not of immediate interest. He was infamous during his years as an agent for not squandering his presence on any client who was not earning major money and for representing people he had never met. He loved his children, but he was not going to let them disarrange his fast-paced life.

Slim had been asked to assume a burden that for the most part should not have been hers or hers alone. The larger problem was that this mothering of teenagers was far from her thing. She loved the glorious, glamorous, glittery surface. That was where she lived. She had no stamina and no taste for this part of life. If Leland expected Slim to pick up the parenting slack, he was sorely mistaken. That, she made it perfectly clear to him, was not part of the bargain.

Leland was working on a movie of Hemingway's short novel *The Old Man and the Sea*. While the book was a huge bestseller, regarded as a classic even in its own time, the tale of gnarled fisherman Santiago battling one-on-one in a boat with a giant marlin was not necessarily the stuff of epic cinematic drama or box-office success, and the writer Peter Viertel was having his own titanic battle working on the screenplay with Hemingway. A worried Leland knew of his wife's special bond with the aging writer, and he asked her to fly down to Cuba to check things out.

Slim had seen the best of Hemingway. Now she saw the worst: a nasty, intemperate man abusing his latest wife, Mary Welsh Hemingway, comparing her invidiously to Slim. The darkly handsome Viertel, a novelist and nonfiction author Slim had met in Los Angeles, was the only bright spot on that misguided visit. Viertel had a well-deserved reputation as a ladies' man, but he was working for Slim's husband. For that reason alone, he should have had the good sense to leave Slim alone. But he didn't—and she was more than willing.

Tired of the tedious duty with Leland's children and days fraught with little but anxiety, Slim was delighted to forget her "real" life back home and romance the handsome screenwriter. She told Viertel that her relationship to her husband "had become a companionate one." Fifty-three-year-old Leland had almost died several times, his life was full of stress, and maybe he wasn't interested in sex so much any longer. But in telling her lover about this, she was stripping her husband of his manhood.

At the end of her life, when Slim was writing her autobiography with the help of three writers, she was reluctant to talk about her affairs. She could not talk about Clark Gable because there were untrue rumors that Gable was her daughter's father, and she was not about to call attention to that. It would have sold books to write about Frank Sinatra, but he was a family friend who dropped into the house at will, and it wasn't the kind of relationship, as short-lived as it was, that a lady publicly discussed. Other relationships were likely so truncated or unpleasant that they did not deserve to be memorialized. So, she settled on writing only about Viertel, with whom she had a romantic tryst that did not make her look too bad. Three days sounded about right, though Viertel claimed the affair had actually lasted for six months.

Slim did not have the husband she once had. Leland had an immensely complicated professional life. He had no time for Slim the way he had when he was wooing her. She needed the attention, the acclaim, the admiration for her beauty . . . and her husband just wasn't giving it to her. "Slim was naturally very bright," said Annette Tapert, who wrote her autobiography. "She was sometimes *too* bright for somebody who wasn't doing anything." As bored as she was, affairs were a way to get attention and fill her nights with intriguing moments.

Leland knew much of what his wife was doing. He was an astute judge of human character, especially in women. One had to assume that on some level, he knew his wife was cheating on him, but she had exhibited a measure of discretion, and he had not felt diminished.

More so than Slim's affairs, an even better distraction from the unpleasant aspects of her life was spending time with Truman. When she was around him, she had no choice but to focus on Truman and his world. And what could be better in February 1958 than going off to Russia with Truman, Cary Grant, and the producer Sam Spiegel, who was showing several of his films to Russian audiences? After ten days in Moscow, Grant and Spiegel flew to Leningrad, but Truman insisted on taking the overnight train, and the intrepid Slim was happy to go along. It was cold and dark on the Red Arrow, but it was an adventure, and she had no complaints.

Some people thought of Truman as this pathetic, untrustworthy little gossip who spent his days doing little but passing on the most savage of tales. It was true there was no worse gossip than Truman, with his trove of ugly stories, but that was only part of him. "He was such a mercurial, many-colored, many-sided person, like a big mirrored ball with light hitting it at different angles," said Slim. "But inside that ball was a really extraordinary mind; he was one of the three or four brightest people I've ever known in my life." He seemed to have read every book worthy of reading and could segue seamlessly from one esoteric subject to the next. It was a delight just to sit there listening to him.

From Leningrad, Truman and Slim flew to Copenhagen. It was a peculiar experience traveling with Truman. He would one day be as famous as any movie star, but that was still years off. For most people, he was simply as strange looking (and acting) a person as they had ever seen. Wherever he went, people turned and looked at this bizarre apparition, having no idea what to make of him.

"No one loves me," Truman said on their last evening in Copenhagen. "I'm a freak. You think I don't know that? I know how difficult it is for people to adjust to what I look like and how I sound when they first see me. It's one of the reasons I'm so outrageous. I'm an *object*. I'm a *centerpiece*, not a figure of love, and I miss that. There's not an awful lot to love."

After years of marriage to the powerful and influential Leland and a lifetime as the most magnetic beauty in any room, Slim had gotten so full of her sense of power and position that she thought she could say and do almost anything. But when she decided in a fit of pique and frustration that she wanted to tell Leland of her affairs, her friend Leonora Hornblow tried to talk her out of doing such a foolish thing. But Slim did not listen.

Why did she do it? It wasn't out of a sense of guilt. Guilt wasn't one of her emotions. Hornblow thought Slim spoke out of sheer egotism. "She was so vain she wanted him to know how irresistible she was," Hornblow said. Slim was, after all, reaching the watershed age of forty. She was very aware of that, and she feared her famed beauty was fading.

Leland turned pale. He got up and left the room, saying nothing. But his actions could not have spoken louder. For years, he had tolerated her put-downs and sharp tongue as part of the price of marriage. He'd stayed faithful to her as well. But he could not stand this.

As far as Slim was concerned, everything was just fine. She'd said her piece, and in October 1958, she was excited about her upcoming trip to Munich with her husband, who was negotiating with Baroness Maria von Trapp for her life rights to what would become the hit musical (and later movie) *The Sound of Music*. As Slim was planning the trip, Lauren Bacall called to ask if Slim could leave early and meet her in Madrid. A year previously, Bacall's husband, Humphrey Bogart, had died, and this seemed like the kind of thing a friend should do for the recently widowed actress. Leland had no objections to Slim's early departure; he would meet her in Europe in a few weeks.

Just before Slim set off, Babe called and asked for a favor too. The first few days that Slim would be away in Europe, Babe's friend Pamela Churchill was going to be in town staying with the Paleys in their Manhattan apartment. Would Slim mind if one evening Leland escorted the British woman to a Broadway play?

Like everyone else, Slim knew Pamela Churchill's reputation. Since the early 1940s, when Pamela was married to Prime Minister Winston Churchill's son, Randolph, she had had a staggering array of affairs. Although not as beautiful as Babe or Slim and far shorter,

Pamela had luminous skin that looked like it had been nurtured in the London fog, and she possessed a manner that men found irresistible. In the years that followed her first marriage, she had dated and been "kept" by some of the most powerful men in the world, but her curse was that none of them wanted to marry her. So, despite Slim's jealousies and suspicion, what was the big deal if Leland sat for a couple of hours next to Mrs. Churchill in a Manhattan theater?

After all, it was unthinkable that Leland would leave her for this little woman who men passed around like a party treat.

Several months later, in February 1959, shortly after Slim returned to New York after a week at the Main Chance health spa in Arizona, Leland told her they were going to a dinner party at the apartment in Carlton House, where Pamela was staying. Upon arrival at Pamela's place, the first thing Slim noticed were dozens of Sterling Silver hybrid roses on every free surface—the same flowers her husband always sent her. During the evening, Pamela exhibited a strangely proprietary air toward Slim's husband; when she asked Leland to get the ice bucket, he jumped up at her command and knew just where to find it, as if he had gone for it many times.

Slim had her dalliances too, of course, and it was no big deal if Leland had his—though it was discouraging that he couldn't do it with someone better. Slim did not see how her behavior might have driven her husband toward Pamela.

Leland had been going through a string of failures in his business life that certainly hadn't helped the marriage either, but things seemed to be turning around on the work front. Later that year, with the success of the Broadway musical *Gypsy*, which opened in May 1959, her husband was back on top, and money was falling on them like a spring rain. These were good signs. All it would take to bring her husband back into the fold was to get him off alone on a European vacation.

Leland agreed that they would spend a few days in Paris and Madrid and then a whole month in an apartment in Venice at the Gritti Palace. A few days before they set out on what was to be in essence a second honeymoon, Leland said he had business to finish and she should head out alone. That hadn't been the idea, but Slim flew to Paris.

Truman was having lunch at a Manhattan restaurant when he saw Leland and Pamela at another table. Pamela had such a reputation that wives might be advised to lock up their husbands when the British siren approached the edge of town. However, this was neither breakfast nor dinner, but merely a benign midday meal. In all innocence—a rare status for Truman—he went up to the couple and kiddingly said he was going to write a tell-all note to Slim. "As a matter of fact, with my usual gaucherie, I *did* write Slim asking if she knew her husband was running around with the notorious Mrs. C," Truman said. His joke, however guilelessly made, proved alarmingly prescient.

After a few days in Paris, Slim went on to Madrid to await her husband. At her hotel was a message from Leland saying he would be delayed even longer, for most of another week. When Leland finally arrived in Madrid, he had no time for white roses or pleasantries. "I think we should have a talk," he said. "I think we should take a sabbatical from one another for a few weeks."

Leland wasn't good in ending bad things, whether a play, a movie, or a marriage, and he couldn't say straight out that their marriage was all over. But Slim knew it was. As soon as her husband left, she began crying uncontrollably.

Slim sailed away on the producer Spiegel's yacht and managed a short affair with an available Spaniard, but nothing could dull the pain. When after a few months Slim flew back to New York, she headed out to the home in Manhasset. Pamela had already been out to the house, placing red stickers on the items of furniture she wanted in the divorce settlement.

6

The Notorious Mrs. C

NOTHING ENLIVENED TRUMAN'S days better than a delicious scandal. As much as he felt sorry for Slim losing Leland, it was all wonderfully divisive and exciting. Everyone Truman knew took stations on either side of the grand social battlefield. Babe and her sister Minnie vowed to fight eternally against "that bitch" Pamela, while Babe's other sister, Betsey, stood in support of the soon-to-be new Mrs. Hayward (despite the fact that Pamela had slept with her husband, Jock Whitney, during World War II). Truman was convinced Betsey took Pamela's side simply because she was relieved that she no longer had to fear that the British seductress would come again for her husband.

There was hardly anyone in Truman's social world as notorious as Pamela, and that made her even more intriguing. Truman was going to anoint her a swan—a black swan, perhaps, but a swan nonetheless. Truman thought about sex the way Pamela did. It had very little to do with morality at all. Although Truman was not a big fan of one-night stands, sex was something one did as often as possible with any available partner or partners. Pamela was a little different. She did it only if it might advance her position in the world.

Pamela was clearly the kind of character Truman wanted in *Answered Prayers*. Just chronicling her affairs would have filled the pages of a book. "We spent a lot of time on yachts together," said Truman. "Anybody becomes a confidant on a yacht cruise, and I think I've lived through every screw she ever had in her life. Believe me, that's an Arabian Nights tale of a thousand and twelve! She's interesting because she has fantastic taste and she knows everything about everything, but she has absolutely no intellectual capacities at all. She's some sort of marvelous primitive. I don't think she's ever read a book, or even a newspaper, except for the gossip column. I guess it's because she comes from one of the oldest families in England, the Digbys, and they figured they didn't have to learn to read or write."

Pamela was brought up in the countryside of southwestern England, a region that was like a landscape painting by John Constable. Lord and Lady Digby lived in Dorset in a grand manor house overseen by twenty servants.

During the Great War, Pamela's father exemplified the highest ideals of the British aristocracy. The youngest commander of the Coldstream Guards, the lean officer led his soldiers into battle. He was twice wounded, and the French honored him with the Croix de Guerre. Lord Digby had thickened since his youth. The hefty gentleman might have lost some of his weight if he had lifted a hoe once in a while, but that was decidedly beneath him. He appeared almost dotty at times as he roamed Minterne, the 1,500-acre family estate, with a box of his beloved chocolates under his arms.

Lady Digby was a handsome, stately woman perfectly fitted to be married to the eleventh Baron Digby. For Pamela, Lady Digby sought nothing less than what she had achieved: marriage to a rich, high-born gentleman. Pamela was the oldest child, but the rules of primogeniture laid out that her younger brother would inherit the estate and the title. If Pamela did not find a worthy husband, there were nothing but dispiriting possibilities out there—from tutoring positions to becoming the aging spinster aunt.

Upper-class British women were not educated so much as groomed. She must not learn so much that she became dissatisfied and opinionated, interjecting herself into manly conversations that were none of her business.

There appeared to be no danger of that with Pamela. When it was time for her and her younger sister, Sheila, to go to boarding school, her parents chose Downham, a school in Hertfordshire that had a reputation as a finishing school rather than for its academics. Pamela felt right at home. She was social and outgoing and had no interest in bookish things.

When Pamela went up in the hills to wander with her dogs, she dreamed of what might be. She told herself, "When I am grown up, I will leave this place and I will live in a city." But if she were to leave the country and make her own way in the world, it was not going to be on the strength of her looks. Pamela was so plump that her face was like a round bowl. When people wanted to praise her looks, it was to her reddish-brown hair and her lily-white, luminous skin they turned rather than to her figure.

Pamela's next major activity was to make her debut and to be presented before the king and queen. She managed the elaborate curtsey before the monarchs, but she was less than a success with the weeks of balls and parties that were the essence of a deb's life. Although her parents had provided her a stable of the finest ponies, they were unwilling to spring for even one of the splendid gowns that many of the other debs wore.

If Pamela had been thin, she might have looked less dowdy in her inexpensive dresses. She dealt with her insecurities by projecting an aggressive, outgoing manner that only made people move farther away from her. Some men thought she may have been signaling sexual availability, but that didn't mean they were interested. There is no cruelty like teenage cruelty, and a number of the young women shunned Pamela. One of her few friends was Kathleen Kennedy, the daughter of the American ambassador. No matter how forlorn Pamela felt, she kept on smiling . . . though a friend recalls Pamela breaking down in tears after one party.

After the disappointment of her debut, Pamela might have headed back to the family estate in Dorset and given up on London. But no way was she going to retreat into a narrow provincial life. At whatever cost, she was going to make it in the Big City.

It became obvious to Pamela that she needed a mentor to lead her where she wanted to go, and Olive Baillie fulfilled that role exquisitely. The Anglo-American heiress was married to a member of Parliament. Thanks to Baillie's fortune, the couple lived extravagant lives. Their gem was the medieval Leeds Castle in Kent, where on weekends, Lady Baillie invited an eclectic group of politicians, artists, and writers to stay. She took a special concern with young Pamela, who was delighted to be spending time with accomplished figures twice her age.

For the first time since she began riding horses, Pamela saw something she really wanted to learn. She saw how Baillie had created an elaborate social world, with herself at the glittery center. Leeds Castle was the stage where her chosen actors played out their roles. Baillie liked talkers and had little room for conversational wallflowers. Each weekend was a new adventure, one in which no one quite knew where things would go. It showed that with money, taste, and social daring, one could create a whole world.

Lady Baillie had lovers. That was part of her model too, and many of the guests changed partners and beds. Although still a teenager, Pamela was coming to understand that bourgeois morality was for the unadventurous—and she decidedly wasn't that.

Pamela realized that sex could be a useful device for getting what she wanted. She wasn't beautiful, but she was young, and that was often enough—especially when she was so adept at projecting sensuality. With her torpedo bosoms and ample derriere, her nickname was "the dairy maid," and there was ample speculation over whether the dairy maid delivered. Maybe she was far from an intellectual, but she had lived the social life of the British country gentry, and she could talk with almost anyone worth talking to, keeping the conversations bouncing animatedly along.

Within a short time, Pamela metamorphosed from an obvious provincial into a sophisticated, quick-spoken woman who seemed far older than her years. She dressed better and, exuding a certain sexuality, appeared far more attractive.

Pamela began the first of her affairs with older married men. They tended to be more thankful than men her own age, had far more to talk about, and had the money to be generous. Pamela had no qualms about taking gifts and cash from men. If they wanted to give it to her, why not?

It was all terribly amusing, but in the quest for a husband, it was not great to be viewed as worldly far beyond her nineteen years with a dance card full of lovers. Some of her contemporaries were already married, but there was no gentleman asking her to be his wife. When Germany invaded Poland and World War II began on September 1, 1939, the weekend parties at Leeds Castle ended, and with them the easy frivolity that had propelled Pamela's life. She got a small apartment in London and a job as a French translator.

One evening when Pamela had hardly settled down in her new life, she received a phone call from Randolph Churchill. Everyone knew of his father, Sir Winston Churchill, who for years had been preaching the evil menace of Hitler's Germany to a nation that for the most part had not been listening.

Randolph was a subaltern in the British army on leave in the capital. He was infatuated with the actress Laura Long. She was not available, and he was looking for a night's entertainment. A mutual friend, Mary Dunn, suggested he call Pamela. Dunn described her as a "red-headed tart." He hadn't expected Greta Garbo or Marlene Dietrich. A red-headed tart was worth a call.

"What do you look like?" Randolph asked Pamela on the phone, subtlety not being one of his virtues.

"Red-headed and rather fat, but Mummy says that puppy fat disappears," Pamela said. That was Randolph's version years later, and it may be a twisted, disgruntled memory, but it sounds about right.

When a salesperson isn't sure she has the top-grade product, it's often best to undersell.

Randolph was as fat as Pamela, larded down with booze and rich eating, but as a man his weight was unworthy of comment. His very first evening alone with the "red-headed tart," he asked Pamela to marry him. The tall officer was impressive in bite-sized doses, and she said yes. These were not star-crossed Shakespearean lovers come together in the darkness of war. Randolph told a friend in Pamela's presence he was marrying her because he feared he would die in the war and wanted to leave a male heir. As far as Randolph was concerned, Pamela was little better than a broodmare.

Pamela knew little about her husband-to-be, and her agreement to marry him was even more peculiar than his. Up to that point, she had devoted her life and ambition to marrying the proper man. No matron on the verge of spinsterhood, she was still a teenager and did not have to jump impetuously into this marriage. It had little to do with what most people called love. But she soon realized that this was not just a marriage to Randolph but a marriage into one of Britain's greatest families. The high point of the wedding at St. John's on October 4, 1939, was the presence of Randolph's father, the newly named First Lord of the Admiralty.

Randolph had gotten it into his swollen head that he was going to die in the war. In the next months the newlyweds moved from posting to posting as Randolph waited for a call to combat that did not come. That made him even more irritable. This itinerant, rootless life would have been difficult even in the flush of first love, but there was none of that. Almost any other groom would have waited a decent interval before resuming his womanizing, but Randolph was not about to give up any of his pleasures.

Displaying fortitude and patience, Pamela tried to make the most of her troubled marriage. When she became pregnant early in 1940 and Randolph went off to training camp, she moved in with her in-laws at Admiralty House, spending weekends with them at their Chequers estate. No question that it was socially advantageous to be spending time with the British politician on the verge of leading his nation in the greatest struggle of the twentieth century, but it was far more than that. The Churchills treated her in the intimate, sensitive way that her parents had not.

Winston liked having a pretty young woman around him, but beyond that, Pamela was special because she was a listener. That was no small matter. Other people pretended to listen, but often their minds wandered, or they sat figuring out what they would say in response. Pamela truly focused on the person before her with all of her attention, drawing the speaker out—though Winston needed no incentive to tell his many tales.

That spring the Germans invaded France, and Pamela's father-in-law, Winston Churchill, became prime minister. Even as Nazi bombs rained down in the London night, personal life continued.

Sometimes a pregnancy brings a troubled marriage together, but not this time. Randolph was incapable of being emotionally solicitous of anyone beyond himself. When Pamela gave birth in a four-poster bed at Chequers on October 10, 1940, Randolph was off in the arms of one of his lovers. But at least he had the son he had long desired.

Pamela lost the weight she had gained during her pregnancy and transformed herself into a stunningly attractive woman. On her newly svelte body, her ample bosom appeared even more pronounced. Seeing no reason to tell her in-laws that she planned to divorce their son, she spent the weekends with the Churchills, often dining with world leaders and top British officials.

German planes unloaded their deadly cargo anyplace at any time. No one in the great city was free of the threat of death from the sky. Not hunkering down in fear, Pamela was exhilarated by the danger. Feeling as alive and free as she had ever been, she found these years "the most exciting time in my entire life."

Most of the upper-class women of Pamela's generation were brought up like her. Poorly educated, they were set up to have the same lives their mothers had. But the war thrust them into whole new worlds. Many of them went to work in factories and hospitals. Legs that had known silk stockings now wore wool socks. Whereas before they had gone to the beauty parlor for the latest styles, they now pulled their hair back in Victory Rolls. It was next to impossible to get new lipstick, so they melted down the old. And forget mascara. Shoe polish would do. They lost the narrow snobbishness they had thought so chic and had become far more complex and interesting than they ever would have been without the war. As for Pamela, the war merely elevated her concern for the things she had always cared about.

Pamela dressed provocatively and went out most evenings. It was only a matter of time, and probably not much of that, before she would have had a memorable affair. There were men everywhere, her possibilities endless.

In mid-April, Pamela attended a dinner at the Dorchester Hotel for Adele Astaire, who had begun her life dancing with her brother, Fred, and was now married to Lord Charles Cavendish. Pamela was aware enough of political realities to know that one of the other guests, W. Averell Harriman, the head of the lend-lease program, "was the most important American in London."

Without a successful lend-lease program bringing a vast armada of ships, weapons, and foodstuffs across the Atlantic, Great Britain would almost certainly not be able to sustain its fight against Nazi Germany. Averell was a peculiar choice for this crucial mission. When in the post–Civil War period, his father, Edward Henry "E. H." Harriman, built the Union Pacific into a great rail line, he was vilified as a robber baron. His son was a Yale gentleman, a generation removed from his father's entrepreneurial zeal and energy. Although Averell aspired to become a politician, his persona was as animated and exciting as an undertaker. An unlikely Democrat, President Roosevelt was unwilling to give Averell a powerful role in the New Deal. Undeterred, he pushed himself forward to be given this important position.

As soon as the forty-nine-year-old official arrived in Britain in March 1941, Averell was hurried out to Chequers to meet the prime minister. Averell was so important to the British war efforts that Winston invited him out each weekend, where the American enjoyed the intimate family-like atmosphere. It was on one of those occasions that the lend-lease representative probably met Pamela.

This dinner at the Dorchester was almost certainly the first time Pamela spent much time with Averell. Even if he had been ugly beyond measure, the important American official would have been worthy of interest. But Pamela said later that she found him the most beautiful man she had ever seen. Most twenty-year-olds would not have swooned over a man in late middle age, but Pamela had a thing about far older men. It wasn't just that she was looking for a father figure. She truly liked men that her contemporaries would have side-stepped as elderly. The fact that he was married was of no more consequence to her than whether he liked jam on his crumpets. It was war, and people did what they wanted with each other whenever they wanted to do it.

With her astute understanding of the male psyche, Pamela knew precisely what she was doing that evening. Although she never dropped her demure veneer, she more than Averell instigated their relationship. It was a bold and cunning move. Pamela was right when she said the affair "could have gone the other way," proving overwhelmingly destructive.

Winston adored his only son. He didn't forgive Randolph his faults—he didn't see them. What was he likely to think if he learned his beloved daughter-in-law was having an affair with Averell Harriman? The prime minister might keep it quiet, though he would likely never think of Averell or Pamela the same way again. It was also possible that Winston would be so angry that he no longer could work effectively with the lend-lease representative. Even if the prime minister was willing to condone the affair for the sake of the war effort, there was the possibility of a scandal that would light up newspapers on both sides of the Atlantic.

When the air raid drills and the German bombers were heard in the London sky that evening, Pamela accepted Averell's invitation to join him in his ground-floor suite. By that act, Pamela made it clear what she was willing to do. It was up to Averell. Over the years he had indulged in all kinds of affairs. As long as he was quiet about it, his wife said nothing. But this was different. Having an affair with Churchill's daughter-in-law would be a provocative and dangerous business, capable of setting back his all-important task. But Averell had an heir's sense of entitlement and Pamela had set it up brilliantly. If he wanted to spend the night with this gorgeous young thing, he was going to do it.

Pamela soon proved to be highly useful to Averell. Despite his intimate contact with the British leaders, he understood little about the power dynamics of London and the people key to his mission. Pamela not only knew them personally, but she had shrewd insights that no one in the American embassy could possibly match. In this relationship, Averell was the one who had the learning to do, with Pamela as his savvy teacher.

Within a few weeks, Averell and Pamela moved out of the Dorchester into a splendid Grosvenor Square apartment where the American ambassador also lived. Averell's twenty-three-year-old daughter, Kathleen, came to live with her father. The two young women bonded like sisters, Kathleen showing no apparent discomposure that her father was sleeping with her new friend.

With Averell's money and access to American food supplies, Pamela gave dinner parties like practically no one else in London, the room full of ranking officers, high officials, and important visitors. The courses kept coming, one after another. Where else could one have salmon and oysters and thick steaks, the kind of food the average rationed British citizen did not see on her dinner plate until after the war?

No question about it, this war was fun if you were in the right place. There was, however, a slight glitch when Randolph came home on leave, infuriated that he had been cuckolded by a man he had met in Egypt and considered a friend. He saved most of his anger not for the wife he despised or for Averell, who was bedding his wife, but for his parents, whom he believed had promoted the affair by inviting the adulterous couple to Chequers for weekends.

Pamela had long before learned to tiptoe around her husband's rage. Instead of risking his pulling down the temple by going public, she agreed she would move out of her wonderful apartment and limit the amount of time she spent with Randolph's parents. She had another reason for changing her residence. Averell's wife, Marie, had learned of the affair. She was having her own relationship with the bandleader Eddy Duchin, but she feared her husband's newest affair would rise so high into the public consciousness as to ruin her reputation as well as her husband's.

Averell had a rich man's stinginess. He could have paid for every dinner he ever ate, but he turned the business of not picking up checks into performance art. Thus, it was astounding that this parsimonious multimillionaire set Pamela up in a lovely apartment and started paying her £3,000 a year ($178,000 today), a rich stipend that continued years after their affair ended.

With a free apartment and ample money, Pamela had everything she needed to live the life she thought was her right and privilege. But there was a downside to this game as well. A man who had an elaborate series of lovers was generally esteemed, but a woman doing the same thing was shameless. Pamela thought she had gotten away with her affairs, but men were more vicious gossips than women, and they savaged Pamela mercilessly.

The legendary polo player Tommy Hitchcock Jr. had come to London in the army air corps. He heard the rumors about Averell bedding Pamela. Tommy called his nephew, who was also a pilot, and asked if the story was true.

"I don't really know, but I wouldn't be surprised," the man said.

"Why not?" Tommy asked.

"Let's just say if she had as many pricks sticking out of her as have been stuck into her, she'd be a porcupine."

The story made the rounds of the clubs and the bars. The tale traveled even further. Truman appropriated the line for the narrator of "Unspoiled Monsters," one of the chapters of his novel *Answered Prayers*.

With his lifestyle, Truman was hardly one to condemn Pamela's promiscuity. He saw sex as the place where humans were at their most intimate and vulnerable. As an author, that endlessly fascinated him.

When Truman arrived in Paris for the first time in the summer of 1948, he was living a bohemian life far from the world of the social elite. To him, the city was so exciting, it was "like living inside an electric bulb." Beyond that, everything was cheap, and he kept his hotel room so full of flowers it was like a garden. He learned to ride a scooter and drove around Paris like any other young Parisian. He had dinner with the gay French writer André Gide and vowed that he had sex with another writer, Albert Camus.

Truman arrived in Paris to wondrous acclaim. His novel, *Other Voices, Other Rooms*, had been published in January to bestselling success. Like most first novels, *Other Voices, Other Rooms* had a large autobiographical element. It was his life in Monroeville, peopled by Southern grotesques and blown up into something full of menace and shadow and poetic truths. In one of the first novels with openly gay characters, the Truman-like main character Joel comes to terms with his sexuality in part by talking to the transvestite Randolph.

The characters offended a number of establishment critics, but it was impossible to deny that Truman had the most stunning powers of observation and a richly lyrical style. Even the largely unimpressed *New York Times* reviewer admitted that the twenty-three-year-old novelist was "precocious, self-confident and genuinely gifted." Despite the prevailing idea that Truman was carried forward on the shoulders of adoring critics, *Other Voices, Other Rooms*, like much of his work, received mixed reviews.

The author photo on the back jacket generated almost as much attention as the book. In the provocative picture, Truman lies back languidly with a come-hither look. Truman's fame traveled as far as Paris, where Denham Fouts spotted the stunning book jacket photo. When Denham saw Truman's photo, he sent him a blank check with one word written on it: "Come." The story may not have been true, but it was a good story that enhanced Truman's provocative reputation, and when he arrived in Paris, he went to see Denham.

In certain circles, Denham was something of a legend. A beautiful young man born and raised in an aristocratic family in Florida, he decided early on that work was for the ugly. He would live well, based on the kindness of strangers. And so he did, moving from barons to princes to all kinds of upscale Europeans. It was a glamorous but cynical life, and by the time Truman met the thirty-four-year-old Denham, he was a sour, drug-addled shadow of his glory years.

Truman was both fascinated and frightened by Denham. After being thrown out of his Paris apartment, Denham died later that year in a Roman pension. When Truman wrote *Answered Prayers*, he could have made the narrator a character like himself. Instead, he created P. B. Jones, a shrewd hustler like Denham and precisely his age at his death.

Early the next year back in New York, Truman met thirty-four-year-old Jack Dunphy at the party the writer Leo Lerman held every Sunday evening in his Manhattan apartment. Jack became the one sustained love of Truman's life, an intimate friend, loyal and devoted beyond measure. Jack had chiseled, manly good looks fit for a cowboy dancer in *Oklahoma!*, which is precisely what he was in the original 1943 Broadway production. His wife, Joan McCracken, was one of the stars. When Jack was called into to the service during the war, his wife was unfaithful and their marriage ended.

Jack was a man of absolute loyalty, and this betrayal was devastating to him beyond measure. He wanted to be a writer, not an actor, and his grief was assuaged somewhat by the publication of his first novel, *John Fury*, set in the Irish slums of Philadelphia where Jack grew up. Although the book did not have the stylistic originality of *Other Voices, Other Rooms*, it received fine reviews and suggested that Jack might have a successful literary career ahead of him.

Jack said that if his ex-wife had not cheated and he had stayed married, he never would have slept with a man. That was probably true, but he fell hard and fast for Truman. Despite his attraction, Jack felt a certain trepidation about getting involved with the bestselling author. Success had turned Jack's wife into a preening, self-involved caricature of herself, and he knew Truman might head down that same glittery, ultimately self-destructive pathway.

Jack and Truman were so different. Jack was a loner. He couldn't stand parties and interminable dinners. Truman never saw a party invitation he cast aside. Jack did not trust people and thought many of Truman's acquaintances were there to take advantage of him. Truman didn't care. He was having a wild time.

The idea that two ambitious writers could happily live together was a stretch, whatever their sexes. But in these early years, the love and affection between Jack and Truman was a halo over their lives.

Pamela was far more circumspect than her critics imagined. There was nothing Byronic about her, no out-of-control, crazed romances, no mindless trysts with stable boys. She appraised men the way a gemologist evaluated diamonds, making a close examination to determine their precise worth.

Only men of power and substance intrigued her. There was the immensely rich Jock Whitney, only recently married to one of the Cushing sisters. As a champion polo player, Jock was known for riding his pony recklessly against his opponents. Jock was just as daring off the field of play. In the war, he served in the Office of Strategic Services (OSS), the precursor to the CIA. When he was captured in France, he jumped off a prisoner train and made his way back to the Allied lines. A far more generous man than Averell, Jock was so taken by Pamela that he started sending her regular stipends.

Then there was General Frederick Anderson Jr., chief of the Eighth Air Force's Bomber Command, whose wife and two children were back in Washington. There was also likely the British air chief marshal Sir Charles Portal, who had a wife and two daughters and wrote Pamela love letters.

Pamela was savvy enough about the world of power to be a worthy conversational partner with almost anyone. Not only was she a superb listener, but she remembered what she heard and knowingly evaluated its importance. That was one of the primary reasons Churchill often still called on Pamela, finding her a useful source unlike anyone else.

Pamela's affair with Averell had cooled to warm ashes by the time he left London in October 1943 to become ambassador to the Soviet Union. He did not have the gumption to tell her until just before he left, and though she knew he would never marry her, she considered it "a big, big blow."

The world of men that was her universe was out there as always, and within two months Pamela had found her next important lover, the CBS radio broadcaster Edward R. Murrow.

Pamela had learned long before that emotional intimacies were seductive. She befriended the handsome thirty-five-year-old journalist with poignant tales of how much Harriman's leaving had hurt her. These made her vulnerable and inviting, and soon they were in each other's arms.

Murrow was the most admired reporter in London. During the Battle of Britain, his stark, compelling reportage convinced many Americans that Great Britain must not be left to die alone.

Frequently Pamela accompanied Murrow in the middle of the night to Broadcast House and sat there listening as his stunning word pictures evoked the war for Americans. When the light went off, he was far from the personable radio personality known by his listeners. Often withdrawn and depressed, he wasn't part of the sparkling wartime nightlife that many of the other correspondents enjoyed. His wife, Janet, was with him in England, and until Pamela he had not been involved with other women.

Of all Pamela's lovers, there was nobody like Murrow. He was not a rich heir. His parents had been dirt-poor farmers, and he had never forgotten his upbringing. When the Nazis were defeated and peace finally won, he hoped to see a more equitable society. Ed saw in Pamela precisely what he thought was wrong with the British elite. "You're spoiled," he told her. "Everything is easy for you. You were too much adored at too tender an age, and you don't understand what real life is."

Pamela's affair with Ed continued fitfully onward, even after Janet became pregnant and gave birth to a son, Casey. Pamela was obsessed with Ed. She became the aggressor, unable to countenance the idea that he might choose to live without her. Emotionally out of control in a way she had never been over any other man, she flew to New York to try to reignite their romance, but it was all over for Murrow.

Ed had a new career at CBS News in New York and a renewed family life, but what did Pamela have? The glorious excitement of the war was over. So was her great love of those years. She had nobody, and she was nothing without a man.

"In my life, I have always lived with men, for men, through men," Pamela said. She could not go a week without a man without feeling diminished. It wasn't that she was obsessed with sex, but her relationships with men defined her. It was a frightening way to be. She needed someone new, and she needed him soon, and she needed him desperately.

People assumed that with all her lovers, Pamela was a woman of wanton sexuality who gave men who shared her bed pleasures they could not find anywhere else. That simply wasn't true. She told several people that she didn't particularly like sex. It was little more than an obligation, a sweaty ritual that she could not avoid.

When Pamela was in New York, she took up with Stanley Mortimer, whose estranged wife, Babe, was on her way to becoming Mrs.

Bill Paley. Stanley was handsome enough, though his money was not of the magnitude that intrigued Pamela, and their relationship did not last very long. That was just fine, because Averell had come back to London as the new ambassador, giving Pamela a reason to return to the British capital. Pamela was hardly settled into her new routine when President Harry Truman called Averell back to Washington to become secretary of commerce. He was gone, but his annual stipend, which allowed her to live a life of luxury, continued until 1950.

Pamela was once again without a man. London was no longer the place for her. The Labour government was hostile to a stratified society in which people like Pamela sat at the top. She thought she deserved a full measure of credit for bringing American and British leaders together during the war; her critics had a less charitable opinion of her actions.

Pamela decided that Paris would be her new home. In the aftermath of the war, aristocratic Parisians and other wealthy Frenchmen asserted themselves anew in a vibrant social world devoted to pleasure in all its forms. In such a world, Pamela was a natural. Her son was no impediment to Pamela's new life. Little Winston stayed in London to be brought up largely by his nanny.

In Paris, Pamela attended the grandest social events. One evening she was a guest at the Grand Prix Ball, an annual event for the highest social circle. The host was thirty-six-year-old Aly Salomone Khan, whose immensely wealthy father was the spiritual leader of Ismaili Muslims in India and Pakistan. The diminutive, swarthy playboy prince had been brought up in manner and style to be indistinguishable from a member of the British upper class. He was incredibly generous, bankrolling the ball and giving the lady guests Hermès scarfs and perfume, but to some of the guests he was still a "wog."

Aly got even by sleeping with the wives and women of the anointed. He used a technique he called "Imsak," which allowed him to make love all night long; if he had not had a cent, his bed would probably not have been empty. He went from rose to rose, pollinating away, never stopping at one flower for long.

The ball was an occasion for Aly to seek his newest conquest, and that evening it was Pamela. She was a little plump for his taste, with the beginnings of a double chin, but there was something uniquely striking about her.

7

A Tub of Butter

PAMELA COULD NOT have lived for so many years the way she did without having an astute understanding of what her lover was thinking. In that respect, it was good for her that so many men were unable or unwilling to hide their feelings. A character of endless whims, her paramour Aly could turn from a lover in an instant.

When Pamela flew with Aly on his two-engine plane to his ten-bedroom estate on the French Riviera, she assumed everything was fine. And so it was when Pamela arrived for what was supposed to be a lengthy stay.

When Aly saw a sex goddess on the screen, his reaction was to wonder how he could have her. Thus, when Rita Hayworth arrived at Hôtel du Cap down the road in Antibes, seeking to reconcile with her husband, Orson Welles, Aly had other ideas. With Pamela camped out at his estate, Aly flew off to Spain with the actress, who he would marry the following year. Pamela usually knew when to say goodbye, but she was not about to leave and make it easy for this man who dismissed her without a thought.

Aly was so solicitous of his guests that everything continued the same way whether he was there or not, including the lunch buffet, with its extravagant mix of foods. Pamela could not sit in her room bemoaning her fate. However melancholy she felt, she had to eat, and she walked out on the balcony overlooking the Mediterranean where the other guests sat having lunch. As she did so, a motor launch pulled up to the dock and two men got out.

Pamela was a connoisseur of the male form, taking pleasure in looking at attractive men, but she had rarely seen a man like the one walking up the stairs. He was so handsome that it was natural to assume he used his looks to make his living. He could have been an actor or one of the Roman gigolos who sidled up to American tourists on Via Veneto. That was the kind of dark, dangerous beauty he had.

"My name is Gianni Agnelli," he said. The twenty-seven-year-old heir to the Fiat auto fortune was a year younger than Pamela. Unlike many inheritors who hunkered down within their wealth, Gianni lived a life of endless daring. Of all Pamela's previous lovers, the one he most resembled was the intrepid Jock Whitney. Shortly before his grandfather Giovanni died in 1945, the Fiat founder told Gianni that before he took over the reins of the company, he should enjoy himself, and he was doing just that.

Gianni had been an officer in the Italian army during the war. He served part of that time in Russia, where he was wounded twice and lost a finger to frostbite. He now drove the roads of Italy and France in his sports car as if in a road race, heedless of any laws. On the Riviera, he was famous for jumping out of a helicopter and swimming ashore to Hôtel du Cap. It was the most dramatic of entrances, foolhardy and challenging, and nobody ever forgot him.

The Fiat heir was not a man who waited when he wanted something. He had hardly met Pamela before he invited her to sail with him to Capri. As intriguing as the invitation was, she felt it best to have a friend with her. Her choice was Gloria von Fürstenberg, a member of the floating world of the postwar international set. This was not a society that cared much about the backgrounds of those they associated with, so long as they had a commodity of value: beauty, wealth, or power. Gloria had beauty, and as soon as she married her fiancé, Loel Guinness, she would have wealth as well.

But Gloria's son came down with measles, and at the last minute she could not join the party. So Pamela dumped young Winston off on a friend and set off alone on Gianni's sailboat, the *Tomahawk*, thus beginning the strangest and most emotionally complicated of her many affairs. In her cabin that first night, a glass fell, cutting her face, an omen if ever there was one.

Pamela was used to luxurious circumstances, but even for her, Gianni's life was unique. His massive apartment in Rome was part of an ancient palace, while Villar Perosa, the family estate outside Turin, was a magnificent residence. It wasn't just the sheer size or opulence of these homes that was so special but rather the ornately eclectic style, honed over years of wealth and investment. It was the family signature.

Gianni would one day be revered as the greatest businessman in Europe. He had an astute understanding that one of the keys to power was personal relationships at the highest level. That was one of the reasons he was attracted to Pamela. Sleeping with a gorgeous woman who had been Winston Churchill's daughter-in-law was, as he put it, "not bad." She had listened and learned, and she had connections and insight useful to him that he would not get easily anywhere else.

The affair wasn't about love. "You fall in love at twenty," Gianni said. "After that, only waitresses fall in love." Like the rest of his play-boy friends, he liked to bed the most beautiful women—actresses, models, starlets, luscious bimbos—and move on briskly to the next. He had the life he believed every man wanted, and he wasn't going to change for anyone. And he never did. "Everybody's a playboy," he said. "Everybody tries to be one, some manage it, others don't."

Gianni did not want Pamela to spend much time anywhere near the Fiat headquarters in Turin. His sisters were endlessly protective of their beloved brother, and in Pamela they sensed a predator come to devour what was not hers. Her crime was wanting to marry Gianni and be a good wife.

The Agnelli sisters were not the only ones who were skeptical. Gianni's carousing buddies were brutal in their assessments of women, and they would have found it a cause for endless amusement if he had married this divorced Protestant who carried with her dual baggage of a child and a discolored reputation. She simply wasn't the kind of woman one married. "Pamela's a geisha girl who made every man happy," said Truman, who met Pamela years later when she was living in New York City. "They just didn't want to marry her."

Gianni enjoyed his moments with Pamela, but he didn't really live with her. He flitted in and out in the wild rush of his life. Pamela had a sophisticated awareness about men and their ways, and she surely understood her position in her lover's life. And yet for five years, against the most extraordinary odds, Pamela worked to draw Gianni to the altar. She did so in part by providing invaluable services to him. She became in effect his majordomo, managing the part of his life he wanted managed. He was used to hanging out with a pleasure-obsessed, coke-sniffing set whose primary attributes were their looks and their money. She brought together eclectic, sophisticated groups of worldly guests, and he valued her for it.

But it wasn't just high-minded pursuits they shared. No one topped Gianni in his devotion to gossip. Pamela had long been adept at harvesting such material, and she frequently called her lover to tell him the latest and darkest secrets of the most feted people in the world. He loved it.

In his way, Gianni treated Pamela spectacularly well. For two years he rented Château de la Garoupe on the French Riviera for her, and then he purchased La Leopolda, the most extraordinary estate on the entire French coast. When Pamela wasn't down on the Mediterranean coast, he provided her with a luxurious apartment in Paris and all kinds of gifts and other perks.

Before meeting him, Pamela dressed in the predictable pattern of upper-class British women of that era. It was as if she expected a rainstorm at any minute and she had to be ready. That would not do around her stylish Italian lover. Gianni set Pamela up with Balenciaga and Dior, and she left their ateliers cloaked in the latest styles.

As generous as Gianni was to Pamela, she still had to deal with those around him who thought they were serving him by treating her badly. Pamela and Gianni slept in separate bedrooms. His Greek friend Peter Zervudachi brought hookers into her bedroom and left traces so she would know they had been there. His four sisters never let up, but the worst of it was Gianni's younger brother Giorgio, who shot a spate of bullets through her bedroom door at Villar Perosa. It wasn't a serious attempt to kill her, but it terrified her and exposed the Agnellis' psychological wounds.

Their father had died when he was decapitated by the propeller of a seaplane. Their mother died ten years later in an auto accident.

Gianni fled this tragic past with a frantic life, acting as if yesterday did not exist and tomorrow might never come.

It was a mark of how serious Pamela was about marrying Gianni that she decided to convert to Catholicism. It wasn't that hard to convert from one faith that mattered little to her to another faith to which she appeared to give little credence. There are always casualties in such matters. In this case, it was young Winston who would be deemed illegitimate if his mother got an annulment so she could become Gianni's Catholic wife.

In 1948, Pamela was in the midst of learning about Catholicism when she discovered she was pregnant. Her new faith taught that abortion was a sin, but Pamela's concerns lay elsewhere. It was the most crucial moment in her affair with Gianni. If she bore his child, whether or not he married her, he would have to take care of them forever. But Gianni saw the pregnancy as a threat to his freedom, and that threat trumped his faith. Nothing was going to take away his freedom.

Gianni insisted that Pamela have an abortion. She was conflicted, but ultimately she believed that if she agreed to it, Gianni would feel indebted to her and they would be ever closer to marriage—her ultimate goal from this liaison. It didn't occur to her that he might not want to spend his life with a woman whose presence reminded him of his complicity in this act.

Gianni accompanied Pamela to Lausanne, where she was going to have the procedure, but he was not about to squander his time waiting for her. Instead, he traveled 211 miles to the Villa d'Este hotel on Lake Como. The next day, half-sick and disoriented, Pamela joined him. Instead of being even momentarily solicitous of her, Gianni bragged about the beautiful model he had bedded the previous night.

Pamela had accepted that Gianni would have other lovers. She had given up so much of herself to be with him, but what was left? At La Leopolda, she oversaw spectacular dinner parties with animated conversation and notable guests. And when the company left at midnight, her coked-out, manic lover would head out in his Ferrari with his carousing buddies to the casino at Monte Carlo for gambling and to pick up women for his pleasure. And who was this woman standing alone at the entryway? Whoever she was, there was anger within her that she dared not acknowledge.

One evening in August 1952, Gianni and Pamela were attending a black-tie event at La Leonina, an estate just down the coast. He had no patience for overlong social events and had the shortest of attention spans. So, he left early. Pamela did not know it, but he had not left alone.

Pamela arrived back at La Leopolda in the early-morning hours to find her lover in bed with the stunning Anne-Marie d'Estainville. It wasn't just this betrayal. It was a lifetime of betrayals encapsulated in this moment. She rushed toward them, screaming taunts, trying to strike them. Her screaming was so loud, her emotions so profound, that she was soon spent, and she left them there.

Always playing the gentleman, Gianni offered to drive Anne-Marie home. He probably drove even faster than usual as he contemplated what had just happened. Although he knew every turn on the road skirting the Mediterranean, he was high on cocaine, the drug that propelled him on what he called his *"grande nuits blanche"* (grand white nights). He made a wrong turn and smashed into a butcher's truck containing three working-class men trying to make a living. Almost anyone else would have suffered serious legal consequences, but he was Gianni Agnelli, the prince of the Côte d'Azur, and like everything else untoward in his life, it was all quickly covered up.

Gianni suffered the worst injuries, a cracked jaw and a leg broken in nine places. The doctors wanted to amputate, but he said no and spent a laborious nine months in a Florence hospital recuperating.

Pamela hovered as close to Gianni as she could, expressing her profound concern. His sisters worried about their impulsive playboy brother marrying the British siren. As far as they were concerned, this notorious woman would be a stain on their family that would be impossible to wash away. They knew that she was having an affair with the Greek shipping tycoon André Embiricos, and they smelled hypocrisy.

The sisters felt they must peel their brother away from Pamela. The best response was to dangle some delicious alternatives in front of Gianni's eyes as he lay there for many months, unable to resume his playboy ways. To do so, one of the sisters, Cristiana, invited the elegant young Marella Caracciolo di Castagneto, a Neapolitan princess, to Turin.

Having some sense of what was up, Marella canceled a sailing trip and hurried to the northern Italian city. Soon after she arrived, Cristiana brought her to Gianni's hospital room. Six years his junior, Marella had had a crush on Gianni from the time she was a teenager. The few times they had come together, he had hardly noticed her.

Although Gianni's sisters wanted their brother to marry her, Marella knew that he had a bachelor's soul and would have to be led blindfolded to the wedding altar. Thus, she either let herself get pregnant or it was just one of those accidents.

For Gianni, Marella's pregnancy was the same dilemma he had

faced with Pamela Churchill a few years before (and, likely, other times in his wild bachelor life as well). In this instance, he knew he could not ask Marella to have an abortion. She was a much more suitable match for him than Pamela had ever been. And eventually he knew he would have to marry, to father a male heir to carry on the Agnelli name and the Fiat industrial dynasty. Although it was not quite as crude a reasoning as Randolph Churchill marrying Pamela in hopes of having a son before he died in the war, it was hardly Demetrius and Helena in Shakespeare's *A Midsummer Night's Dream*.

Marella and Gianni married on November 19, 1953, on the outskirts of Strasbourg in the small chapel of Osthoffen Castle. There were only about sixty guests, a minuscule number for an Agnelli dynastic wedding. The twenty-six-year-old bride was three months' pregnant but looked model-thin in her Balenciaga gown as she held on to Gianni's arm. The thirty-two-year-old groom was still on crutches that he handled as deftly as ski poles. In his one-button formal coat and gray pants, he was as model-perfect as his bride. The famous photographer Robert Doisneau photographed the wedding for *Vogue*. Even on this day the eye went to Gianni, and he was the central focus of many of the photos of them together. Some observers thought he looked sullen and displeased, but nobody knew his true feelings.

A smart businessman takes care of people in the right way, and Gianni made sure that things were right with Pamela. He gave her what Truman called "one of the most beautiful apartments in Paris I've ever seen," a Bentley, and a massive settlement. With her modest alimony check from Randolph and possible other money from Jock Whitney, she could live at a high level of wealth and privilege. Pamela did not have grand estates and splendid yachts, but what did that matter when she was invited everywhere?

Pamela was now in her mid-thirties. Her youthfulness still shone, and she was at the age that Truman believed was the beginning of a swan-like woman's true beauty. From now on her beauty would be an act of self-creation that Truman thought should be honored as an artistic achievement. Most women, even if they had the money, did not have the ambition or the discipline to maintain themselves as Truman envisioned, but Pamela did. Her looks were her most precious possession in her quest for a new husband.

This was a serious enterprise. Most Parisian women would have been delighted to have their hair done once a week by Alexandre, one of the premier hair stylists in Paris, in his salon. Pamela had Alexandre come to her home most days. Then there were frequent visits from the masseuses, manicurists, and sales consultants at Dior and Balenciaga, who brought gowns and dresses that she bought by the score. She went nowhere without being exquisitely put together.

Pamela was constantly on the move, traveling generally where there were presentable single men, from evenings in nightclubs and glamorous restaurants to masked balls in Paris, horse races in England, and polo matches wherever the international set lit for the day. Her dinner parties were themselves part of this world, and they were among the most desirable invitations in Paris. Many of her guests found the evenings singularly scintillating, but a few found them boring, nothing but an endless regimen of high-level gossip.

Truman did not travel in Pamela's luxurious style, but from 1949 for the next decade Truman and Jack spent most of the year outside the United States in all kinds of exotic places in Europe and North Africa.

In August 1949, Truman and Jack were living in Tangier, where they celebrated Jack's thirty-fifth birthday at a late-night beach party. Truman's friend, the photographer Cecil Beaton—who would, six and a half years later, introduce him to C. Z. Guest between acts of *My Fair Lady*—had arrived in Tangier just in time to decorate one of the grottoes at the Caves of Hercules with a staggering array of flowers, hangings, draperies, and lanterns. In the next grotto, a group of unseen musicians played the Arab music that Truman had come to love. There was no food to eat, only champagne and hashish.

To reach the beach, the attendees walked on a narrow pathway wending its way down a cliff. The other partygoers handily made their way. Truman was not about to do it. He feared scorpions sitting there waiting to sting him to death. Four strong Moroccan workers ended up lifting Truman onto a litter and carrying him downward. It was far more dangerous than if Truman had walked, and as he sat there like a petite pasha, he kept screaming out, "Goodbye! Goodbye!" It would have been an exotic way for the promising author to die, but the litter made it to the beach. When the party ended, the men carried Truman back up the cliff.

That was a wonderous evening, but for the most part Truman and Jack lived serious, sedate lives. When they first arrived, they inhabited a modest mountaintop house whose corrugated steel roof magnified the summer heat of the North African city. Truman would have loved to move to more congenial quarters, but the nasty truth of his life was that he didn't have much money. People thought if you had a bestseller, you were rich. It simply wasn't so.

Truman wrote in the morning, primarily reworking his set-aside first novel, *Summer Crossing*. In the torrid afternoons he napped or swam and often in the evenings walked with Jack in the Casbah or attended expatriates' parties. He cared for little beyond his writing. At least he got out of that terrible house. Truman wrote his high school English teacher Catherine Woods that he was staying with Loel Guinness in his house in the Casbah, the first time he had any connection with the Guinnesses.

At the end of the year, Truman flew back to New York to give a reading from his short story collection, *A Tree of Night*, at the YMHA on Ninety-Second Street. The largely Jewish audience were used to hearing distinguished authors read from verified literature. They had never heard anything like this little man on a stool speaking in a barely audible voice about places they had never gone and would never want to go. But they loved him. They absolutely loved him.

Truman likely could have made money giving readings and talks around the country, spreading his reputation even further. And he could have stayed in New York to write while promoting himself with the powers that be. But Truman needed the kind of peace and solitude that he found only in Europe. So, in April 1950, Truman and Jack hopped a Norwegian freighter to Palermo, Sicily, and from there took the train to Taormina, a seaside town across from the toe of Italy.

When Truman and Jack arrived, the writer Donald Windham was there to greet them. Truman and Donald had become friends previously, and he helped them find a small villa just outside town, where D. H. Lawrence lived for two years in the twenties. These were two of Lawrence's most productive years, and that was a positive omen.

Once Truman and Jack hired a teenage girl, Graziella, to clean and prepare lunch, the two authors settled down to work. Truman had largely given up on *Summer Crossing* and was beginning work on a new novel, *The Grass Harp*, in which he reworked many of the themes in *Other Voices, Other Rooms*.

Their neighbors included a group described as the "Edwardian queens," who had lived there since World War I. The many visitors who descended on the town included the heiress Peggy Guggenheim, who came for a lengthy stay. Boisterous and loud, she insisted upon attention. Then there was Eugene O'Neill, Christian Dior, Jean Cocteau, and other notables.

Truman's mother and stepfather also descended on Taormina. Nina was on the wagon. She had an edge to her, as if she could not help thinking about a drink. Jack despised her, a sentiment she fully shared about him. He considered her "nothing but a hillbilly from the South, a pushy climber who only wanted to be in the New York Social Register."

Jack's anger toward Nina was not so much about her as it was about Truman. Nina had overwhelmed Truman with affection in some kind of grotesquely exaggerated Southern way. Then time and again she abandoned him physically and emotionally. Truman was a respected, successful writer, but to his mother he was still just a gay man, not the kind of son she deserved.

Jack saw how obsessed Nina was to get in "Society." She and Joe spent money they did not have trying to reach some mythical place among a class of people where life would be singularly beautiful. Jack was antisocial and so hardly the best guide to party life, but he thought Truman had some of his mother in him. He salivated to be around certain people and get to certain venues. It was one thing about Truman that Jack couldn't stand.

These were just minor distractions. Truman and Jack spent most of their time together in the best year of their love. When Jack looked back on their time in Taormina, he recalled one evening standing near the bandstand of a nearby town. The orchestra was playing arias from Bellini and Verdi. Above the sound of the music from a house high up above, Truman called out, "Jack . . . ! Jack . . . !" It was a fierce entreaty, a measure of how much Truman needed Jack. Once they left Taormina, that sound was heard no longer, or if it was heard, it did not mean the same thing.

Jack worked as hard as Truman on his own writing, but it wasn't going anywhere. A man of less character would have taken out his frustration on Truman, but that wasn't Jack. He was proud that when they left Sicily, Truman had completed his short novel.

When *The Grass Harp* was published in October 1951, it received the best reviews of Truman's career. In a typical critique, *The New York Times*'s Orville Prescott called it a "vast improvement" over *Other Voices, Other Rooms*, a novel he considered a "sinister and rather sickening excursion into a hot-house world of baroque symbolism and festering and decayed beauty." Truman had ditched the homosexual themes and added a dollop of Southern sentimentality, and Prescott loved it.

Pamela was rich, beautiful, and available, and it was not long before she fell upon her next serious lover. He was Baron Elie de Rothschild. The businessman and banker carried one of the most famous names in France. Although not as handsome as Gianni, the dilettantish Rothschild had lean, attractive features. He had gone off to war in

1939 with what he said was "a horse and a saber" and was captured by the Nazis. He tried to escape, and had he not been an officer, the Nazis probably would have killed their Jewish prisoner.

Other men were paying so Pamela could live her splendid life, and Elie could enjoy her pleasure with little investment. The Rothschilds had been France's leading Jewish family for generations. Most of them were well mannered and cautious in their public demeanors. Elie was different. He could be staggeringly rude and vulgar. Had he not had the name and fortune he did, he would not have been invited to many of the places he went.

Since Elie insisted that the couple keep their relationship as quiet as possible and not go out together in public, his conduct did not much matter to Pamela. As secretive as they tried to be, it was inevitable that Liliane de Rothschild learned about her husband's relationship. Though Elie had had previous affairs, Liliane sensed that this was more serious. She was a highly cultured, sophisticated woman but did not have the image of the kind of woman Elie wanted on his arm. Pamela, who could be crueler in her observations about women than men, said she looked like an "old toad."

Elie should have been particularly sensitive to his wife. Liliane had just given birth to their daughter, Gustava, when her beloved sister, Thérèse, and her stepfather died, and her grieving mother collapsed. It was overwhelming, and for a long time Liliane saw no one. And as she mourned, she knew her husband was out there somewhere with Pamela.

Liliane trailed Pamela's chauffeur-driven Bentley through the streets of Paris in her Austin Mini. Pamela had the nouveau riche attitude that you associate yourself only with whatever is most expensive. She would never have driven an Austin Mini. As for Lil-iane, she was a Rothschild, and she could drive whatever she wanted wherever she wanted—and this day she wanted to drive straight into Pamela's Bentley. And that was what she did.

Pamela could not understand why Elie didn't leave this crazy woman and marry her instead. But Elie avoided any talk of marriage. Pamela was approaching the watershed age of forty, and she was not about to squander her time doing little but tearing off the months on her calendar. She did the only thing she knew how to do to get herself out of uncertain circumstances: she took on new lovers.

One of Pamela's affairs was with Albert Rupp Jr., an American who had married an automobile heiress. Rupp spent his wife's money as if he had earned it himself. He paid for Pamela's hotel room when she came to New York, bought her jewelry, and gave her cash.

For the 1957 Christmas holidays, Rupp arrived in St. Moritz with his family, while Pamela was also in the same hotel. Mrs. Rupp went to Pamela's suite in the afternoon and found her husband in the bedroom with the notorious Mrs. C. That was an unpleasant moment, but what ended the affair was Rupp's erratic behavior. Her lover was an alco-holic, and Pamela dropped him shortly before he killed himself.

Pamela had been playing this game of romance her entire adult life. She had accumulated a measure of wealth, but in all those years she had only lived a few fitful months with a man, first with her hus-band, Randolph, and then with her lover Averell. The others had been like Elie, coming and going as they pleased. She had gained a reputa-tion as a woman you did not marry. If you had money and a certain way about you, you could have her without that formality.

Pamela had not lived for love. In none of her romances had she given herself up for a man. She had sought privilege, status, and riches, and she had almost always sought men who could give her what she wanted. Pamela thought that would lead to marriage, but it never had, and after all these years, there was a measure of quiet desperation in her quest.

So when Pamela met the highly successful movie and Broadway producer Leland Hayward in New York, she knew this was her chance. Leland was going through a tough patch in his marriage to Slim, and he was completely overwhelmed with the pressures of his work. He also knew little of Pamela's past. To him, the name "Churchill" still resonated with magic.

After a few weeks with Leland, in which he became utterly smitten with her, Pamela understood the urgency of her situation. Although fifty-five-year-old Leland wanted to marry Pamela, he wasn't her first choice for a husband. Elie was. After all, the French baron was fifteen years younger, far richer than Leland, and had a title other than "producer."

Pamela went to Elie and said that Leland wanted to marry her, but she wanted to marry Elie. He had made it clear to her in so many ways that he was not going to divorce his wife to marry her. The fact that she had finally found someone willing to marry her changed nothing. Not only did the Frenchman say no, but he left angry at her attempted emotional blackmail.

Leland was all that was left. At Pamela's age and circumstance, Leland was likely a last chance for the kind of life she wanted to live. And so, forty-year-old Pamela sold her Paris home for a king's ransom of $500,000 ($4.3 million in today's dollars) and made her way to New York City.

Once Pamela married the just divorced Leland in a Las Vegas civil

ceremony in May 1960, it was time for the new Mrs. Hayward to begin to live the way she and her husband deserved to live. Taking almost half the money from the sale of her Paris residence, Pamela
bought a fifteen-room apartment in one of the most prestigious ad-
dresses in Manhattan, on Fifth Avenue and Eighty-Third Street, right
across from the Metropolitan Museum of Art. Using her new husband's money, she spent roughly as much decorating the home as she
did buying it.

With Leland on her arm and one of the most splendid apartments
in Manhattan as her abode, she set out to show the New York social
world that it dare not ostracize her. What better way to begin than to
give a dinner party for the Duke and Duchess of Windsor? The royal
couple were regulars at soirees at Pamela's Paris residence, and it was
no stretch inviting them.

Americans went gaga over royalty. Even Pamela's most intransi-
gent enemies among the Manhattan set would salivate over an invitation to dinner with the duke and duchess. But why give them that
opportunity? As Cholly Knickerbocker's column pointed out, the
party in March 1961 "was noteworthy because it was attended exclu-
sively by leading theater names and no socialites."

The following week, Pamela gave another party. Since Pamela had
been a girl, she had been written about in the papers. So, of course,
she wanted the party to be covered in the proper way. To do so, she
invited the rotund, ebullient party promoter and social columnist
Elsa Maxwell, who wrote at only two speeds: half gush and full gush.
As the guest of honor, Pamela chose a couple she had known in Paris,
Loel and Gloria Guinness.

Gloria was no mere New York socialite but a sophisticated member of the international set. Her pink Balenciaga gown was set off by

an incredible array of emeralds from the Guinness safe at the Waldorf Astoria.

That evening the Haywards' new apartment was full of many of the leading theatrical figures of the day, including Laurence Olivier, Jerome Robbins, and Moss Hart. Not only was Henry Fonda there, but his actress daughter Jane came along as well. Mary Martin had become a star playing in the Hayward-coproduced *South Pacific*. These days she was playing on Broadway in another Hayward-coproduced musical, *The Sound of Music*.

After dinner Mary walked up to the piano and sang a number of songs. Afterward, Ethel Merman got up. She was going out in a road company of the Hayward-coproduced musical *Gypsy*, and she sang some of the songs she made famous in a voice that could have cracked the flutes of champagne. It was an incredible evening devoid of the usual stuffy socialites, and the new Mrs. Hayward had put it together beautifully.

Truman saw how Pamela was making herself part of what he thought of as "his" New York world. Not only did he make her his friend, but he considered her the newest of his swans. Others who had turned their backs on Pamela twirled around toward her, in part because she seemed so good for Leland. A traditional wife was rare on the East Side of Manhattan, but that was what she was, doggedly watching out for her husband. Babe had said she would never talk to the husband-stealing Pamela, but even she was impressed. "I can see that Leland has fallen into a tub of butter," she said, and so he had.

To her new husband, Pamela was nanny, nurse, and lover all wrapped up in one extravagant package. Slowly and definitively, she took over Leland's life, leading him away from his show business friends toward her international set.

Pamela wanted a weekend house in the country. Slim had commandeered the Manhasset house in the divorce, and Pamela was not about to head out there. Leland was rich, but he didn't have the money to buy a grand estate that would allow her to compete with the Paleys and the other mega gentry. Money went far further in Yorktown Heights, forty miles north of the city. There the couple acquired a property that Pamela transformed into an English country house that she named Haywire.

Few artifacts scattered around Haywire memorialized Leland's extraordinary career. By the looks of the place, he could have been a British gentleman who had spent his days riding to the hounds and kibitzing at his club. Leland had no apparent problem with that. He was proud of his wife's previous marriage to the son of Britain's great wartime leader, as was Pamela, who insisted on being called Pamela Churchill Hayward.

Pamela was an energetic woman bubbling with life—and once she got her two homes set up, she needed something else to do. Without ever having worked seriously in her life and devoid of knowledge of business and economics, in October 1963 she opened the Jansen Boutique on East Fifty-Seventh Street, selling antiques and reproductions. Although anyone would have predicted that it would turn out to be a dilettantish indulgence that Leland would have to subsidize, Pamela proved to be a natural businesswoman. The shop was a major success. She probably could have expanded into a whole series of stores, but Leland was beginning to suffer serious health problems, and in May 1967, she felt she had no choice but to sell.

It should have been expected that Leland would begin to have difficulties. A few months before he married Pamela, his ex-wife Margaret Sullavan committed suicide. A few months later, his daughter Bridget did the same. As he dealt the best he could with these personal tragedies, his professional life took a dramatic turn for the worst. He had been arguably the most successful Broadway producer in America, but now nothing worked.

Slim conjectured that her former husband's failures might have had something to do with Leland leaving her, but more likely he did not have the energy any longer and had lost his sure touch for the cultural marketplace. He had always imbibed heavily, but now he had become what by any measure was an alcoholic, nursing Jack Daniel's through the day, until by evening he was gently slurring his words.

Leland had always had an extravagant lifestyle fueled on the millions of dollars poured into his coffer first from his actor clients and in recent years from one successful play after another. The money was no longer there, but he still had the same lifestyle. When he and Pamela went down to Florida to visit the Guinnesses, he was so taken by Loel's helicopter that he purchased a two-seater version that he flew to work. The couple had what most people would have said were spendthrift ways, but this was their whole identity. To live on a lesser scale was to live a lesser life.

When Leland had a series of strokes, Pamela brought him back from the hospital to die at Haywire. She hired several Franciscan priests to help her minister to her husband, but a great burden fell on her, and she handled it with dignity and aplomb. When sixty-eight-year-old Leland died on March 18, 1971, she invited a large group of his show business colleagues and social friends to their home for the wake. As she had in Leland's last weeks, she handled this day with class as she bid him goodbye.

During their eleven years of marriage, Pamela and Leland had run through most of his money, and she was left almost bereft financially. There was only one way she knew how to survive—through the largesse of rich men—but she was fifty-one years old now, and the patina of allure that had drawn men to her was not so strong any longer. But she was a player, and she had no time or inclination to spend her days in endless mourning.

The very month after Leland's death, Pamela went off to Palm Springs to stay with Frank Sinatra. The singer was only a friend, but in the winter the California desert resort was full of as many millionaires as palm trees. From there Pamela flew to England, suffering the indignity of flying coach. With no money to stay in her preferred suite at Claridge's, she suffered the further indignity of bunking with her son, Winston, in a tiny bedroom in his apartment. These misadventures were evidence she really did not need that a middle-class life was not for her.

After spending enough time in her beloved London to realize it was no longer the city for her, she went off with Gloria and Loel Guinness on their yacht for a Mediterranean cruise. Gloria had not bothered stocking the larder with rich, eligible gentlemen along with other delicacies, and Pamela left before the cruise was over. In early August, she flew back to New York to take up residence once again at Haywire.

"Truman claimed that she [Pamela] came off the [Guinness] boat very depressed," said Brooke Hayward, Leland's oldest daughter with Margaret Sullavan. "And they talked one morning and he said, 'Well, listen, Pamela. What about Averell Harriman? Let's remember, Marie died a year ago. Kay Graham [the publisher of *The Washington Post*] is giving a big dinner. He's going to be there. Call her. She's an old pal of yours and go.'" Kay later said this did not happen, but she would not want to be seen as a secret matchmaker manipulating the seventy-nine-year-old widower.

Pamela arrived early for the dinner at Kay's Georgetown home. When Pamela saw that she was placed next to Averell, she insisted that she be seated back-to-back with him. Most women would have been delighted to be seated next to their quarry, but this way all evening long poor Averell had to keep twisting and turning his head to talk to the one woman at the party with whom he wanted to converse. That was the last time Averell ever had to turn his head to talk to Pamela.

Averell was spending the week in his Georgetown mansion and flying up to his estate on the North Shore of Long Island at Sands Point for the weekend. Peter Duchin; his wife, Cheray; and their children were spending the summer at Harriman's house. Peter had been brought up like a son by the Harrimans, and he was family. Shortly after Kay's dinner, Peter received a phone call from Pamela, who invited herself up for the weekend. Averell seemed delighted, pulled out of the emotional doldrums.

Peter was a bandleader. Saturday night was money night, and he had a gig that evening. Cheray had an invitation she couldn't change, so Averell and Pamela were alone in the house. When Peter got back at one thirty in the morning and went to turn on the light on the porch to pour himself a drink, he heard a scream. "Jesus wept!" yelled Averell, a non sequitur if there ever was one. There lay Pamela and Averell on the sofa, their clothes in disarray.

Everyone went back to their bedrooms, and Peter thought this extraordinary evening was at an end. But a few minutes later, a loud crash reverberated through the house. When he jumped up and ran into the corridor, Pamela was already there, saying that a lamp had fallen down. In the morning, she told a different story.

"It wasn't the lamp. It was Averell. He fell through the window."

"He what?"

"He walked all the way around the outside of the house in his slippers and pajamas. But the poor darling forgot about the screen."

Pamela never did say where Averell was walking.

About a month later, on September 27, 1971, six and a half months after Leland's death, Pamela married Averell in a small ceremony in Manhattan. Eschewing a honeymoon, the couple flew immediately to Washington, where Pamela set out to transform Averell's life.

It was not enough just to bring in expensive decorators to change the stodgy, antique-ridden home into something with a certain pizzazz. The great house and everything else around Averell had to be stamped with her image. It was Harriman money that had built all this, but she was Mrs. Harriman, and the new era had begun. Through the house she placed her imprimatur in the form of the Digby family's convoluted crest, which included an ostrich holding a horseshoe in its teeth and two chained monkeys and beneath it the family motto. Pamela put the crest on needlepoint pillows that were placed all over the house, stationery, and matchbooks that many guests took home.

Not all the political figures and socialites who came to the Harrimans' for dinner knew enough Latin to realize that the Digby family motto—*Deo Non Fortuna*—meant "From God, Not Fortune." Anyone who knew Pamela's story would have thought the words should have been reversed.

8

Gloria in Excelsis

ALONG ONE SIDE of the bar at Miami Beach's Fontainebleau hotel ran an enormous glass wall, behind which patrons could watch people swimming underwater in the pool. It was decidedly more interesting than most lounge acts, and first-time visitors found it fascinating. Among them one evening was Truman, who sat on a barstool next to Gloria Guinness, a regular on the Best-Dressed List, and Eleanor Lambert, the fashion impresario behind said list.

Gloria was used to drinking flutes of Dom Pérignon, not piña coladas, but she was a player. As the threesome sat relishing the scene, they saw a swimmer urinating in the water. Then they noticed swimmer after swimmer doing the same thing, so much so that the pool should have been flushed, not drained. Lambert was so disgusted she wanted to leave. Truman and Gloria thought it was just about the most amusing thing they had ever seen and sat there joyously watching the performance.

Gloria and Truman were in Miami for the first Cassius Clay–Sonny Liston heavyweight championship fight in February 1964.

Boxing was not a sport for the Beautiful People, but the media portrayed the contest as a battle between good and evil: the rope-a-doping young challenger from Louisville against the gnarly ex-con from Philadelphia whose own family called him "the King of the Beasts." Gloria was covering the fight for *Harper's Bazaar*.

When Gloria and Truman walked down the steps to their ringside seats at Miami Beach's Convention Center, they looked as if they had dressed for a christening. Gloria was five feet nine and a half inches tall, and with the added height of her heels, she stood above most in the massive crowd. She wore a black raw-silk suit, simple in its elegance, that reached up just to her throat, setting off a neck so long it hardly seemed human. Her facial features were all delicately rendered, her hair was pitch-black, and she was by any measure a beautiful woman. No one would possibly imagine she was even close to fifty-one years old. Truman considered her one of his swans, and she did appear an exotic bird that had landed ringside by mistake and would soon fly off again.

The photographers had come to take pictures of the fight, but some of them were so drawn to Gloria and Truman that for the first couple of rounds, instead of shooting the drama within the red velvet ropes, they focused their cameras on the spectacular couple at ringside. Liston failed to come out for the seventh round, in one of the most controversial endings in boxing history. There was much to write about, but neither Gloria nor Truman ever bothered, and it remained just another unique evening for the two friends.

Gloria was all about money. "There are certain women, and a few men too, who, though perhaps not born rich, are born to *be* rich," Truman wrote in one of his notebooks for *Answered Prayers*. "By and large, these persons are artists of an odd variety; money, in

astronomical amounts, is their instrument—they require it as a vio-
linist requires a violin, a painter, paint. Without it, they are creatively
impotent; with it, they fuse material elements—from food to fine
motors—into fantasies that are both visible and tactile. In other
words, they know how to spend dough; but in a manner that, while
morally arguable, is at least aesthetically valid. The Duchess of Windsor is such a person; and so, to cite other examples from so-called
'real' life, are Mrs. Harrison Williams, Mrs. Paul Mellon, Mrs. Loel
Guinness."

To be one of Truman's swans, it wasn't enough that a woman be
elegant, beautiful, and rich. She had to be amusing, and of all his
friends, no one was more amusing than Gloria—sometimes too
amusing. For the most part, the ultra-rich have literal minds, and
they find excessive wit dangerous, even subversive. That was a lesson
that Gloria never cared to heed.

In the years when Jackie Kennedy was married to Aristotle Onassis, Gloria and her husband, Loel, were invited on a ten-day cruise
with the couple on Onassis's splendid yacht, *Christina O.* The Guinnesses flew into Cozumel that first morning from their winter home
in Acapulco and took the tender out to the yacht.

Onassis insisted on perfection. So did Gloria, but she didn't make
such a big deal of it. That defeated the whole idea. She simply had to
tweak the shipping magnate just a little. As Gloria stood around the
pool having a drink with the others, she turned to Onassis and said,
"I am very disappointed with you."

That was a phrase Onassis rarely heard. He turned toward her,
wanting to know what he had done to offend her. "There is no yogurt
on your boat," she said. What was a Greek without yogurt?

Gloria's attempt at wit fell to the deck. Onassis called an aide and ordered one of his Olympia planes to fly to the United States and bring back yogurt.

The Guinnesses lived as well as Onassis. They had an almost stultifying array of homes. There were two residences in Acapulco, a grand home in Paris, an estate in Normandy, a house in Switzerland, an apartment at the Waldorf Astoria in New York City, a grand mansion just south of Palm Beach, a yacht, and a ten-passenger plane to take them from home to home. Over the years, Truman went to almost all of these places, but nowhere more frequently than Gemini, their Florida residence.

The 62,200-square-foot main house stretched across the barrier island from the Atlantic Ocean to Lake Worth. It did so by burrowing under A1A, the north-south highway. The massive living room where the Guinnesses' guests gathered was literally under the road, just another unique thing about the sixteen-acre property. Truman stayed in his own little guest house along the 1,200-foot-long stretch of private beach.

Gloria and Truman could have talked half the night, but when the witching hour of 11:30 arrived, Loel told them that everyone had to go to bed. Gloria and Truman begged him like children asking to stay up beyond their bedtime hour, but Loel did not listen, and off everyone went to their bedrooms.

When another of Truman's swans, C. Z. Guest, heard about Truman's visit to Palm Beach, she insisted Truman stay in her apartment rather than twelve miles down the road with Gloria and Loel. It was not as difficult a trek as C.Z. made it out to be. The Guinnesses had their own helicopter to whisk their guests around, after all. But nonetheless C.Z. wanted Truman with her.

If Truman had been a rag doll, the two women would have torn him apart in their quest for his presence, but he was distressingly real. Trying to play King Solomon, Truman agreed to spend a few days with C.Z. before heading south to the Guinness estate.

To show who had true authority in this matter and all matters, when Truman was there, Gloria decided to give the party of the season. Usually she preferred dinner parties for no more than twelve, where conversation was the thing, but that evening she decided to give a soiree around the pool and out on the lawn and invite *everyone*. As Gloria saw the world, *everyone* meant the Duke and Duchess of Windsor. She adored them, especially the duke, whom she considered the "last impulsive and adventurous dresser in the masculine world of fashion." Once she had the duke and duchess, she invited the crème de la crème of Palm Beachers. And so, when the evening arrived, *everyone* was there—everyone but Mr. and Mrs. Winston Guest. They were not invited.

Gloria set lots of tables around the pool, with just enough candlelight to make the ladies look their best, and two different large tables for the food. There she presented her guests with both cold food and hot food, a giant tin of iced caviar, cold chicken salad, baked ham and imported pâté, French onion soup, scrambled eggs, German sausages, and candied fruits. And there was this gay mood that cast its light across everything. That was as much Gloria's creation as everything else.

Of all Truman's women friends, none was a person of such mystery and complexity as Gloria. Her Mexican birth was as hidden and debated as so much else in her life. There were rumors that she had been a B-girl in Mexico City, hustling in the bars. The allegation amused Gloria. Her real story was far more interesting.

Gloria's journalist father, José Rafael Rubio y Torres, was a

supporter of the reformist president Francisco I. Madero, the batter-
ing ram of the Mexican Revolution. Gloria Rubio y Alatorre was born
in Guadalajara on August 27, 1912, at the beginning of the struggle.
The next year, Madero was deposed, arrested by his enemies, and
murdered as he was being transported between jails. That was what it
meant to lose in a time of revolution. Leaving his family behind, Gloria's father fled into exile to the United States, where he died in 1916.
Over a million Mexicans died in those years of atrocity and bloody
revenge. That was the measure of Gloria's childhood, where the heavy
hand of history intruded everywhere.

Gloria's memories of her childhood were not about the arbitrary
march of history into her life but of her mother and the nuns. "Early in
life, I knew only two influences: good and evil," she wrote. "My
mother, the Church, the nuns with their words and actions always
strict, virtuous and clear (and at times intolerably cruel) were, so I was
told, the only *good* influences I would know in my life. I was later to
discover that this was not so far wrong."

Young Gloria deplored the oppressive weight of the Church on
her life. Her meager protest was to fall asleep saying the rosary. Gloria's aristocratic mother, Maria Luisa Dolores de Alatorre y Diaz-
Ocampo, and her daughter went to live with relatives on their grand
haciendas, but the revolution reached into the countryside, taking
away land and giving it to the peasants. Her mother and the nuns did
not lead Gloria to God, but they taught her the essential lessons of her
life. One of them was that the mind and the hands must always be
busy.

When her mother was not praying, she was working, much of the
time making Gloria's clothes. Her mother could have purchased
store-bought clothes, but that did not impart the lesson she was

teaching. As Gloria watched, she cut the cloth and stitched the garments together with immaculate precision, creating clothes so finely made, it was said, that they could be worn inside out.

Like Truman, Gloria was a stunningly observant person who had perceptions that were almost perversely idiosyncratic. Who else but Gloria would see the holy sisters of her childhood as fashion plates? "No dress or custom will ever be as safe, or as beautiful, or as well thought out as any one of the many different habits of the many different orders to which nuns belong," Gloria wrote. They always dressed the same, and they were always perfectly fashionable.

Señora Alatorre was astounded at her daughter's beauty—it was as if a seed had been carried on the wind from distant reaches and sprouted miraculously in the soil. "Gloria, you are the most beautiful girl in Mexico, *and* you are smart," her mother told her. "Never settle for anything in life that is second-best. You don't have to. You can have whatever a woman can want in this world." Hearing that the first time was flattery. Hearing it twenty times was an admonition, and a challenge.

Gloria saw how her beauty intrigued men, acting a magical talisman that could get her what she wanted. But it was also a dangerous gift. In 1933, twenty-year-old Gloria married forty-seven-year-old Jacobus Hendrik Franciscus Scholtens, the Dutch-born superintendent of a sugar factory in Veracruz. He was over twice her age and one of a breed of foreigners who the Mexicans believed were exploiting the wealth of their nation. Scholtens had money and status, though, and for Gloria was a way out—or so it seemed. But the marriage was a failure, and after two years, she divorced and headed, almost penniless, to Paris.

All Gloria had was her beauty and her youth, but rightfully

handled, that could get her almost anywhere. That was especially true in Paris, where individuality was praised above all other values—and no one had seen anything like Gloria. She did not think she was as unusual as the Parisians did. "I knew how to sing and to dance," Gloria wrote in *Harper's Bazaar* in 1968. "But what Mexican girl grows up without singing and dancing? And my hair was black and curly, and my eyes were black and almond-shaped, just like other Mexican girls. But here, in Europe, hardly anyone had ever been to Mexico or had bothered to read much about it."

Gloria turned this lack of knowledge into her secret weapon. "It was this very ignorance that made my own particular struggle for happiness and success a very easy and enjoyable task," she wrote. She re-created herself as an irresistible character, exaggerating the parts of her background that Parisians adored. People, particularly men, went crazy for her Mexican accent. So why not drive it right over the top? And her grammar when speaking French—well, sometimes she made mistakes. Why not up that too, make her speech a convoluted journey through a field littered with broken syntax? Men loved that. She was this engagingly bizarre character whose utterances were the subjects of wry amusement. She seemed like a comedienne, and she was gorgeous.

"Do all Mexican women look like you?" the men asked.

"Yes," Gloria replied.

"I don't believe it. It's too good to be true."

Next to food, nothing mattered more to Parisians than the way they dressed. Most had limited wardrobes, but they did a remarkable job of looking stylish and presentable. Years later, when Gloria was on the Best-Dressed List, she probably spent $250,000 a year on her clothes, at least $1.5 million in today's money. She had almost nothing to spend on clothes during her Paris years, but she managed to appear spectacularly well dressed. She knew that style was a natural gift, and you did not have to have money to dress well.

"A woman's best friend is not a diamond but a little black suit," Gloria wrote in *Harper's Bazaar* in 1963. That was practically all you needed. After all, if you had that little black suit and knew how to use it, you could eventually obtain a slew of diamonds.

Gloria made some money as a model, but that alone did not merit her entry to venues of the haute elite. It was her beauty matched with her extraordinary sense of style and a wit that she used like a scalpel. With her unerring ability to sniff out the wealthiest, she found her way into a new set of grandiose people.

There were maharajahs from India, merchant princes from South America, rich nobles from Italy, American expatriates, and myriad others whose only common denominator was their money. They traveled the world in their own closed circle. They worked at nothing so assiduously as outdoing one another. Gloria's father would have likely found them a race of bloody parasites, but Gloria was intrigued. This was not the Old Society, with its quiet deference and discretion. This was something bold, new, and audacious.

In 1935, Gloria married a man who fit perfectly in this new international set, Franz Egon Graf von Fürstenberg-Herdringen, a divorced thirty-nine-year-old German count with a young daughter from his first wife. The marriage gave Gloria the title Countess Fürstenberg. Count Fürstenberg frequented the highest rank of society in the Third Reich. The Fürstenbergs were one of the oldest German families, with a Gothic Revival castle in Westphalia as well as homes in Berlin.

Gloria gave birth to a daughter in 1936 and a son three years later.

As the Nazi theorists saw it, Gloria's Mexican blood fouled a pure Aryan line going back centuries. When Gloria married, the Aryan racial laws had not yet been cast in concrete, and being married to such a highly placed husband, Gloria had to be accepted. If one could forget the appalling politics, it was a fascinating time to be living in Berlin. Gloria was a new bride during the 1936 Olympics, when Hitler showed off Germany's capital. In the years following there were gigantic parades celebrating Hitler, the streets lined with hundreds of thousands of cheering Germans applauding the triumph of the thousand-year Reich.

When the war started with easy victories in the west, life got even better as the bounty of those countries flowed east. Champagne arrived from France, cheese from Holland, chocolate from Belgium, silk stockings from Paris. But that was not all that flowed into Berlin. As most of the men went off to fight, four hundred thousand *Zwangsarbeiter*, or forced laborers (more than 10 percent of the city's population), arrived. To the Germans, it was deeply troubling having these outsiders all over their prized city, and many Berliners were profoundly suspicious of these foreigners.

For the first time in her life, Gloria had the money to buy the clothes that she felt were her destiny, but where could she wear them with her husband off fighting on the Russian front? It bothered her that she received so few letters, but it was the most vicious of wars, with little time for genial correspondence. If the Russian soldiers did not kill a man, the brutal cold would do the job. Gloria was alone with her two children in a foreign land in the midst of a cruel war. By 1943, British bombers had begun to pummel Berlin day after day, including 1,800-kilogram bombs that could render an entire block into rubble.

The worse it got, the wilder the nightlife grew—and the heavier the drinking and use of amphetamines. It was this world Gloria embraced. It was a choice that some women made in London and Moscow as well as in Berlin, a decision that other women considered a double betrayal to the vow they had made on their wedding day and to the blood-tinged struggle of which their husbands were part. But guilt was something that never troubled Gloria.

"I heard from my husband infrequently and spent every moment in the interim driving myself mad with worry, worry that I would hear he was missing or dead," she said. "I started to go out at night to take my mind off it. I guess I got lost in the social whirl—it was easy. There were a dozen parties every night then, even while the bombs fell. . . . We danced and sang and flirted and wore the best we had. It was wild—wild."

Gloria was not hanging out in lowlife bars where soldiers on leave drank themselves into stupors and puked in the street. As always, she had a gift of finding her way to elite circles. Her well-born companions drank as much as the poor soldiers and had ready access to amphetamines. They partied as if life might end in a burst of flames and blood, not an unreasonable assumption in Nazi Germany.

At one of those parties Gloria met Walter Schellenberg, a high-ranking Nazi official. In his black Secret Service (SS) uniform, Schellenberg rightly believed that he looked "dashing and elegant." Tall and thin, he appeared a Teutonic version of Gary Cooper. An ambitious man in his early thirties, Schellenberg had joined the SS because he believed it was full of "the better type of people," not the brown-shirt thugs of the Sturmabteilung (SA), who fought pitched battles in German cities. Once inside, he jumped at the opportunity to join the Sicherheitsdienst (SD), the special security and intelligence division within the SS overseen by Reichsführer Reinhard Heydrich.

Gloria would never forget what she was wearing the evening she met the spymaster: "a pure white off-the-shoulder sheath—one diamond on a platinum chain." Nor would she forget how Schellenberg looked at her body. "Well, he gawked like a baby," she said.

It was a dangerous thing for Schellenberg to develop a relationship with Gloria. He was well protected, but he had seen how things could change in a minute, resulting in a career and life destroyed. He had already used a full measure of chits to marry his second wife. To get a marriage license, he had needed to submit an *Ahnenpapiere*, a certificate of racial heritage, and with his fiancée's Polish mother, it was impossible. He went to Heydrich to ask him to intervene. The reichsführer's investigators discovered that Schellenberg's fiancée's aunt was married to a Jewish mill owner. That should have killed it right there. Although Heydrich felt that the fiancée's lips and eyebrows were "exaggerated," clearly displaying her inferiority, he went ahead and authorized the certificate. But Schellenberg paid a high price—Heydrich now owned him.

Schellenberg had a way with women. During his escapades in Paris, he had an affair with the couturier Coco Chanel and may have recruited her as a spy. Other involvements with foreign women took place when Heydrich came up with the idea of Salon Kitty, an upscale Berlin brothel in which everything in the house would be secretly recorded. Schellenberg was deputized to set up the establishment, which was staffed with cultured prostitutes from all over Europe, including a number of upper-class Germans. It was amazing what men would say in the throes of lovemaking, and the operation was a major success.

As for Gloria, she was an amazingly seductive woman. Men would do things for her they would not do for anyone else. During their affair, Schellenberg took her places where only the Nazi elite ventured, places she could not have gone to otherwise. But there came a time in ravaged Berlin when Gloria decided enough was enough. Not only did she want to divorce her husband, but she wanted to leave Germany and take her two children with her. In arranging Gloria's exit, Schellenberg was taking an enormous chance. Her husband was still alive. If he came back and found his wife and children gone, who would he blame and what revenge might he take?

But as the end of the war drew near, Schellenberg had more immediate concerns. To disguise his own bureaucratic role in the murder of European Jews, he set out to save a number of them, and he tried to negotiate an end of the war.

No one in the Nazi leadership likely traveled as much as Schellenberg. Madrid was one of his favorites and for good reason. Neutral Spain was a cauldron of espionage. Beyond all the Nazi clandestine operatives interspersed throughout the city, there were seventy to one hundred Germans in the military sector housed in buildings that were part of the German embassy.

On one of his trips to Madrid, Schellenberg headed out to the Plaza de Toros de Las Ventas to watch a bullfight from *barreras de sombra*, a prized seat in the shade. Next to him sat Gloria, still married to her German husband. The ladies at the corrida were all dressed to the nines, but no one equaled the countess. Her blue suit trimmed in red and stunning hat drew attention to her.

Schellenberg always had two bodyguards somewhere nearby to protect him. If, somehow, they failed and he was captured, all he had to do was to pull out his artificial tooth, removing the poison that would kill him in thirty seconds. If that did not work out, he could turn to his large blue signet ring, which held a capsule of cyanide.

A few rows back in the grand arena sat Aline Griffith, a young spy for the OSS, there to see her first bullfight. Even spies needed diversion, and everyone said what the matadors did in the ring was pure art. As Aline prepared for a spectacular afternoon and waited for the first bull to enter, the American woman looked down a few rows and saw Schellenberg, her agency's greatest nemesis, sitting with Countess Gloria Fürstenberg.

Aline had been tracking the comings and goings of the exotic new arrival. While she was living with her two children in two rooms at the Palace hotel, Gloria's beauty attracted all kinds of men, not just the types who could have been spies but also such company as the Egyptian Ahmed Fakhry, the son of Ambassador Mahmoud Fakhry Pasha.

Gloria did not appear to have much money, but she dressed in a manner that brought attention to her wherever she went. That was a strange thing for her to do, since Aline was convinced that Gloria was likely a Nazi spy. It wasn't the height of spy craft to hang out in public with Germany's spymaster.

Sometime after that Sunday afternoon, Aline met with Gloria, who had had enough of the Nazis and was looking to work for the Americans—and what a story she had to tell. "One night after the opera, I was at a party when Schellenberg walked in," she said. "That was the beginning. In a month I was dining with Himmler and even Hitler himself."

Gloria was trying to sell herself to the agent as a person of value, and she likely exaggerated her closeness to the Nazi elite. When Aline looked back on those war years, she was convinced that Gloria was no great spy but had "become a messenger for the Gestapo in return for being allowed to leave Berlin with her children."

In the aftermath of the war, there were about eleven million

Europeans displaced from their native countries, shuttled away in camps or shuffling along distant roads with dazed eyes. Gloria and her children could easily have been forced to join their ranks, but she had this mysterious way of arriving in places that she had no right or reason to be. Gloria became engaged to the young Egyptian Fakhry, whose father at that point early in 1946 was the foreign minister in the Cairo regime.

That attachment likely gave Gloria the money that allowed her to fly to Paris, where, at a restaurant early in April 1946, she met Duff Cooper, the British ambassador to France. The aristocratic diplomat liked women with his wine and wine with his women, and he was as much a connoisseur of one as the other. He was totally taken with Gloria, his wife and his mistress be damned.

In Paris, Gloria had the money to act the way she wanted to act. She thought it was absurd to think of money as the root of all evil. It was nothing more than "a very convenient medium of exchange" and ridiculous that "nobody is willing to admit liking or enjoying money." It was like water, and one couldn't live without water. In Paris she was positively drowning in money, so much so that she gave a glorious party with all kinds of food and drink, beautiful women, men with their wives and mistresses, a scene that reminded Duff of something out of Balzac. The ambassador tried to do nothing to offend his jealous mistress, who accompanied him to the party, but Gloria was so demonstratively loving toward him that there was little he could do. Later that evening he told his mistress that it was all over between them.

The next evening, Gloria and Duff had dinner in a private room at the petite Auberge du Fruit Défendu. Afterward they went upstairs to one of the bedrooms. "For the first time Gloria gave herself to me,"

Duff wrote in his diary. "I don't think I have ever loved anybody physically so much or have been so supremely satisfied."

The ambassador was giddy in love, so much so that he dismissed the warnings when he was told that "Gloria was a Gestapo agent in Spain during the war and that it was monstrous that I should go to her house." When she said it wasn't so, well, it wasn't so, and he went enraptured to her home. "I never heard nightingales singing so loudly as those in the trees under her window, and was never happier," he noted in his diary.

Duff found Gloria the most incredible mix of contradictory characteristics. She was both "wonderfully intelligent and wonderfully ignorant." She knew nothing about the political world that was at the center of the ambassador's life, but she endlessly fascinated him. It was disappointing a few weeks later when she called from the airport to say she was on her way to America. She did not tell him, but she was traveling across the Atlantic to go to Mexico for a proxy marriage with her Egyptian lover.

When Gloria returned, the new Mrs. Fakhry was as interested in carrying on her affair as before, but for Duff the profound passion was gone. "She said I was no longer in love with her, that I merely wanted her physically," the ambassador wrote in his diary. "What she meant was that I was treating her like a tart, which indeed I am."

That December Duff learned that Gloria had left Paris, taking her two children and their governess with her. She was to meet her new husband in Marseille and travel from there to Kenya. "I suppose it is all for the best," Duff noted in his diary, "but I shall miss her very much."

That seemed to be the end of it, but Gloria was not going to live forever in the hinterlands of Africa. She returned to Paris a few months later and had lunch with Duff at the Hôtel de Crillon. She was pregnant and doubly happy, since as she told Duff, her husband had inherited a great deal of money and a house in Switzerland, where she intended to go to have her baby.

Duff next talked to Gloria seven months later. She was back in Paris and apparently had lost the baby. If that wasn't difficult enough, the French authorities said they had "*mauvais renseignements*" concerning her and were throwing her out of the country. It almost certainly had to do with her role during the war. Duff had his deputy approach the minister of the interior, who in the end said Gloria could stay.

Gloria's third marriage lasted only three years. Without money or prospects, what was this mother of two in her late thirties going to do? She had long since had a way of gravitating toward the rich and powerful, and she did it once again when she met banking heir Loel Guinness. While Gloria was partying in Berlin among the Nazi elite, Loel was flying fighter planes in the Battle of Britain with such distinction that the French named him an officer of the Legion of Honour.

Loel's father had died recently, leaving him $200 million ($2.39 billion in today's dollars), making him one of the richest men in the world. That fortune would have made almost anyone nervous about a penniless interloper, and Loel was of a suspicious nature.

Loel had learned to be mistrustful for reasons that were as much personal as they were political. In 1935 he had returned from a trip to Australia to find his first wife ensconced in a Paris hotel suite with Aly Khan, the playboy son of the leader of millions of Nizari Ismaili Muslims, who himself would later have an affair with Pamela Churchill. In those years, Loel was a member of Parliament, and the divorce was one of the most publicized scandals of the decade. For Loel's second marriage, he was the one caught cheating, and that marriage also ended in divorce.

Most inheritors of great fortunes worry that people will try to take away a cut of the money that they have acquired in a windfall of good fortune. It is almost impossible that Loel would have married Gloria without limiting what part of his money she might obtain. None of that negotiation was ever made public, and in April 1951, they married in Antibes, France.

9

"She Is"

FROM THE DAY thirty-eight-year-old Gloria married Loel, Gloria had a single-minded goal: to sit atop the swirling social world that she'd gained entry to just before World War II, and which was again picking up steam now that the war was over. Although forty-four-year-old Loel was a member of the British establishment, the Mexican-born Gloria had no European social background. And she had, of course, trafficked with Nazi war criminals; that was a stain that was hard to wash off, no matter how beautiful and accomplished she was. Almost anyone else from her background would have acted repentant, fawningly obsequious to her social betters and studiously copying the behavior of those whose company she sought. That was not Gloria. She had no self-doubt and made no fumbling gestures as she took what she considered her righteous place in this world. It was as if her entire life, every episode, good and bad, had been in preparation for this moment.

The settings, of course, must be exquisite. That began with the Guinnesses' Paris residence, located on Avenue Matignon near the

Tuileries Garden. It was called an apartment, but it was in fact larger than many houses. The entrance off the elevator led to a vestibule with an imposing Louis XV console. To the right a long hallway led to two bedrooms and a terrace, where Gloria loved to entertain cherished friends. Straight ahead was the dining room with its eighteenth-century wallpaper. On the left was the grand salon, a mammoth room with ceilings that reached more than twenty feet and walls covered with brown velvet.

The apartment was furnished with an eclectic mix of antiques that in someone else's hands might have seemed a hapless mishmash, but in Gloria's hands worked perfectly. Then there was the wine cellar, as good as any in Paris. Even the food was a challenge to convention. One favorite dish was a baked potato as big as a small melon, stuffed with butter and caviar.

Gloria could invite the likes of the Duke and Duchess of Windsor over to such a sumptuous home, as she did in 1955—making sure the evening was duly noted in the society columns, of course. The twice divorced duchess was a woman of immense social ambition who used not just her husband's lineage but fashion and the image she created as the engine of her advance. She largely dominated the engagements that were the central focus of her and the duke's lives. Gloria did much the same in her marriage. She was the dynamic, intriguing force outshining her husband, a man who appeared sometimes the captive of a world where he did not belong.

Gloria had an immediate rapport with the duchess. For the royal couple, the Guinnesses were a delightful addition to their voluminous social calendar. To Gloria, their friendship was far more important. Befriend the duke and duchess and you were deemed welcome in the highest reaches of international society.

The following year the Guinnesses had dinner with the duke and duchess and the playwright Noël Coward at the Hôtel de Paris in Monte Carlo. The Belle Époque hotel stood next door to the casino, and Gloria insisted they gamble a bit. Coward managed to lose £100, which put him in a foul mood. On the drive back up the coast to their villas, Coward found the duke's conversation "completely idiotic," the absurdity enhanced by his deafness. Gloria didn't care. She would have propped the duke up in the back seat of the car and listened to his endless blathering for hours, as long as she could say that she was socializing with the former king. She became so close to the couple that two years later she invited them to stay with her in the Guinnesses' Florida home.

The day would come when Truman would be welcomed in the circles that Gloria frequented, but in 1951, he was living modestly in Taormina, devoted to little beyond his writing. One day that spring a determined man showed up in the Sicilian town. His name was Arnold Saint Subber, and he was the Tony Award–winning producer of *Kiss Me, Kate*, the Cole Porter musical that was still running on Broadway after two years. The thirty-three-year-old producer had come all this way because he was looking for his next big hit, and he wanted it to be Truman's novel *The Grass Harp*.

Truman knew nothing about the uniquely complicated process of writing a successful play. But he was as broke as ever, and a hit as big as *Kiss Me, Kate* would take care of his financial woes. Truman jumped boldly into the role of playwright, never contemplating that this endeavor could end in disaster.

The out-of-town tryouts gave all kinds of indications that things weren't right, but when *The Grass Harp* opened on March 27, 1952, Truman was in a blithely optimistic mood. As the celebrities started arriving at the Martin Beck Theatre, he stood across the street with the producer, watching them get out of their limousines.

The reviews were decidedly mixed, as if the critics had seen two different plays that evening. Brooks Atkinson of *The New York Times*, the dean of New York drama critics, called it "a beautiful play," but on the other side of town at the *New York Daily News*, John Chapman wrote, "I don't know what it's about." Unfortunately for Truman, most theatergoers saw the same play as Chapman did. There was ample blame to divvy up for the failure (Cecil Beaton's sets, for one thing, were absurdly overwrought, looking nothing like life in a Southern hamlet), but Truman's play itself had to take most of the blame. *The Grass Harp* closed after a month.

Even before the final performance, Truman and Jack were sailing back to Taormina so Truman could return to his forte: writing novels, novellas, and short stories. But Saint Subber had not given up on Truman. He would go on to produce many of Neil Simon's most successful plays, and he believed in Truman's talents as a playwright. An immensely social person, Truman loved the collegial aspect of playwriting, and he was ready to try his fortune again. The producer plucked one of Truman's short stories, "House of Flowers," and announced it fit for a musical.

Truman had written the story back in 1948, when, on a trip to Haiti, he had hung out at the whorehouses that lined Bizonton Road, listening to the whores tell their tales. The story of Ottilie, a "lovely light color(ed)" seventeen-year-old prostitute, the queen of

Port-au-Prince's Champs-Élysées brothel, did not seem likely to appeal to churchgoing tourists from Minneapolis. But the producer implored Truman to adapt the tale into a play.

That fall, after beginning work on *House of Flowers*, Truman and Jack drove north in their little Renault to spend the winter in Rome. Truman took so much baggage he could have been Napoleon invading Russia. On top of the trunks and suitcases in the back seat, their blue terrier, Kelly, yapped out the window.

As busy as Truman was, it wasn't just Broadway that had come calling. With his quick, acerbic wit, Truman was a natural writer of dialogue—a fact not lost on the Hollywood community. While he and Jack were in Rome, film producer David Selznick hired him to try to save the execrable script for the movie *Indiscretion of an American Wife*, a Montgomery Clift/Jennifer Jones picture that ended up being an utter failure despite (not because of) Truman's contribution. Undaunted, Selznick gave him full rein on the script for the soon-to-be-classic caper film *Beat the Devil*, loaded from beginning to end with Truman's marvelous lines ("The only thing standing between you and a watery grave is your wits, and that's not my idea of adequate protection").

Truman could have gone to Hollywood and likely become a top screenwriter, but that wasn't what he wanted. Instead, in the spring of 1953, Truman and Jack packed up their things and drove to Portofino, a quaint fishing village on the Italian Riviera that was becoming a tourist spot for wealthy visitors who had to be wherever the chic gathered. And so they came, the famous and the celebrated, the powerful and the rich. Truman was almost as much a tourist attraction as Castello Brown, the castle above the town. He did his work during the day, but in the evenings, he was the center of one scintillating party after another. Truman wrote David Selznick, "I can't tell you what Portofino's been like the past August—really rather fun, if you just abandoned yourself to it," which is precisely what he did.

Jack didn't find it "really rather fun" hanging around these pretentious arrivals who were seeking nothing but their own amusement, in doing so driving Truman away from the writing that was his life. There was a cautionary tale in the case of Truman's raven. One day when they were living in Sicily, the servant girl Graziella brought Truman a bird with clipped wings. He named the bird Lola and placed it on the floor with his two dogs. Lola ran around pretending she was a dog. Even when her wings grew back, she did not fly.

Truman took the raven to Rome, where he and Jack were living in a high-rise apartment building. One day, when a big cat jumped at Lola on the balcony, she jumped off into the air. At that moment, when she could only live if she reverted to her true self, she could not do so, and so she died, smashed against the concrete.

Was Truman pretending he was something he was not, and one day when he sought to return to his true being, would he not be able to get there?

When the winds of autumn bore down on Portofino, Truman and Jack packed up once again and drove to Switzerland to visit Charlie Chaplin and his wife, Oona, who Truman had known since they were teenagers. From there they drove to Paris to stay until January, when they planned to sail home on the *Queen Mary*.

Truman and Jack were both going through troubled times with their writing. Jack was despairing of his future as an author. Truman was his own best critic, and when he read the pages of *House of Flowers*, he knew it wasn't good. Once he got back to a cold New York winter, he would have to sit there week after week rewriting this play that he was obligated to finish.

New Year's Eve 1954 came and went, and when it was about time to pack up once again for the sail across the Atlantic, Truman's stepfather, Joe, called from New York to say that Nina had ingested a bottle of Seconal and descended into a coma. He called again soon afterward to say Truman's mother was dead.

Joe and Nina's jerry-built house was already crumbling before her death. To maintain the lifestyle that Nina had insisted upon, Joe had been pilfering money from his Wall Street firm. When his employer discovered nearly $100,000 missing (close to $1 million today), he was fired and a criminal investigation begun. In 1955, Joe would plead guilty to forgery and grand larceny and spend a little over a year in Sing Sing prison.

Nina and Joe had bought their way into café society. With their money gone and their names disgraced, Nina was gone too. She had a husband who needed her and a son with whom she had not fully reconciled, but she felt she had no reason to live.

Truman flew home to attend the ceremony at Frank Campbell's on Madison Avenue, the funeral home where all the best people had their services. He was full of the most overwhelming series of emotions—sorrow, anger, love, remorse, hate, bitterness—all mixed together. That was his mother's bequest to her only son, these horrifying feelings that would never fully leave him.

Four and a half years later, Truman came up with the idea for *Answered Prayers*, a novel about women who had their dreams of riches fulfilled and for the most part ended up with the taste of ashes in their mouths.

The Guinnesses' family tree looked like a bramble bush. Loel's twenty-four-year-old son Patrick fell in love with Gloria's eighteen-year-old daughter Dolores from her marriage to Count Fürstenberg. This meant that Patrick was marrying his stepsister. In October 1955, the whole family was in Paris for the wedding. Fürstenberg had survived the war, and he was there to give his daughter away. Also there that day was Princess Joan Aly Khan, Patrick's mother, who had gone on to marry and divorce Aly Khan. It was all maddeningly complicated—and that was only part of it.

Gloria was developing social relationships that rarely left her and Loel truly alone. When the Guinnesses went down to the Riviera in the summer, they rented a grand home on the Mediterranean. The day started around noon for drinks on the deck of the Guinness yacht. Then the captain sailed off to one island or another, joined by a flotilla of other yachts. The boat dropped anchor and sat there, with the crew serving more drinks, until the ship headed back to port to dock by four (and no later). Time was needed to change and be ready for cocktails and the dinner party, wherever it was that evening.

Since she was a child, Gloria had understood the role of fashion in a woman's life. Now that she had the money to buy whatever clothes she wanted, she tackled the process of shopping and dressing with immense seriousness and great gusto. It wasn't just the dresses that mattered but the whole ceremony of presenting herself to the world in the best possible light. Her clothes did not define her. She defined her clothes.

All of Truman's closest women friends were on the International Best-Dressed List at one time or another, but none of them had as intimate a relationship with fashion as Gloria did. "Gloria, Glorissima . . . the ultimate in elegance," *Women's Wear Daily* headlined in a front-page story in 1962. "Effortless, gracious, interested—in the theatre, art, music, literature, people, living," the fashion daily wrote. "An inspiration to fashion designers—one of the few women to influence Balenciaga . . . a great personal friend of Castillo . . . the dream of Bohan, Givenchy, St. Laurent and others, who adore her."

It irritated Gloria that once Jack Kennedy was in the White House, First Lady Jacqueline Kennedy was almost universally considered the best-dressed woman in America. Jackie stood ahead of Gloria on the International Best-Dressed List, a position that Gloria felt was absurd.

Gloria had a rapier wit and savage opinions that she knew she must keep to herself, but sometimes she just *had* to say something. Four months after the assassination of President Kennedy, Gloria attended a Manhattan dinner party. A guest mentioned the president's widow, who was viewed as a saintly figure beyond reproach. Gloria mocked the idea that Jackie represented some ideal of elegance. She went on like a prosecutor presenting a bill of accusations, each one more vivid than the last.

Among the other guests was Diana Vreeland, the editor of *Vogue*. Her banker husband, Reed Vreeland, was there too, and he felt he had to come to the former First Lady's defense. "You come out of Mexico," he said, confronting Gloria in a way almost no one had ever done, "are received by all of us Americans, and you have the

impertinence to criticize the wife, the widow of our president. You . . .
You . . ."

The infuriated banker was not so much challenging the veracity of
what Gloria said as attacking her nationality, and Gloria responded
with her own volley of verbal blows. The fisticuffs reminded one jour-
nalistic commentator of the recent Clay-Liston championship fight,
with Reed doubtlessly the noble Clay and Gloria the dark criminal
Liston. Eventually, dispassionate heads separated the combatants so
the dinner party could continue.

Gloria got a measure of vindication a number of years later, when
Jackie was married to Onassis and the couple came to dinner one
evening in Florida. Onassis had married the most desirable woman
in the world, but that evening he was having his doubts about that
judgment, especially when he compared her to Gloria. "You look terrible," he told Jackie. "Look at how Gloria looks. . . . Look at you.
You're a mess."

"I know—I got dressed in a hurry," Jackie said. It was not an ex-
cuse Gloria ever would have made.

Gloria not only wore clothes wonderfully but created whole new
fashions. She wore one of the first black mink coats. She did the same
with turbans. Sometimes she skewed the fad of the moment with a
deft feint of her tongue. For a while the Chanel suit was as ubiquitous
on the exalted women of the international set as the Mao suit in
China and as immune from criticism—except, of course, from Gloria. "Chanel suits are for Switzerland," Gloria opined, turning the
small Alps nation into the West Virginia of Europe. "I could not possibly wear them in Paris where everyone else does. They are adorable,
though, for lonely mountain roads."

Gloria was at her most intense and focused during the annual showing of the new collections during the torrid days of August. It was important enough to her that she flew in and out of Paris on the Guinness plane from her home in the cool heights of Epalinges, Switzerland. Whatever collection she saw, from Balenciaga to St. Laurent to Givenchy, she was in the front row in the most desired of placements. This was not only because she purchased so much but because the couturiers admired a woman who was in some ways one of them.

Remembering all her mother had shown her, Gloria did not just buy a dress. She first touched the stitching and appreciated the cut until she understood precisely how it all came together. It mattered how things were made. Quality was everything. These clothes were living things to her. She almost never had them ironed. That was desecration. It worked just fine to hang them up properly in a damp warm room.

Gloria loved it when Truman showed up, be it to one of her parties or for a stay at one of her homes or for a cruise on the yacht. The only caveat was that sometimes he would bring along Jack, who could hardly contain his aversion for being there.

Truman had a predilection for straight men whom he sought to introduce to the true faith. Jack loved Truman with fidelity and moral passion. He was appalled at Truman squandering his time and talent on what he considered gaudy, glittery rich folks who had nothing to give him but their trivial gossip. He believed if Truman went far enough down that road, he could destroy his stellar career.

Jack loved to ski. It was a measure of how much Truman cared for his lover that the couple spent some of their winters in a rented house in Verbier, Switzerland, where Jack skied most days. One evening the Guinnesses drove over from their home. Truman wanted everything to be just right, and he cooked dinner and chose the proper wines.

Jack was in one of his moods. He turned toward Loel and said, "What the fuck are you doing here, you big fat Nazi?" Loel had flown innumerable missions against the Germans. It was Gloria who had trafficked with the Nazis, and although that was not brought up, the false claim hung over the evening.

To those who had known Gloria when she walked alone along the boulevards of Paris in the thirties, if they saw her now, deferred to and lauded wherever she went, they might have assumed that she had everything. Perhaps she did have everything, but everything was no longer enough. A woman of focused ambition, she decided that she wanted to be a writer, and she began working at it with the diligence of a starving artist working in a garret.

Gloria wrote a play that a producer agreed to bring to the London stage. "I did a play once and it was going to be produced in London, but my husband didn't let me," she said years later. "He said I would leave him alone for weeks on the road or whatever you call that. He said, 'I don't want to spend my weekends in Manchester and Birmingham.'" In the end, Gloria decided, "I'd rather have the husband than the play."

Whether the play was any good or not, it was certainly a worthy accomplishment. And it threatened Loel as nothing had before in their marriage. He said she must cease and desist and devote herself to her wifely duties.

Loel was jealous of his wife. Wherever they went, she stood at the center of the light, an ebullient presence discoursing provocatively on whatever subject was at hand. If she became acknowledged as a playwright or published the novel she was writing, he decided, she would be impossible.

One of Gloria's friends who observed Loel's attitude toward his wife was Mary Wells Lawrence. As head of a major advertising agency, Wells successfully competed against men at a time when few women reached executive positions. She observed her friend's plight with special poignancy and insight. As Wells saw it, Gloria "desperately wanted to have a career, and she was trapped and humiliated by her husband. Everything she did was marvelous, but nothing was hers. She used to say, 'I'm a well-dressed housewife.'"

For tax purposes, the magnificent Guinness jewels were owned not by Loel personally but by the Guinness corporation. When the couple went to a formal affair, he opened the vault and gave his wife a diamond necklace or earrings to wear. When they returned late that evening, she handed them back and he locked them in the safe until the next time. That was the way it was with everything in their lives. He was merely loaning things to her that she might one day have to return.

Gloria had built an incredible life with Loel. She had come to think of it as hers. But it wasn't, not if Loel chose to take it away. If she wanted her days to go on as before, she had no choice but to turn away from her writing.

Just as Gloria was in the painful withdrawal from her dreams, *Harper's Bazaar* came to her and asked her to do a four-times-a-year column for the monthly. It wasn't like seeing your name on a marquee in the West End or the cover of your novel in the window at the Doubleday store on Fifth Avenue, but it was something. She could do it without upsetting Loel or dramatically interrupting her life.

To Gloria, fashion was not just clothes, it was a philosophy, a way of seeing. Life was about dressing well, acting well, and living well. Judgmental to a fault, she filled her columns with authoritatively pronounced opinion on anything that crossed her vision. When she wrote about what made a person chic, she was in some measure describing her own being: "They are original without being beginners, exhibitionists without being pompous, insolent without being patronizing. Immodest but never vulgar, observant but not inquisitive, immoral but not obscene and notorious but not infamous."

Gloria had a low opinion of the male sex. As a beautiful young woman, she'd seen lusty, salivating, boastful males desperate to get what they wanted and willing to say or do whatever it took to get their way. As a result, she developed her own personal theory of what propelled history, a thesis tied in some measure to what Truman had written about the swans in his 1959 essay in *Harper's Bazaar*.

"God created Eve so that men could create money, and it is through the wants of Eve that the world has kept on moving," Gloria wrote in one of her essays. "Eve is intelligent. She knows that youth has to be replaced by something if not as wonderful, at least as desirable, and she has chosen perfection, and so well has she achieved it, that to him, she is still the same girl, but oh, so beautiful! So much so that he feels uncomfortable and when looking at his bank statement, right down insecure. But then, one can't have everything, and Eve has become a very valuable asset in his business and social life, and although he lacks in imagination, he swims in ambition."

Men, she felt, had no imagination and were in some ways dupes to God's epic scheme. Because of their ceaseless lust, grand enterprises grew, great ships crossed the seas, and skyscrapers rose into the skies. Women were there to receive the fruits of their labor. Her theory was hardly more flattering to women than it was to men—and it was about to run headlong into a new generation's changing ideas and mores.

As Gloria painfully realized, the sixties were a bad time to be growing old. Legions of youth came prancing onstage carrying their psychedelic banners, mocking everyone over thirty, and declaring that the only true fashion was fashion forged in the street. "Damn Those Young Girls!" she headlined one of her columns, and that was precisely how she felt. Damn the arrogant self-assurance of youth. Damn the perfection of their skin and their figures. Damn the abomination of the miniskirt. She had tried one and was sick at the way her legs looked. What did these young girls know about a woman of a certain age with "the slightest little bit of fat and wrinkles on her knees beginning to show?"

What could Gloria do but mock youth, writing that she had been "absolutely delighted to rid myself of good manners, bras and bad conscience," though none of that was true. She was full of envy and anger at those who pushed her aside, but there was sadness too. "I can't help but feel sorry for the younger ones—the ones that will have to face the seventies amidst all the glittering moral squalor that has become so fashionable," she wrote.

But while she railed against the changing times, the fashion establishment embraced her writing. In 1967, Gloria received the first Penney-University of Missouri Award as America's best fashion journalist. She knew the ballroom at the Waldorf would be full of fashion journalists and industry executives, who would look at whatever she wore with detailed professional concern. To seek the outfit for such an important occasion, she went to André Courrèges in Paris.

Courrèges was originally trained as a civil engineer, and his streamlined clothes were the essence of sixties hip. Courrèges invented the go-go boot and deserved partial credit for the miniskirt, items that perfectly defined what Gloria hated about cursed modernity. That she wanted to wear the designer's clothes on her fashion day of days was extraordinary. Still, she didn't want to look like she thought she was a teenager. Nor did she want to resemble friends who dressed in little but Courrèges. She had never ordered from Courrèges before, but she did this time. He personally fitted a cream coat and navy dress with a flaring skirt. She matched that with a beige hat from Balenciaga. It all worked perfectly together, a chic outfit for a woman of a certain age.

Gloria flew from Paris in the Guinness plane to New York to accept her award. Anyone who saw Gloria that day would assume this woman lived a life of splendor. Who could have imagined that she saw herself as a squatter in her life, owning nothing and belonging nowhere? Only a few understood, like Mary Wells Lawrence, who considered her friend "the saddest woman I ever met."

10

A Guest in the House

O N A COLD evening in March 1956, Truman ventured out of his Brooklyn apartment to travel to Broadway's Broadhurst Theatre to attend the opening of *My Fair Lady*, a new musical by Alan Jay Lerner and Frederick Loewe. CBS was the major backer, and Truman's friendship with Bill and Babe Paley was likely the reason he had a coveted ticket to a play that had created such a buzz even before its first performance.

From the moment the curtain opened on Eliza Doolittle, a Cockney flower girl spewing out uncouth, largely unintelligible lingo as she attempts to sell her bouquets in London's Covent Garden, the New York audience was enchanted. They watched as the phonetician Professor Henry Higgins (Rex Harrison) turns Eliza (Julie Andrews) into an upper-class young woman who speaks the King's English. The play was set in London, but it was a very American theme. A person can be anything she wants to be if she tries hard enough and has the right instructor.

As Truman sat in the theater that evening, he was a little like Eliza himself. Babe had been his Henry Higgins, and what she didn't teach him, he had largely taught himself. At the end of the first act, when a triumphantly transformed Eliza dances among the blue bloods at the Embassy Ball, Truman could have been her escort.

Between acts Truman walked across the street to a crowded bar charged with excitement. *My Fair Lady* was already being lauded as the most important opening of a musical since *Oklahoma!*, thirteen years before. The bar was jammed, but amid the patrons he spotted his friend Cecil Beaton, who had designed the costumes for the musical and was enjoying one of the best evenings in his life.

Standing next to Beaton was a woman who transfixed Truman. When he saw this elegant, beautiful woman with a magical aura, he was transported. It was the rarest of sightings, and he remembered it the way one recalls the beginning of a great love affair.

Truman mused lyrically that he saw Lucy "C. Z." Guest "shimmering in the blue smoky light. Her hair parted in the middle and paler than Don [*sic*] Perignon, was but a shade darker than the dress she was wearing, a Main Bocher [*sic*] column of white crêpe de chine. No jewelry, not much makeup; just blanc do blanc perfection." No wonder the women who were the subjects of Truman's tributes adored him.

That adoration did not begin that evening. C.Z. could wilt roses with her imperious stare, though she preferred to do it to men who had the audaciousness to seek her attention. This evening she had no interest in squandering those few minutes talking to this strange little man who only came up to her breasts, a part of the body in which he had decidedly no interest. When Beaton introduced her to Truman, she responded with what the author took as "ice cream reserve."

Truman did not become friends with C.Z. that evening, but soon Truman learned "that lurking inside this cool vanilla lady was a madcap, laughing tomboy." His newest friend was a Boston Brahmin, a member of the old American aristocracy. There were only about six thousand of them, and when she was growing up in the thirties, they practiced rituals and customs that even then were becoming anachronisms in upper-crust Manhattan and its environs.

These proper Bostonians had a reverential belief in the old and settled. They might have a grand house on Beacon Hill and a splendid North Shore summer home, but they must never be seen as showing off. That meant they were comfortable wearing a twenty-year-old suit and driving a ten-year-old car. They purchased quality, and quality lasted forever in cars and clothes—as well as in people. Everyone who mattered knew that, and everyone knew everyone. That made things simple.

C.Z. was born Lucy Douglas Cochrane in Boston on February 19, 1920. Her nickname came about because her sister could not pronounce the word "sister" and started calling her "Sissy," which evolved into C.Z. In elementary school, C.Z. was so distracted and loud that a later generation of physicians might well have diagnosed her with ADHD and put her on meds. When she was ten years old, her teacher noted on her report card that she "needs to be very busy or she will gain superficial social superiority." To C.Z., there was nothing superficial about social superiority. It was more crucial to life than Latin or algebra.

C.Z. spoke in a Brahmin accent. Americans who had never visited London often thought these Bostonians were speaking in upper-class British accents. But these hybrid tones sounded as if they were native to an isolated island in the North Atlantic.

Brahmin Boston was an enclave of privilege where C.Z. learned almost nothing about the ravages of the Great Depression. The thirties were a terrific time to be reaching maturity if one had money and thought the poor deserving of their fate. Things were cheap, and the rich love bargains just as much as the poor.

When C.Z. was a teenager, her mother sent her down to Fermata, a school in South Carolina for well-brought-up young women. The teachers were not about to furrow the brows of their rich charges with heavy learning, but even the light curriculum was too much for C.Z., who far preferred riding to studying. In all her education and family training, she never learned such mundane business as cooking a meal or changing a sheet. There were servants to do that, and the less one knew about it, the better.

Although C.Z. was accepted in Boston society, she was far from a pure-blooded member of the Brahmin world. The problem was not her father, Alexander Lynde Cochrane, who had Scottish roots that went back to the land's greatest hero, Robert the Bruce. Cochrane was an investment banker and a full-fledged member of the Boston upper crust. Two years after he died in 1928, his widow married another wealthy Bostonian, the lawyer Dudley L. Pickman Jr.

The problem, as far as Boston saw it, was C.Z.'s mother. Vivian Wessell was a New Yorker. If that had not been shocking enough, she came from a theatrical family. Before her marriage, she had sung in operettas, while her own mother had traveled the country as an accompanist and musical impresario. It was one thing to sing a song or two in the library after dinner or play a bit of Strauss on the piano, but being paid to perform onstage before an audience was beyond déclassé. There were few things worse than a professional *anything*.

To the old Bostonians, blood defined everything. If it was lacking or tainted, sooner or later it would show up like a latent illness that strikes in its own good time. That time, as far as C.Z.'s family was concerned, happened when C.Z. and her older sister, Nancy, made their debuts.

Their debuts so horrified traditionalists that the Society chronicler Cleveland Amory spent a long paragraph in *The Proper Bostonians* writing about the debuts in 1936 and 1938, which "by the strictest Boston Society standards, [were] extremely outlandish affairs." The author described in telling detail the things the family did to offend the sensitivities of a city that had embraced them.

The young women in the First Families generally made their debuts on Friday evenings in the fall at the Country Club, known by outsiders as the Brookline Country Club. The Cochrane sisters' debuts were held not at the Country Club but at the Pickmans' forty-room Stanford White mansion on Commonwealth Avenue.

Not content with yanking Nancy's debut out of its rightful place, Amory wrote that the "home was entirely transformed into a Paris street scene, complete with sidewalk cafes, lampposts and twinkly stars." If that wasn't insult enough, two years later, for C.Z.'s ball, "the home became equally unrecognizable, the entrance hall being transformed by a vigorous array of potted trees and plants into a garden scene and the dining room being hung from top to bottom with gold satin looped up with mountain laurel and hemlock boughs."

To make matters even worse, the guests danced until dawn, something that never would have happened at the Country Club. The only solace, as Amory quickly pointed out, was that Mrs. Pickman was a New Yorker and hardly responsible for her social ineptness. Her assault on revered customs did not end with her daughters' debuts. Mrs. Pickman gave parties that combined classical musicians with jazz artists, Broadway performers with players of Brahms. To the traditionalists, it was mixing champagne and beer, but it showed the youthful C.Z. that there was an inviting world beyond the gates of old Boston.

No teenager in Boston was written about in the press more often than C.Z., and the stories chronicled all the pleasures of her privileged young life. She loved to ride, and what could be better on an August day than taking the jumps on a spirited horse at the annual field day at an Ipswich estate? Theater was quite the thing, as were the symphony and the opera . . . as long as you went opening night, when your presence and dress were sure to be noted in the morning's *Boston Globe*. Not just a spectator, C.Z. played in tennis tournaments and was in the ballet in the skating extravaganza starring the three-time Olympic champion Sonja Henie at the Boston Arena.

C.Z. had no interest in plebian sports such as baseball and football, but hockey was worth watching, especially if it was the Harvard boys defeating Princeton at Boston Garden. The Boston Bruins, the city's professional hockey team, were sport at a different level. As C.Z. and her sister walked to their rinkside seats, hoots, whistles, and screams came in tribute to the gorgeous Cochrane sisters.

C.Z. was rumored to be dating a number of the players, an endeavor so far beyond the pale that it was only whispered. To the moralists of the Old Society, it did not matter whether the rumor was true. Even attached falsely to her name, it was a badge of shame. C.Z. was not the only debutante behaving in ways unthinkable to their mothers' generation, but like everything else in her life, she did it in a more flamboyant way.

One evening in December 1936, C.Z. and her mother went to the Colonial Theatre to watch a young actress, Katharine Hepburn, starring in *Jane Eyre*. The classic novel by Charlotte Brontë is the story of a plain English governess defying everything society set out for her, overcoming challenge after challenge. The actress onstage was doing the same. As the daughter of progressive parents, she had been pushed by her mother to attend Bryn Mawr College, where she began acting. In the years since then, Hepburn had had some major successes and equally dramatic failures. If some admired her abilities, others mocked her as talentless and manly. Her career in Hollywood had plateaued, and touring with *Jane Eyre* was a way to work again in a meaningful way.

C.Z. had a secret desire to be an actress herself, a double reason for her to be at the Colonial that evening. Although Hepburn was a child of privilege, that was where the similarity between the two women ended. Hepburn understood that the price of success was paid in hard currency, and she was willing to pay it, even if it meant spending the Christmas season in a hotel room in a city far from home. But life had taught C.Z. a different story. Everything had been given to her. That was just the way it was, and it was the way it *should* be.

What set C.Z. apart from most of her fellow debs was not her height but her beauty. When *The Boston Globe* ran a picture of her at a debutante party wearing a floor-length, shimmering, vertically striped, low-cut gown and elbow-length gloves, the image was reproduced in papers all across America, from Billings, Montana, to St. Petersburg, Florida. Her looks were such that she won the title North Shore's Prettiest.

Beauty had been C.Z.'s magic wand all her life. All she had to do was to wave it and she got what she wanted. As a little girl, adults looked at her and praised her in a way they did not children who had more common looks. As a debutante, her dance cards were always full, and men were always there pursuing her. Combining beauty with wealth, she walked where she wanted to walk and got what she wanted to get.

The attention C.Z. attracted wherever she went did not just happen. She dressed to maim, always stylish with a soupçon of sexiness but never quite vulgar, never over-the-top. It took money, lots of money, to always wear a different stunning outfit, but money was only the beginning. Yes, it took style, but style wasn't enough either. Beyond that it took a certain theatrical energy to project oneself onto the world.

No longer a post-debutante but a young Bostonian lady, C.Z. knew that her next preordained endeavor was to marry properly and begin the cycle all over again with her own daughters and sons. That may well have happened if World War II had not intervened, changing life even for women in Boston Society. In ordinary times, C.Z. would have considered it far beneath her to do such a pedestrian thing as take a job, but with the war she joined a volunteer organization, the Massachusetts Women's Defense Corps, and spent her days at the defense center.

That left C.Z.'s evenings free. At whatever theater or club she entered, there was that rustling of attention that showed she had achieved her desired aim. At the opening of *Winged Victory*, a show to benefit the Army Emergency Relief Fund, any number of stars had flown in for the evening, from Sergeant Gene Autry to Greer Garson. But when C.Z. walked down the aisle to her seat wearing a black satin dress with a narrow band of lace highlighting the low neckline and black stockings, there was a tremor of excitement as if a Hollywood queen had entered the theater. Youth, beauty, attention . . . that was the game, and it was a fierce competition.

Determined to succeed not just in the society ballrooms but also

Twenty-three-year-old Truman Capote was a stunning-looking young man when his first novel, *Other Voices, Other Rooms,* was published in 1948.

It was a second marriage for both when Barbara "Babe" Paley married CBS mogul William S. Paley in 1947.

Nancy "Slim" Gross married Hollywood director
Howard Hawks in 1941. Gary Cooper was the best man.

Nancy "Slim" Gross married
her second husband, producer
Leland Hayward, in 1949.

Pamela Harriman married her first husband,
Randolph Churchill, in 1941.

Pamela Harriman married her second husband, Broadway producer Leland Hayward, in 1960.

Gloria Guinness in a
white crepe dress by
Lanvin Castillo in 1963
in her Paris apartment.

Gloria Guinness wearing
an off-the-shoulder dress
by Schiaparelli.

Truman Capote escorting
Babe Paley (right) and Gloria Guinness.

Mrs. Winston "C. Z." Guest wearing a party dress of white Italian pique by one of her favorite designers, Hattie Carnegie.

Mrs. Winston "C. Z." Guest in Palm Beach with her poodle in 1962.

Donna Marella Caracciolo di Castagneto's wedding
to Giovanni Agnelli in 1953 in Osthoffen, France.

The Italian princess Marella Agnelli
was considered one of the most
beautiful women in the world.

Truman Capote escorts his dear friend Lee Radziwill through the New York social scene.

Lee Radziwill with her sister, Jacqueline Onassis,
and friend Rudolph Nureyev.

Mrs. Winston "C. Z." Guest dancing with Truman Capote at Studio 54.

Truman Capote turned the disco
Studio 54 into his respite from reality.

on the stage, C.Z. got herself a theatrical agent and took whatever gigs she could get, including a job appearing onstage with Slydini, the magician. Her interest in show biz got a decided boost when she began an affair with the movie star Victor Mature, who had begun his Hollywood career touted as a super Tarzan figure. Mature had joined the Coast Guard and was sailing out from Boston on the North Atlantic guarding convoys.

For the first time, C.Z.'s name reached the national gossip columns. "Victor Mature to wed Lucy Cochrane when divorce finalities permit," the gossip columnist Walter Winchell wrote in June 1943. The actor was already divorced, and his marital status was not the reason the couple never reached the altar.

Theater was in the family blood, and before C.Z.'s older sister joined the Women's Army Corps, she acted in summer stock alongside a number of well-known performers. When C.Z. decided to become an actress, she was not going to start out in some crummy theater in the hinterlands. She wanted to go right to Broadway.

C.Z. did not have to go out to hustle connections. They simply appeared before her in her natural habitat. In Boston she met the theatrical producer Lee Shubert, who arranged for her to be in the chorus line in *Ziegfeld Follies*, the long-running Broadway revue. The show had its first run in 1907 and featured scores of tall, dazzling chlorine-blondes who did little but walk down a staircase wearing elaborate costumes. There were not so many young women in the latest version, but they still were what drew the audiences, not the jokes of the comedian Milton Berle. In January 1944, the show was nearing the end of its run, and though nobody was going to buy a ticket just to see the long-legged C.Z., it would be good publicity to have a twenty-three-year-old Boston socialite as one of the Ziegfeld girls.

The most unusual aspect of C.Z.'s theatrical life was not her performance but that she lived in a suite at the Ritz-Carlton hotel. As it was, she lasted no more than two months before she left to understudy the ingenue role in a new comedy, *Mrs. January and Mr. X*. Although C.Z. was taking acting lessons, she had yet to speak a single word on any stage. Thus, she may have been fortunate that the play flopped and she never once had to play the role.

Truman had little luck with plays either. When *House of Flowers* opened on Broadway in December 1954, the reviewers were no kinder than many of them had been to *The Grass Harp*. The critics took personal umbrage at Truman, and that was a frightening thing to any author. John Chapman of the *New York Daily News* began his review, "It is too bad, and possibly disastrous, that Truman Capote conceived the first scene of 'House of Flowers' out of a dirty little mind." Brooks Atkinson of *The New York Times* ended his review, "He [Truman] lacks the flair of the real troubadour of sex. Maybe we should forget about the brothels. They are getting to be a bore."

House of Flowers closed after a modest 165 performances, but it rocketed Truman's fame to an even higher level. The fancy folks Jack called "the peacocks" were more interested than ever in having him around, and he was more interested than ever in being around them. Truman went off to Jamaica with the Paleys and flew out to Los Angeles to stay with the Selznicks before flitting up to Boston with Audrey Hepburn and Mel Ferrer to see Julie Harris starring in *The Lark*. And he started hanging out with Marilyn Monroe and having dinner with Jackie Kennedy when her husband, Senator John F. Kennedy, was not in town. Wherever Truman went, he was wildly entertaining, spinning his mesmerizing tales.

Jack wasn't the only one upset with all the time Truman was spending around such people. John Malcolm Brinnin was a well-known poet and the head of the Poetry Center at Manhattan's YMHA. John saw himself as a protector of literature, not in a snooty, overweening way but out of profound concern. He greatly admired Truman as an artist. On a holiday in Portofino in the summer of 1955, John picked up a copy of *Time* magazine and saw a picture of Truman dancing with Marilyn Monroe. The image epitomized what John thought had gone wrong with his gifted friend, and he sent him a postcard: "Was *this* the Portrait of the Artist as a Young Man? Joyce's motto was, Silence, exile and cunning. What's *yours*?" He signed the card: "Reader of Time."

Truman didn't get it because he didn't want to get it. He wrote John back, "I have done nothing to deserve your misguided candor."

No matter how much time Truman was squandering with his rich friends, his talent had not diminished. That December he joined a company of *Porgy and Bess* traveling to Leningrad and Moscow to write a story for *The New Yorker.*

Truman's idea of paradise was a group of intriguing people isolated together for an extended period. Whether it was actors stuck together in a hotel in Italy or a troupe of Black actors traveling eastward together across the frozen heartland of Russia in the "sleek collection of dark green cars" known as the Blue Express, it was people knocking against one another, creating all kinds of drama. To bring this vividly alive, it took an observer who saw, heard, felt, and tasted everything before him and committed it to the page. It took discipline and attention to everything that was happening.

The author was an omnipresent observer missing nothing. Almost any other journalist would have focused on the significance of the first American cultural exchange since the birth of the Soviet Union, the importance even greater because the actors were Black. Truman focused on what he observed with his all-seeing eyes.

"If the Russians were stunned, they were not alone," Truman wrote, describing what happened opening night in Leningrad at the end of the first act. "Several of the American journalists huddled together, comparing notes. 'It's not going over,' a baffled Dan Schorr complained to a bewildered Time-Life photographer. And Mrs. Bohlen, following her husband up the aisle, was poignantly pensive. Later she told me the thought behind the expression: 'I was thinking—well, we've laid an egg. Now what are we going to do about it?'"

Some people said that Truman's story *The Muses Are Heard* was satirical—but if it was, it was gentle satire, never taking away the dignity of the subjects. Published first in *The New Yorker* and then as a short book, *The Muses Are Heard* announced Truman's emergence as one of the best narrative nonfiction writers of the day.

Truman and Jack generally spent their summers in Europe, but in 1956 they decided to take a house on the Connecticut shore at Stonington, a conservative redoubt that in its way was as exotic as Tangier or Taormina. Overseas, Truman was just another crazy American. In Stonington, he was the strangest thing many of these people had ever seen.

Truman announced himself to the community by doing such things as wearing pedal pushers without underpants, exposing his most intimate possession to public view. When he went swimming, he wore not a bathing suit but underpants, including a pair that had large ants printed all over it. And when he went downtown, he wore a

blue T-shirt so short that it exposed his bare midriff. This was unusual enough that the shopkeepers peered out at this bizarre creature. The town's children, always looking for diversions, followed
Truman, shouting foul things at him.

All kinds of writers and editors were summering in the environs,
and there were frequent dinner parties. Truman brought three pairs
of glasses with him. The other guests knew that when he put on the
darkest pair, it heralded the arrival of his best and most outrageous
stories. "It was quite apparent that he couldn't lie properly unless his
eyes were covered," said the writer David Jackson.

Truman didn't need dark glasses to talk about the high point of
the summer: when the DuPonts sent a boat for him and he spent the
day at their estate on Fishers Island. "I have to go over to Fishers and
see my magnates," he said, dismissing his current company as if they
were hardly worthy of him.

That fall, Truman and Jack moved into a basement apartment in a
Brooklyn Heights town house. Truman showed guests the whole
house, intimating that the entire, multifloor building was his residence and that he had restored and decorated the entire building
himself. He did this without wearing dark glasses.

One of Truman's neighbors was Norman Mailer, who had inherited from Ernest Hemingway the mantle as America's leading macho
author. Mailer thought that writing was like fighting a boxing match;
in order to "win," you had to knock your opponent out. That was not
the way Truman saw it, and by rights the two men should not have
been friends. But above everything else, both of them appreciated
literary accomplishment, and they grew to admire each other.

One day chancing into each other in the neighborhood, they decided to have a drink. Truman was wearing what Mailer described as

"a little gabardine cape . . . looking like a beautiful little faggot prince." Truman could have dressed in a manner that did not advertise his sexuality, but then he would not have been Truman. The two authors entered the first drinking establishment they came to on Montague Street, an Irish pub. It was 3:30 in the afternoon, when hard drinkers were already hard at work.

In those days before gentrification, an Irish pub was a decidedly working-class affair. Most good Irish Catholics did not want gays in their churches or their schools—and they sure as hell did not want them in their pubs. Mailer feared he might have to fight their way out. But Truman was the mark of coolness. He walked straight through to the back of the bar and sat down.

Mailer thought if he had to live like this, he would be pulsating adrenaline from morning to night and would "die of adrenaline over-flow." But this was Truman's life.

Her theatrical career may have been on hold, but C.Z.'s nightlife siz-zled. Victor Mature was still her man, and when he was in town, they were together. C.Z. had never experienced the tedious, often de-meaning process of trying out for parts and risking rejection. She knew the right people in the right places, and she did not have to de-mean herself by hustling to get ahead. It was at a Manhattan dinner party among talk of other things that the Hollywood producer Dar-ryl Zanuck met C.Z. and signed her to a film contract at 20th Cen-tury Fox. Just like that, she was off to Hollywood with plans of becoming a star. It was her due, after all.

As C.Z. arrived in Los Angeles, Katharine Hepburn was back in town as well. In the romantic comedy *The Philadelphia Story*, she had played to type as a socialite. The popular Academy Award–winning film showed that there might be room for C.Z. to play roles that hardly stretched her. But she still had the minuscule attention span that she had in elementary school. Not realizing that "overnight success" often happens after years of work, she was totally unprepared to spend the time it might take to hone her craft and find her place in the Hollywood ecosystem. The auditioning process was often humiliating, nothing but rejection after rejection, and she began to lose interest in acting as a profession.

Though C.Z. quickly played out her hand in Hollywood, her evenings were far from boring. Much of the time she was with the Australian-born swashbuckling star Errol Flynn. The actor was almost twice her age and married, and her affair with him suggested how far C.Z. had traveled from the chaperoned world of a Boston debutante. She eventually got an uncredited role in *Diamond Horseshoe* starring Betty Grable and Dick Haymes, but that was it. After spending no more than six months in her abortive film career, C.Z. left for Mexico City, where she took up with a devastatingly handsome bullfighter.

There were few things rarer in Mexico City than a blond beauty, and C.Z. attracted stunned attention wherever she went. One of those who saw her and was mesmerized was the painter Diego Rivera, who asked to paint her in the nude. The finished painting was placed above the bar at Ciro's, a leading club, where patrons could sit drinking palomas or margaritas, admiring the nude body of a Boston Brahmin. By then C.Z. had left the city for good, not the least bit distressed that she had left part of herself there.

C.Z. may not have been an actress, but she was incredibly

photogenic. One of those mesmerized by seeing one of her photos was Winston Frederick Churchill Guest, an heir to the Phipps steel fortune. His mother had married Frederick Edward Guest, a first cousin to Winston Churchill, and Winston Guest had been brought up both in England and the United States. The dual fortunes had been so large and so long-standing in the two families that they existed in their own alternate, upper-crust reality.

Although the British-born Winston had taken American citizenship, he was as much British as American, and he and his family had a decidedly British approach to wealth: namely, they did not care if you did nothing as long as you did nothing well. Winston had no qualms about his wealth, and he did pretty much what he wanted to do. And one of the things he wanted to do was to meet the blonde in the picture.

"You can have affairs, God knows I've had plenty," said C.Z. "But you marry someone from your own environment." Those fervent nights with movie stars and hockey players were fine in their place, but these were not the kind of men one wedded. If she married Winston, she would be embracing not only him but an entire way of life.

Winston was the perfect model of what C.Z. had been taught a man of her class should be. Of course, he was rich. That was a given. The forty-year-old had strong, masculine good looks and was an imposing six feet four inches tall. With his degrees from Yale and Columbia Law School, Winston could have done almost anything. He owned an airline in Mexico City, but he was primarily a gentleman amateur and could play almost any sport well. Not only had he won club titles in tennis and golf and an international pigeon-shooting championship, he was one of the greatest polo players of his generation.

Only a rich man can afford a string of polo ponies and traveling around the world to matches. As great as he was at his chosen sport, Winston's talent as a horseman was known primarily among a sophisticated group of the wealthy elite, and that was the way he wanted it. He did not want vulgar fame, his image reproduced endlessly in newspapers, his name shouted by the masses. Winston lived totally within his world, socializing and playing sport among the anointed.

There was another key to Winston's ideal of a gentleman, and that was physical courage. Early on in World War II, Winston had flown to Cuba to be a member of Ernest Hemingway's crew on his boat, *Pilar*, armed with machine guns and depth charges, sailing the Caribbean looking for Nazi submarines. After that experience, Winston was almost turned down by the marines because he had lost part of his trigger finger in a hunting accident. In the end, Captain Guest shipped out to the Pacific, landing in Chungking, China, fulfilling what he took as a gentleman's mandate in Shakespeare's words, "seeking the bubble reputation in the cannon's mouth."

Winston's mother was a woman of intrepid spirit and the key to almost everything her son did. When he was two years old and the family was living in a mansion in the English countryside, the building caught on fire and Mrs. Guest rushed back into the house barefoot to rescue Winston and his younger brother, Raymond. In the twenties, Mrs. Guest was so enraptured by Charles Lindbergh's flight across the Atlantic that she sought to be the first woman pilot to replicate his feat. If her son and other family members had not adamantly opposed Mrs. Guest, she likely would have been the first woman to fly the Atlantic and one of the most famous women of the age. Instead, she backed Amelia Earhart in her successful flight. In her sixties, Mrs. Guest traveled to Africa to hunt lions.

Mrs. Guest had heard about C.Z.'s infamous nude picture and may have had her doubts that her beloved Winston should marry such a woman. But C.Z. was comfortable in Mrs. Guest's world and aware of all its subtleties. After talking to C.Z., Mrs. Guest put no impediment in the way of her and Winston's marriage, which to almost everyone seemed a perfect match. As for the notorious painting, Winston purchased it for 15,000 pesos ($3,075 at the time) and stored it in a back room in the family's fifty-five-room mansion on Long Island, where it was unlikely anyone would see it and be struck by the resemblance to the *grande patronne.*

Winston had been previously married to a Woolworth heiress, with whom he had two children, but when he met C.Z., he was decidedly free. Winston would inherit much of his mother's fortune, while C.Z. came from enough wealth that she could not be accused of marrying her fiancé for money.

C.Z. had been brought up to view her wedding as the most important social occasion in her life. It was to be done with panache and elegance, witnessed by all the people who mattered and a few who did not. Winston wanted none of that. The couple flew to Havana to Hemingway's country estate to be married by a notary on March 8, 1947. The renowned author and the polo-playing heir were good friends, and whatever twenty-seven-year-old C.Z. may have expected, the wedding was as much a reunion as it was nuptials.

11

A Time of Reckoning

C.Z. WAS USED to being the center of attention. Part of it was her beauty, which drew people to her for reasons good and bad. And despite her lack of formal schooling, she had a quick wit and sharp repartee. But beyond that, she had this relentlessly upbeat spirit that made her pleasurable to be around . . . if she fancied you worth her time.

For most of her early adult life, C.Z. had run away from life as a socialite, traveling as far from her Boston background as she could. (If she had journeyed much further away, in fact, she would not have been invited back.) But it was this bold spirit that also gave her a real kinship with Winston's intrepid mother, who had rebelled (in her own, rather safe way) against the formalistic life of a grand heiress.

Winston was likely drawn to C.Z. in part because she had his mother's adventurous spirit. That was fine in a lover, but not in Mrs. Winston Guest. Ultimately, he wanted a traditional upper-class wife who would never step beyond the bounds of propriety.

Winston abhorred public attention, and he insisted that C.Z.

batten it down and figuratively walk a few paces behind him. But C.Z. did not stand back easily or well.

The early years of her marriage were full of tension—tension that reached the breaking point and soon became distressingly public. The couple had been married scarcely a year when the gossip columnists started writing about a troubled marriage. This went on for several years; in 1952, the syndicated columnist Earl Wilson wrote: "The Winston Guests are doing their brawling in the boites these nights."

But eventually the two settled into married life. Perhaps it was her Brahmin, stiff-upper-lip upbringing that steadied them. "I always thought when you married it was for life," C.Z. said. "You had to stick with it and be brave and cope with the problems." When C.Z. was asked how she stayed married to Winston, she did not talk about love, companionship, loyalty, mutual interest, or children but something far more mundane and impersonal: "Manners have been very important in keeping us together," she said.

What C.Z. called "manners" went far beyond not drinking from the finger bowl. It was social behavior unique to their class. Growing up with servants, C.Z. and Winston were rarely truly alone. They learned to project a public persona that did not change that much even when they were truly in private. They treated each other with endless civility but not necessarily intimacy. To someone brought up in a middle-class home, this might seem stifling and unreal, but it was real to them. Such conduct protected them, saved them from unpleasantness and strife, and kept life moving along with some measure of equilibrium.

C.Z. knew what she could do with her life. The only question was how well she would do it. "Style is about surviving, about having been through a lot and making it look easy," C.Z. said. Style was the essence, and by the time Truman met her in 1955, she had achieved a presence that made her one of the social leaders of the new generation. She was the woman you wanted at your party, preferably with Winston, but by herself was just fine.

Not long after C.Z. met Truman, she invited him to Palm Beach as a houseguest. That was one definition of friendship, and the eternally observant Truman arrived to see how C.Z. lived. Palm Beach had been the winter home of the American elite since the early years of the twentieth century. Winston's parents had completed their place on the island in 1916, and there was no grander estate. Running from the ocean across almost half the island, Villa Artemis was an island within the island.

Truman's fondest memories of that first visit were not a dinner party at the Everglades Club or a stroll along Worth Avenue, but C.Z. walking the dogs each morning on the beach. It was not just one or two dogs but nine or ten, a United Nations of dogs—from purebred English mastiffs to mutts so pathetic that no one but C.Z. would have rescued them. There was a Labrador with a patch over one eye that looked like a pirate's dog, and exotic breeds, including an Egyptian saluki, an obese Pekingese struggling to not be left behind, and a three-legged Mexican hairless that Winston had brought back from one of his trips to Mexico.

When C.Z. threw a stick of driftwood out into the surf, the tripod of a dog rushed into the water, bringing the wood back in his teeth. "Ah, good boy," C.Z. said, hugging the Mexican hairless. "Old soldier. My old soldier."

It may not be true that C.Z. loved dogs more than people, but it was indisputably true that she would not have walked down the beach with such a motley array of people. Nor would she have invited human versions of the fat Pekingese and the Mexican hairless to one of her parties.

Wherever C.Z. went, people looked at her and made note of her clothes. That had been true since she was sixteen years old back in Boston. Now that C.Z. was married to Winston, her clothes mattered even more. When she walked into Le Pavillon for lunch, or down the aisle at the Metropolitan Opera, or into a Broadway show on opening night, people took note.

As likely or not, C.Z. was wearing a Mainbocher. She had developed a close relationship with the American-born designer Main Rousseau Bocher. After learning his craft in Paris, Bocher arrived in America at the start of World War II, bringing the haute couture world of Paris to Manhattan. Never extreme or exaggerated, Mainbocher celebrated the female form in dresses and gowns that were never overdone. Unlike Babe, C.Z. did not aspire to a model's form. She had a thoroughbred's body perfectly attuned to its functions that allowed Mainbocher to dress her in ways that complemented her figure. She had the confidence to wear what she wanted when she wanted to wear it.

"Many women make their grand entrance at Lincoln Center looking like exotic orchids in diamonds and paint," said the fashion journalist John Fairchild, "while Mrs. Guest walks briskly down the aisle in a pale cream cardigan suit." And who was remembered but the lady in the cardigan suit.

It was a story told again and again. "I remember seeing C.Z. once in Paris, in the fifties," the clothing designer Bill Blass said. "She came into the bar of the Ritz wearing a knee-length tweed skirt, a twin set, and moccasins—and in a time when everyone else was tarted up in Dior's new look, she stopped traffic."

C.Z. was named for the first of many times to the Best-Dressed List in 1952. As she became a regular, opportunities arose. One company wanted her to design and promote their brand of riding shirts. That was a natural fit for the athletic C.Z., but Winston would hear nothing of it. If that was in part his cranky, misogynistic self, he was in some measure expressing the values of his class. "Fashion is appalling to so many Old Money beneficiaries because it carries with it a dreadful reminder of the incredible force and fluidity of the marketplace," wrote Nelson Aldrich Jr. To Winston, the idea of turning what one wore into a commercial construct was beyond appalling.

Although Winston and C.Z. had a residence on Sutton Place in Manhattan, her spiritual home was Templeton, the grand estate on Long Island that belonged to her mother-in-law. The three-hundred-acre estate in Roslyn was one of the largest family properties in America.

It was at Templeton that C.Z. gave some of the most intriguing dinner parties of the era. Although she often claimed she was terminally shy, within her milieu she was a social impresario. Able to draw on an artistic world that her husband barely acknowledged, she brought all kinds of guests to her dinner parties, though never more than twenty-four people at a time.

Of course, Truman was likely to be there, and if he was in the country, the playwright Noël Coward might be at the other end of the table, matching little Truman bon mot for bon mot. The Duke and Duchess of Windsor were everyone's perfect guests. Salvador Dalí had painted C.Z., and the cryptic Spanish artist was a desired dinner partner. The beautiful Marella Agnelli was a friend, and if she was in New York, she would likely be driven out, perhaps with her husband, Gianni Agnelli, the head of Fiat. The Agnellis switched from English to Italian to French with the ease that a Ferrari switched gears. C.Z. was friendly with other prominent socialites of her generation, including Babe, and it would not have been unexpected for the Paleys to drive over from their estate for dinner.

Truman appropriated C.Z.'s snobbish demeanor as his own. "You must be either very rich or very poor," Truman said. "There's *absolutely* no taste in between." Those were sentiments to which C.Z. would have concurred, but the very poor would probably have preferred less taste and more money.

Not to the manor born, Truman was always ready to teach lesser beings how they must behave while studiously ignoring the fact that most of this was almost as new to him as it was to them. People thought you could judge the rich by the vintage of their wine or the number of their homes, but Truman believed what truly mattered was the size of their vegetables: they were tiny. "At Babe Paley's table, or C.Z.'s—haven't you ever noticed how extraordinary the vegetables are? The smallest, most succulent peas, lettuce, the most delicate baby corn, asparagus, limas the size of cuticles, the tiny sweet radishes, everything so fresh, almost unborn."

At C.Z.'s dinner parties, the ambience was unique, and the guests were only part of it, thanks to the setting she had done so much to create. "I'd rather have one French desk than a fabulous necklace," she said. "Or a pair of beautiful porcelain birds. Or a horse." With Winston's money and her time, she made Templeton a destination where the well-known and the well-bred mingled together seamlessly.

C.Z. did many things that got her in the papers. When she entered the arena at the National Horse Show at Madison Square Garden, as perfectly seated as the professional riders who would be her competitors and impeccably dressed in tailored breeches, her blond hair tucked perfectly, she was rightfully a focal point of attention. In 1955, she rode into the grand ballroom of the Waldorf Astoria hotel for the April in Paris ball dressed as General Lafayette on a white horse. The only way she would have created a grander sensation was if she had ridden in as Lady Godiva.

Although C.Z. might parade with the best of them in New York, she was in essence a country girl. Truman said she needed "a home and a husband and dogs and horses and children (in that order)."

Truman was in a quandary. For so long he had been the brilliant young writer full of promise. But now in September 1957 he had reached the unbelievable age of thirty-three, and he still had not written the literary masterpiece that was expected of him. Truman was practically the same age as Norman Mailer, who had not only written *The Naked and the Dead*, a masterful novel about the war in the Pacific, but two other serious novels. By comparison, Truman had written nothing but miniatures. In recent months, he had gone to Japan to write a profile for *The New Yorker* about Marlon Brando. It was amusing and controversial, but hardly the way to enhance his reputation as a serious novelist. He had just completed a novella, *Breakfast at Tiffany's*. He knew it was special, but it was not the immortal tome he knew he was born to write.

In the summer of 1958, Truman and Jack went to the Greek island of Paros, where Truman had the time and the space to contemplate his literary future. An eight-hour boat ride from Athens, the island was a place with few tourists. They were staying in a charming hotel looking down on the sea.

No matter how much he enjoyed Paros, Truman would not feel right until he had come up with an idea for his grand novel. He had done well writing about growing up in Monroeville, but he had pretty much mined that subject out. He needed something new, something big.

Truman loved being around his rich women friends. They had taste and style and lived in an exalted world that banned entry to outsiders. But Truman was welcome. Marcel Proust had written *À la recherche du temps perdu,* a classic novel about the French aristocracy. Truman decided he would do the same about the contemporary upper class based in good part on the stories his rich women friends told him.

Taking out his notebook, Truman wrote down a number of names that probably were potential characters in his novel, including well-known society women of the day, the Duchess of Windsor, and Elsa Maxwell. The Duchess of Windsor and her husband the former king were revered figures in upper-class society. One could hardly write about that world without including the duke and duchess. Elsa Maxwell was a social columnist and party giver and a powerful figure in café society richly deserving of being chronicled in Truman's tale. He mentioned only one of his swans, C.Z., but that did not mean he would eschew immortalizing the others in his masterpiece.

Truman wrote to Bennett Cerf at Random House, saying he was working on "a large novel, my magnum opus, a book about which I must be very silent, so as not [to] alarm my 'sitters' and which I think will really arouse you when I outline it (only you must never mention it to a soul). The novel is called, 'Answered Prayers'; and if all goes well, I think it will answer mine."

That November 1958, Truman published *Breakfast at Tiffany's,*

his first fiction in seven years. The novella told the story of Holly Golightly. Raised an orphan in Tulip, Texas, Holly was barely fourteen
when she married Doc Golightly, a horse doctor and a widower with
four children. The nearly fifty-year-old veterinarian gave his bride
no work to do and bought her subscriptions to the magazines she
lounged around reading. Doc believed he had given his young wife an
enviable life, but she was full of secret longings, and one day she left.

Holly ended up in New York, making her living as an escort for
wealthy businessmen while she scanned the horizon for a rich husband. Truman considered twenty-year-old Holly representative of "a
whole breed of girls who live off men but are not prostitutes. They're
our version of the geisha girl."

Truman told *Playboy* in 1968, "The main reason I wrote about
Holly, outside of the fact that I liked her so much, was that she was
such a symbol of all these girls who come to New York and spin in the
sun for a moment like May flies and then disappear. I wanted to rescue one girl from that anonymity and preserve her for posterity."

Holly Golightly is one of the most memorable female characters in
twentieth-century fiction. In the late fifties, profound changes were
percolating somewhere deep in the American psyche. Readers—
especially women—identified with Holly, who, in a conventional
sense, was amoral. In the evenings she went out with men who gave
her $50 when she went to the powder room. Every Thursday she went
out to Sing Sing prison to deliver secret messages to a mafia don.
Holly considered shoplifting a harmless pleasure.

New York was full of women like Holly, Truman knew—women
who arrived in the metropolis with little to offer to the great city but
their looks and their youth. Some found husbands or careers, but

many of them found nothing but emptiness. As their newness wore off, they either adapted or left the city, lesser beings than when they arrived.

Holly and these other women gave up security to live free lives. "Freedom," of course, was an elusive thing, and many young women thought they would find it in the shape of a rich man. Often, as with Edith Wharton's heroines a half century before, the exact opposite was true.

As Truman tells the story, it is clear from the beginning that things are not going to go that well for Holly. At the end of *Breakfast at Tiffany's*, Holly gets mixed up with a crooked businessman and must leave New York. As she exits the city with not much more than a one-way ticket to Brazil, she asks not for a guidebook or a pamphlet of Portuguese phrases but "a list of the fifty richest men in Brazil. I'm *not* kidding."

When Hollywood purchased *Breakfast at Tiffany's*, that ending would not do. From the moment the two stars Audrey Hepburn (Holly) and George Peppard (her upstairs neighbor) appear on-screen, moviegoers know that no matter their troubles, in the end, they will get together. These two will have the happy ending that so many real women in Truman's own circle of acquaintance did not.

Women like Holly were profoundly dissatisfied with the lives they had been given. "The problem lay buried, unspoken, for many years in the minds of American women," wrote Betty Friedan in 1963's *The Feminine Mystique*, the book that set off the modern feminist movement. "For over fifteen years there was no word of this yearning in the millions of words written about women, for women, in all the columns, books and articles by experts telling women their role was to seek fulfillment as wives and mothers."

Truman's Holly was nothing but yearning. It was a measure of Truman's brilliance that he had seen this longing in the American woman earlier than almost any other author. That analysis was all there, not screaming out in didactic prose, but embedded in the tale. When Holly had her "mean reds" and gobbled Seconal, she felt a little better, but the yearning was still there. It never left her.

Holly was the first of the swans. She did not have their money and had only one Mainbocher dress, but she wanted just what they wanted: a rich husband. And for the most part, it did not work for them any better than it did for Holly.

C.Z. and Winston had reputations for having affairs, but in their world, that was almost standard. So was it in Truman's. He consumed sex like a good meal, and he was always hungry. Beyond that, as an author, he saw sex as the place where humans were at their most intimate and vulnerable, and that endlessly fascinated him.

C.Z.'s daughter, Cornelia, is insistent that her mother was not like Truman's other swans, and it was at home at Templeton that this played out. She did things they did not. As she grew older, C.Z., always full of athletic prowess, continued to play tennis regularly and was as fiercely competitive as ever. Plus, there were large stables, giving C.Z. ample opportunity to ride every day. She had an allergy to horses, but that was not going to stop her.

Growing up on the North Shore in the summer, C.Z. followed Mr. Buffett, her mother's head gardener, as he did his job. She walked around the property and learned from him, watching him more closely than she ever had any schoolteacher. At Templeton, C.Z.

directed the gardeners to weed the soil, prune the flowers, and water what had to be nourished. If one watered too much, the plant died. If one didn't water enough, the plant died too. That was a lesson to be learned by trial and error and never forgotten. These were magnificent gardens, and without her efforts, they would not have been what they were.

When C.Z. said she tended her gardens, she did not mean that literally. She wasn't about to intrude in the servants' world. "I love flowers, and I want to know all about them," she said with obvious sincerity. "But I don't want to take away a job from the gardener. I love horses, but it doesn't mean I have to do the manual labor part."

For C.Z., there was a costume for everything. When she was through gardening, she often changed into a Mainbocher or Givenchy outfit and was driven to some splendid Manhattan event, where she was likely one of the belles of the evening.

Like their parents before them, C.Z. and Winston shuttled their two children, Alexander and Cornelia, off to nannies, governesses, tutors, and maids. It was one thing to have a child curtsey politely in the early moment of a dinner party, preferably speaking both in English and French, before toddling to bed hand-in-hand with the governess. That was all well and good. It was something else entirely if the child stayed there trying to be *amusing* to guests who had no choice but to listen.

C.Z. was convinced that a good governess did a better job bringing up children than a mere mother. "That doesn't mean I never saw them," she insisted to Sally Quinn of *The Washington Post* in 1977. "Of course I saw them. I went fox hunting with them."

Winston felt even worse about his wife's proclivities for publicity when he learned in 1962 that C.Z. was about to be on the cover of

Time magazine in a story about American Society. The fact that C.Z. was willing to pose for the cover photo on the front lawn at Templeton wearing riding clothes suggested that the world of the Old Guard was largely dead. Going with it were many of the last aspects of a society that had admired reticence above all else. C.Z. was not the most philosophical of persons, and this shift did not trouble her in the least. In those days, the cover of *Time* was one of the great honors of American public life, and she was wild to do it. Winston did everything he could to stop the story, but he could do nothing against C.Z.'s energy and will.

Truman found the *Time* cover endlessly amusing. It was the weekly's mid-brow take on what an aristocrat looked like. "Cold. Soignée. The Ice Cream Lady. Maybe so. At horse shows. Or riding to hounds somewhere in Virginia." The magazine was not about to portray his image of his friend "galloping across the countryside wearing cowboy chaps, and a man's shirt with rolled-up sleeves."

C.Z. believed God had placed the rich just where they belonged— at the top of everyone and everything. She was convinced the upperclass was better in every way. "Perhaps more is expected of those of us who are better educated and come from more affluent families," she said. "Because we have learned courage and learned what's right and what's wrong." Watergate was a perfect example of this thesis. "If Nixon had had the proper breeding, Watergate would never have happened."

To do good, the rich did not have to squander their treasures in excessive charity. By merely existing, they did immense good. "Look at the jobs I've given people," she mused. "If you have money and servants then you're helping somebody. If rich people didn't spend money the country would be in much worse shape than it is today."

The goal of women like C.Z. was to spend and to spend royally, and in doing so provide a model to the masses. "What's wrong with women inspiring others to higher standards?" C.Z. asked. "Think of all the beautiful works that Marie Antoinette and Madame Pompadour inspired from artists and artisans." Alas, the artisans and others of their class showed their appreciation by leading the queen to the guillotine.

The spirit of the sixties was a direct challenge to much that C.Z. and the other swans believed. As far as she was concerned, it was sheer anarchy out there. Young women no longer looked to copy the clothes of the elite. They made their own style: capri pants, miniskirts, go-go boots, bell-bottom jeans, tie-dyed shirts, what C.Z. considered one appalling item after another.

C.Z. despised the hippie look and considered those who dressed that way social derelicts. They were not just unkempt and sloppy but grimy. "All those dirty, filthy people," she said. "None of those people wore underwear, no wrappers, no nightgowns." C.Z. did not say how she learned they wore no underwear and eschewed nightgowns, but she was sure she was right.

Young women were beginning to go out in the world and do all sorts of things. C.Z. was a bold defender of a woman doing nothing. She took it as an affront that women would not stay just where they belonged. "All young people want to be something they aren't supposed to be," she said. "I never made any films. I went out to parties with Victor Mature, Bruce Cabot, and Errol Flynn. I played tennis every day and I loved every minute of it."

As the proper lady that she was, C.Z. was always well turned out in clothes appropriate to the occasion. It pained her to see these slovenly hippies showing up at black-tie events in clothes that were a direct assault on anything classy and respectable. Even worse were women of her generation who gave up and dressed no better than bag ladies. At one A-list event, one of the guests was a famous woman who came in a sweater and pants. She had put on a lot of weight and was not so much dressed as tented.

"Oh, C.Z., how great you look and how skinny you are," the woman gushed. "What can I do to look like you?"

"Just eat less," C.Z. said.

The world was changing and C.Z. did not like it. She had been brought up to live a certain way and believe in certain standards, and it was all crumbling away in front of her.

Slim Aarons was a World War II combat photographer who returned to America with no other dream but to photograph the rich and famous. On one of Aarons's many trips to Palm Beach, he took the most iconic photograph of C.Z. at Villa Artemis. C.Z.; her young son, Alexander; a Great Dane; and a poodle stood at the east end of a long white pool with its azure water and Grecian columns. Behind them the ocean was almost as still as the pool, and there was a sense of tranquillity and permanence. In her white shorts and white blouse and impossibly long legs, C.Z. looked as if she could have been a Greek statue that had come down off her pedestal to pose for the well-known photographer.

Part of the understated perfection was that this was C.Z.'s home, and she belonged there. Only it wasn't her home, and Aarons may have had to ask permission to shoot there. The estate had been Winston's mother's, and she had died in 1959. Though Winston had wanted to buy Villa Artemis, he could not come up with the necessary $350,000, and it was sold.

C.Z. and her family took up quarters in an apartment above a carriage house garage across from the estate. She made sure it was well furnished, and as always, her parties were done with endless panache, but it was not the kind of place she and her husband were used to inhabiting. It wouldn't do to complain or to suggest that things weren't what they should be. No, everything must be considered just so, and Truman must be invited down as always.

Winston received $600,000 ($4.5 million in today's dollars) annually from his $30 million trust fund. The stables and racehorses at Templeton took out a big slice, costing $200,000 a year. Still, he should have had plenty to live the upscale style he took as his right. But he fancied himself a businessman, and he was discovering it was not a gentleman's world. Nobody cared that he was a Phipps, and he made some bad deals.

His mother had wanted to be the first woman to fly across the Atlantic solo, but Winston's investments in aviation sank without a sight. His money in American Airlines turned to mush. The Mexican government nationalized one of his airlines, and another one headquartered in Panama went bankrupt—leaving him with bills totaling almost $500,000. He took out $265,000 in bank loans to try to satisfy some of his creditors, $100,000 more on his life insurance, and sold several of his most valuable paintings, including Moro's *Mary Tudor*. He told one of his most aggressive creditors that although his art objects and furnishings at Templeton were worth a million dollars, much of it had already been mortgaged to various banks. That was how bad things had gotten.

C.Z. had not married Winston for his money. It was just there. His wealth existed and was always to exist, everything she wanted forever. Nothing ever needed to be discussed. It was part of the unspoken deal. Only now she and her husband were looking more like any other couple trying to figure out how to pay the mortgage and the monthly bills. In 1963, Winston sold their Manhattan apartment, vowing that he preferred driving in from Templeton. That was the story. Everything was fine.

Edith Wharton wrote about what happened in the haute social world of New York in the early years of the twentieth century if you did not have what you said you had. Back then, if you stopped paying your club dues and gambling debts and tried sponging off others, you were as driven out as if you had been taken to the edge of the city and stoned to death. Nobody talked to you. Nobody looked at you. You did not exist.

Things were no longer quite so extreme, but C.Z. and Winston were in the midst of a process that often preceded some form of banishment. One day in August 1967, federal agents showed up at Templeton to tag paintings, antique furniture, and objets d'art that had liens on them. C.Z. was said to have gone around afterward tearing tags off the belongings, but it did no good. The day came when the items were carted up and hauled off for auction at Parke-Bernet Galleries in Manhattan.

On the appointed day in December 1967, Winston was off quail shooting in the Carolinas, but his attorney, Bradford S. Magill, was there to tell reporters his client was not bankrupt or ruined but was having the sale because "he has several different collections, and now wants to buy more silver."

As nearly a thousand people rustled nervously in front of the grand display, C.Z. reportedly was back in the emptied-out rooms at Templeton. In the years she had been married to Winston, Templeton had become C.Z.'s home as much as her husband's. These 150 lots of items that sold over four hours were not abstractions to her but at the center of her life. They possessed her as much as she possessed them. They had been the treasures of kings and nobles and then the treasures of a great American family, and now everything was being dispersed piecemeal to the world.

The auctioneer brought forth a commode that belonged in a museum, "almost certainly one of a set of four made for Louis XIV." Later he called out "two fine pairs of carved and gilded wood and mirror glass doors" from the early eighteenth century. He noted that the gilded doors "were said to have been the elder Mrs. Guest's favorite possession." What did it say about Winston's emotional disengagement from the whole disheartening process that he could not even manage to save this?

The auction grossed $812,275 ($5.3 million in today's dollars), enough after commissions to stave off Winston's creditors. There was one other lodestone hanging around his neck: Templeton. He sold the three-hundred-acre, fifty-five-room estate in Roslyn, New York, and bought a fifteen-and-a-half-acre estate in Old Westbury, naming the far smaller estate Templeton as if they had never left. C.Z. had her horses and her dogs and her gardens, and she went on as before, never talking about all that had happened.

12

Only Maids Fall in Love

TRUMAN SPENT AS much time as he could with his swans, collecting material that would give *Answered Prayers* a veracity and insider perspective unlike any other modern novel about the rich. In researching his book, Truman fancied that he had entered the inner sanctum of wealth and privilege, but most of his swans fluttered in and out of an international café society in which celebrity, money, and power were enough to gain entry.

When Truman met Marella Caracciolo di Castagneto Agnelli in New York City in the late fifties, that all changed. Born an Italian princess, Marella was not only a member of the European nobility, she was married to Gianni Agnelli, heir to the immense Fiat fortune, the greatest company in Italy—and Pamela's former lover.

Marella was a reader, and she had read Truman's first two books even before she met him. She agreed with his assessment of himself that he was a young genius. He drew her into his emotional lair with this soothing sense of intimacy. Truman soon became what she considered one of her "closest friends, perhaps the closest." In *Answered*

Prayers, Truman intended to rip open the lives of people such as Marella, exposing whatever darkness he found. In the meantime, he would accept their hospitality and, with his almost photographic memory, store away everything he learned.

Truman fancied that he was the singular observer, but Marella also had a concern for detail worthy of a novelist, and she was watching him as much as he was watching her. He would call asking to visit her in Turin. It was as if he was making reservations in a grand hotel. "Is the blue room empty?" he asked, referring to his favorite guest room. When Marella said yes, he would show up with Louis Vuitton trunks as if he had come to stay for months. It was one thing to have such bags to take on a grand European tour in the old days, or on a private plane or helicopter the way Marella traveled—but to schlepp them around the way Truman did was courting disaster. If someone didn't steal the luggage, the trunks would soon become scuffed and soiled. And that had nothing to do with what was inside. When Truman opened the luggage, everything was heaped together like clothes in a gym bag.

In March 1965, Truman journeyed to St. Moritz to spend a few days with the Agnellis. The Palace hotel and the Corvina Club were the winter nesting grounds of the European upper class. Gianni's life from dawn until late at night was full of one hyperactive pursuit after another. His 1952 auto accident left him with a limp, and he skied with a brace on his leg. Given all that, it was amazing how fast he schussed down the slopes. Gianni bored so quickly and definitively that people were afraid he would suddenly turn away from them.

At night, as Truman sat with the Agnellis, Gianni assembled witty, sharp people who told their tales quickly and well. These weren't philosophy lessons, but the evenings were unquestionably amusing, and Truman was a natural with his patter. Even as he accepted the homage of the Agnellis' rich friends, endless flutes of champagne, and hospitality that had no top or bottom, he could not admit how much he enjoyed this. He wrote his friend Cecil Beaton, "It was kinda fun. But what a silly lot they are really."

In St. Moritz, as wherever he ventured, Gianni was the center of the action, his young wife little more than an adjunct. Marella came from a noble Neapolitan family whose roots went back centuries and were far more distinguished than the Agnellis, who rose out of the nineteenth-century Italian bourgeois. Her father, Filippo Caracciolo, was the 8th Prince di Castagneto. Marella's mother, Margaret Clarke Caracciolo, was from Peoria, Illinois, the heiress to a whiskey distillery fortune. As a young woman, Margaret set out for Italy, where she bought a splendid sixteenth-century villa in Florence, shortly afterward marrying her husband.

Filippo's problem, one he shared with many European aristocrats, was that he was running out of money. His grandfather, the Duke of Merito, took such pleasure in balls, galas, and horses that to pay for them he had to sell off much of the family land outside Puglia. That left Filippo dependent on his wife's inheritance to live his life of choice, writing novels and poetry and discoursing philosophically with his friends in the evenings.

When the 1929 crash took away most of Margaret's money, Filippo had little choice but to work. An elegant man with impeccable manners, he was a natural for the diplomatic service. For a number of years, he was assigned to Ankara, Turkey, where Marella experienced a different kind of life. During the war, Filippo was general counsel in Lugano, Switzerland, where he worked secretly for the resistance. Before the war ended, he went to Naples to fight with the underground. Marella's eighteen-year-old brother, Carlo, also went off to Italy to fight against the Fascists. He was captured and could have been executed.

This was the measure of the Caracciolo family. They were far more than tired aristocrats; Marella's father was a hardworking diplomat with a patriotic streak. After the war, Filippo became the deputy secretary general of the Council of Europe, an important position in a continent striving to create institutions that would prevent the wars that for so long had torn Europe apart.

With such parents, Marella was a sophisticated young woman. After studying set design and art at the Académie Julian in Paris, she moved to New York, where she worked first as a model and then as a photographer's assistant. She had been engaged to a French aristocrat, who lost her when he sought to delay the wedding a week so he could go grouse hunting. But having reached her mid-twenties, it was time for the still-single Marella to be a little more philosophical about things like grouse hunts.

Gianni was not a perfect catch. He was a man who did not love and could not love, and in fact he looked on the whole idea as little more than emotional indulgence. To Gianni, even women of his class were in some measure inferior beings and largely interchangeable. That was a common male attitude among Italian men in the early postwar years, though Gianni's views were extreme. He was fond of saying, "Ladies are to be treated as sluts, while sluts are to be treated as ladies." It was hardly a recipe for a great marriage.

The Agnelli family was a world within the world, and Marella entered into their inner sanctum knowing almost nothing about them. Shortly after the wedding, she decided to take an overnight train to Paris to go shopping. When she arrived at the Turin station and entered her compartment, she found towels and sheets with her and Gianni's initials on them, her special soaps and creams, and a vase with fresh flowers. This had all been done beforehand by Gianni's butler, Pasquale, and was an indication of what her life would be like as an Agnelli.

Marella and Gianni lived in two homes in Turin: Corso Matteotti, a mansion in the center of the city, and Villar Perosa, a grand estate in the foothills of the Alps. It was the latter that was the Agnellis' spiritual home, the place that Marella went to learn about the essence of this family. What impressed her most about the mansion was "this sense of being in an enchanted time warp."

In the eighteenth century, Villar Perosa had been the home of various nobility. On a number of occasions, the mansion housed King Charles Emanuele III on his trips to the mountains. In 1853, a Turin merchant, Giuseppe Francesco Agnelli, purchased the estate. Marella believed Gianni's ancestor bought Villar Perosa for two interlocking reasons. Not only was the Piedmont Gothic structure a good business deal but by "its association with important royal figures . . . he would inevitably elevate the social status of the family." That was the Agnellis' true coat of arms: business and social advance linked inexorably together.

Giuseppe's grandson, Giovanni Agnelli, was born in Villar Perosa in August 1866. In 1899, the former cavalry officer became a partner in the small venture that become Fabbrica Italiana di Automobili Torino, or F.I.A.T., Italy's dominant manufacturer of automobiles. A businessman with all the ruthless drive of America's industrial

barons, Giovanni pushed out his partners and began a series of dubi-
ous stock maneuvers that led to his indictment in 1908 and two trials
that he survived. Just before the beginning of World War I, he befriended a young politician, Benito Mussolini, and he was there for
the birth of the Fascist dictatorship that benefited Fiat as much as any
manufacturer in Italy. During the Great War, Fiat produced all kinds
of vehicles and weapons for the Italian war effort. There was even a
submachine gun named the Villar Perosa.

In 1919, Giovanni's son and heir apparent, Edoardo, married Princess Virginia Bourbon del Monte, whose mother was an often acerbic, quick-witted American. A truth teller in a land where that was
often considered an unseemly intrusion, the former Jane Allen Campbell thought her daughter was taking a dramatic step downward.
"You need quite a lot of petrol to wash the Agnelli coat of arms," she
famously said.

Their first son, Gianni, was born in 1921. From a young age, Gianni knew, especially from his grandfather, that he would one day
rule the great automobile empire. His life of privilege, which included
a British governess and a private gymnasium, could not shelter him
from life's misfortune. In July 1935, fourteen-year-old Gianni lost his
forty-three-year-old father when the propeller of a seaplane decapitated Edoardo. His mother reacted by living a wildly dissolute life
with a stream of lovers. Ten years later, she died in an automobile accident next to her trouser-less chauffeur.

The Agnelli family say that Giovanni never believed in fascism
and was only with Mussolini for business reasons. They saw themselves living in an amoral world, and he was only doing what anyone
smart would do. When the Italian dictator came to visit Fiat, Giovanni

wore the Fascist's black shirt. Mussolini named him a senator for life, a title that made him proud. During the Second World War, Fiat produced an endless stream of tanks, machine guns, and vehicles to fuel the Axis war machine, and as it did, Giovanni built his fortune in an unprecedented way.

Gianni studied law at the University of Turin and trained at the Italian Cavalry School in Pinerolo, thirty miles southwest of the city, just as his father and grandfather had done before him. When the war started, he followed in the family tradition, joining as a cavalry officer. He fought on the Russian front during the terrible winter of 1941–42 and was wounded twice. As far as the family was concerned, he had fought with the admirable courage of an Agnelli man. They paid no attention to the unsavory truth that he had been part of the Nazi war machine that invaded Russia and sought to turn the beleaguered nation into little more than a fiefdom of serfs.

When the war turned and Mussolini was deposed, thousands of Italians took off their black shirts and paraded through the streets in white shirts, pretending they had been Democrats all along. The Agnellis were no different. Gianni went to join an Italian regiment fighting with the Allies as a liaison officer.

Around forty thousand Italians were fired from their jobs or suffered other consequences because of their collaboration with Mussolini's Fascist regime, and Giovanni resigned from Fiat. With his impeccable English learned from his British nanny, Gianni was able to ingratiate himself with the Allies and make sure Fiat suffered no further bad consequences for having supplied weapons to the Fascist and Nazi regimes that killed thousands of Allied soldiers.

When seventy-nine-year-old Giovanni died in December 1945,

Gianni might have assumed the leadership of Fiat or at least begun to learn seriously about the company so that one day he might be a knowledgeable leader. But the twenty-four-year-old heir had no interest in either one. He was delighted to have a loyal executive, sixty-three-year-old Vittorio Valletta, take control.

Gianni was named the president of a Fiat subsidiary that produced ball bearings, but he was not about to squander his days worried about little metal balls. For the next two decades, Gianni had other interests. His biographer Alan Friedman wrote: "For someone who is perpetually restless, shrewd rather than intellectual, something of an exhibitionist, and with access to all of the accouterments that an income of $1 million a year can provide [$14 million in today's dollars] nothing could be more natural than to frequent that itinerant class of individuals who in the 1940s were not yet known as such, but would later come to be called the 'Beautiful People.'" This was the man Marella married, a gorgeous but careless profligate consumed with little but pleasure.

Gianni was the ultimate Italian man of his era, so much so that Luigi Barzini's classic 1965 book *The Italians* reads in part like Gianni's biography. Barzini wrote, "The Italians have always excelled in all activities in which the appearance is predominant." So stunningly handsome that both men and women turned to look at him, Gianni was as conscious of his clothing as the most style-obsessed of women. This king of style was unwilling to dress like anyone else, and he created several unique touches. The outer portion of his ties came only halfway down his chest, while the inner part fell almost to his waist. If that wasn't enough to attract attention, he placed his watches over the cuffs of his shirts. In anyone else, these idiosyncrasies would have seemed ridiculous, but this was Gianni Agnelli, and people copied him.

Gianni's attitude toward women was the traditional Italian attitude elevated to the nth degree. He was the model Italian lover. "Some are indeed irresistible," wrote Barzini. "Their charm, skill, lack of scruples and boldness are proverbial." He strutted his stuff on the grand boulevards of Rome and Turin and in squares in provincial towns. "How cocky he looks, how close fitting are his clothes, how triumphantly he sweeps his eyes about, how condescendingly he glances at pretty girls from the corner of his lowered eyelids," Barzini wrote. "He is visibly the master of creation. And what is woman? She was obviously placed on earth to amuse and comfort him, as decorative and unimportant as the dumb girls who aid the magician to do his tricks on the stage. Like all inferior people, she must by every means be kept in her place, for her sake, above all."

Everything focused on Gianni. "He has never said 'We,' but 'I,'" Marella said. "He has a narcissism which is a little infantile." She saw that for her husband "a woman is to be conquered, not to be loved," and Gianni was a man of endless conquests.

In the first months of his marriage, Gianni was present neither physically nor emotionally. Marella was left alone at Villar Perosa to try to make sense of her marriage and her new life. "I spent the first months of my marriage on the sofa reading French novels and wondering what I could possibly do with all that time on my hands," Marella recalled years later. She was pregnant and alone, and she was almost certainly depressed.

Gianni had an almost formal relationship with his bride. He knew something was wrong, but he did not come to her to talk to try to figure out why things were not right. Instead, he wanted her to get busy performing her rightful tasks as the mistress of his homes. He called Countess Lily Volpi, who ran her Palazzo Volpi in Venice with perfect social acumen, and asked the aged countess to instruct his wife on how to manage a house. Marella was no stranger to aristocratic style, and much of what the countess told her was probably redundant. What was new to her was that her husband was clearly not happy with her performance as his wife. "To catch a man all one needs is a bed," the countess said, "but it takes a well-run home to keep him."

Before assuming her duties managing the Agnelli homes, Marella first gave birth to her son, Edoardo, in June 1954. Almost as soon as Edoardo was born, she handed off the baby to nannies and governesses. That was the upper-class way, though like so many things in the Agnellis' lives, they carried this pattern to extremes.

Marella's two children, Edoardo and Margherita (born in 1955), suffered from the lack of emotional resonance and closeness to their parents in their childhoods. Years afterward, Marella discussed mothering with her niece, Marella Caracciolo Chia. "Many women have chosen motherhood over marriage, I did the opposite," she said in a voice touched with remorse and assuming that a wife had to choose between the two.

Marella was hardly a bubbling, maternal soul, but on her own she likely would have proved a far better mother than she was. She clearly felt that to protect her marriage, she could not serve both her children and her husband. "He was not very interested to be a father," she said. "Paternal attention is not very Latin. I think Latin men are so full of charm and intelligence, but there is no man who is more narcissistic than a Latin man." And there was no Latin man more narcissistic than Gianni. He needed an heir, but he wasn't about to share his wife with children running in and out of his life, disrupting everything.

And so Marella set out to become the kind of wife Gianni wanted. It was still not easy for her to define her role. But she soon realized that if she was not going to be his intimate companion, she could at least work to turn their shared environment into a work of art worthy of the Agnelli name. Gianni himself was an astute judge of art, and he was amassing one of the great private art collections of the age. "My central preoccupation was Gianni and creating an environment for our art collection that he could relate to," she said. Part of that involved keeping the house in perfect, pristine order. But as important as that was, it did not take up most of her time. The staff she supervised was practiced (some of them having been there since the time of Gianni's grandfather). Villar Perosa had a timeless quality to it, and it would have been an unseemly intrusion to change things too much.

But the gardens were different. No one had lived in the estate during the war, and the gardens had not been tended. Marella saw a challenge. She brought in Russell Page, the best-known gardener in the world, to help her put her stamp on the estate's grounds. Page was not impressed by what he saw. "The garden was relatively small, entirely enclosed by a high wall and so thickly planted with ornamental conifers and laurels that you might have imagined yourself in a suburban garden in Streatham or Neuilly or Brooklyn," Page wrote in his memoir, *The Education of a Gardener*. He set out to eradicate the embarrassing mediocrity of it all.

The Agnellis' gardener had tended to Villar Perosa for more than half a century. He was not amused to have this pushy Brit who spoke no Italian destroying his life's work. Marella mediated as best she could, and as she grew more confident, she interjected her strong input into everything Page did.

The project grew bigger and bigger, and it took several years to reach completion. Page began by tearing down the walls and opening up the garden to connect it with the thirty acres that surrounded Villar Perosa. He filled this land with an amazing array of botany, everything from beds of roses to bushes sculptured into unique shapes. Beyond this land lay a valley bifurcated by a stream. This too was the Agnellis, and here Page built eleven small dams, creating a number of pools. What he had in the end was no longer a garden but a park.

One day Marella asked Page what happened to his original vision "of creating a spontaneous garden of native plants"? He replied, "Oh, but Villar is different from all other gardens. . . . It is my Shangri-la, my ideal world." That it was for Marella too. She wanted to subdue nature, to overcome it and create something perfect. "No detail within the boundaries of the Agnelli property has seemingly been left to chance or to nature alone," she said.

On the evening that Page arrived in Villar Perosa for the first time, he and Marella stood in the first-floor portico looking out on the gardens. They had struck up such an immediate rapport that they began talking about a subject that was rarely discussed with mere acquaintances: the problems of living with a great fortune. Page designed gardens for some of the richest people in the world, and he saw what often happened to them. He cautioned Marella, "One must learn to serve something higher than us all, because if not, one may easily fall slave to the basest, most material aspects of one's life."

Page's words had a profound impact on Marella, and she set out to "serve something higher than us all." She began by working all those months with Page to create the magnificent park at Villar Perosa. When it was finished, she could have invited local schoolchildren or brought in busloads of Fiat workers from Turin during the sweltering days of August. But that was not something she would ever do. A daughter of the European elite, she never ventured beyond her lofty circumstances and never sought to open her doors to those whom she felt did not belong.

With the overwhelming success of the gardens of Villar Perosa, Marella moved on to what in essence was her life's work, creating at least ten magnificent residences from Milan to Marrakech, from Corsica to Manhattan. Although they were only for her family, this was her way to "serve something higher than us all."

13

===

Divided Lives

Truman wasn't having as much success getting his own new project off the ground. It is unlikely Truman was fully emotionally and intellectually engaged in his new novel, *Answered Prayers*, or he would not have been so intrigued by a small one-column story in *The New York Times* in November 1959 about the murder of a wealthy Kansas farmer, his wife, and their son and daughter.

Violence was about to become one of the major themes of American life. Truman may not have had that prophetic insight, but he grasped he might be on to something important. He planned his career moves like a great general, and he spent that day and a portion of the next thinking about the murder before he talked to William Shawn at *The New Yorker* and got him to finance a trip to Kansas to write a story.

No way was Truman going to travel alone out to one of the more remote parts of America in the wake of an unprecedented mass murder. The killers were still out there, and everyone had a right and a reason to be afraid. He said he was hiring an "assistant researchist," a slightly demeaning term in its own right, but he was also looking for a companion to travel in what he knew would be a world almost totally new to him.

Truman's childhood friend Nelle Harper Lee was the perfect person for the role. They knew each other so well that they had their own lingo and private gestures. Since they were kids, Nelle had her own ambitions to be a writer, but for her it had been nothing but endless struggle. She had finally finished a novel, *To Kill a Mockingbird*, which was going to be published in July 1960. Until then, Nelle had nothing but time.

Nelle brought much to Truman's project. Her father had been a journalist as well as a lawyer, and she would have a rapport with the reporters they met in Kansas. Beyond that, she had studied for a law degree (stopping just short of completion), and she had an understanding of the courts and the legal process that Truman did not have. Just looking at their résumés, Nelle should have been the reporter and Truman the assistant researchist.

When Truman and Nelle showed up in Garden City (population 11,811), in the western reaches of Kansas, he brought with him a trunk full of food in case there was not enough to eat in the American heartland. Worried about his deprivations, Babe sent him a tin of black caviar.

One evening Truman took Harold Nye, a Kansas Bureau of Investigation (KBI) agent, and his wife to see the sights of Kansas City. They began at a lesbian bar, moved on from there to a gay bar, and finished the evening at the Jewel Box, a club with female impersonators. Mrs. Nye had never seen such sights in her life, and she had much to tell her lady friends.

To the Kansans, Nelle said, Truman "was like someone coming

off the moon." Only they didn't dress like this on the moon: he wore an enormous sheepskin coat that looked like it could have been worn by Dr. Zhivago driving his sled through the snows of Russia. On his head, Truman wore a curious pillbox-style hat that could have been appropriated from a Park Avenue matron. His scarf was a long narrow cloth that fell all the way to the ground and trailed behind him.

In his suite at the Warren Hotel, Truman dressed equally extravagantly. One evening when four KBI officers made a call on the author, he was wearing what Harold described as "a pink negligee, silk with lace and he's strutting across the floor with his hands on his hips telling us all about how he's going to write this book."

Thankfully for Truman, Nelle was in the room. The officers understood and liked Nelle and could deal happily with her. She was somebody who could be sitting next to them in church on Sunday, and she ingratiated herself with the officers and townsfolk in a way Truman could not. Once she established these relationships, she worked him into the mix, and they embraced this strange outsider as well.

Thanks to the relationship Nelle and Truman developed with the Clutters' lawyer, Clifford Hope, they were able to go with him and the estate administrator, Kenneth Lynn, to visit the Clutters' home outside the hamlet of Holcomb. On a frigid winter day, they drove up the long driveway sided by Chinese elms to the handsome white house standing tall against the Kansas sky. It was here that Herbert William Clutter, a highly successful and well-respected farmer, was shot to death along with his wife, Bonnie, and their two children, sixteen-year-old Nancy and fifteen-year-old Kenyon.

Much of the furniture had been taken out, giving the home an even more ominous, empty feeling. They went down into the

basement, where Mr. Clutter and his son had been tied up by the killers. They both had been shot in the face, and Mr. Clutter's throat had
been slashed. They also went up to the two upstairs bedrooms where
Mrs. Clutter and Nancy were murdered with blasts of a shotgun.

For his first days in Kansas, Truman had provided a measure of
jocular amusement to the local folk, a diversion from the terrible
times. That was not the Truman Capote here this day. He gravely and
meticulously reviewed the murder scene, taking in everything as he
walked through the empty rooms, writing notes on a pad (and keeping even more details in his head). Nelle was doing the same. There
was a sense of evil in these rooms, inexplicable evil, and that could
not be defined by a few words in a notebook.

It did not take long for the KBI team to track down the two killers,
Richard "Dick" Hickock and Perry Smith, and bring them back from
Las Vegas. The two drifters had been cellmates in the Kansas State
Penitentiary. They confessed almost immediately. The two had heard
a rumor that the wealthy Mr. Clutter had a safe full of money in his
isolated house. They planned to take that money and kill anybody
who was in the house. There was no safe, but that did not prevent
them from carrying out the second part of their plan.

Truman and Nelle waited in the freezing January air in front of
the Finney County Courthouse in Garden City when the two hand-
cuffed killers arrived by car from Las Vegas. In the following few
weeks, Truman had long interviews with Dick and Perry. Dick was a
decent auto mechanic, but he had no intention of spending his life
fixing cars. He found excitement and identity in doing bad things,
and one way or another, he was likely to spend most of his life in
prison. Dick was like other lowlife types, depressing and sad and ordinary, hardly the stuff of literature.

To Truman, Perry was the far more intriguing of the two. Some observers felt that in Perry, a half-crippled runt of a man with a tortured childhood, Truman saw a dark side of himself. There may have been something to that, but Truman also saw a complex, fascinating character. Perry's mother was a Cherokee Indian and his father an Irishman, a mix that played out incongruously on his face.

Perry had gotten in a serious motorcycle accident in 1952. Truman wrote that "his chunky, dwarfish legs, broken in five places and pitifully scarred, still pained him so severely that he had become an aspirin addict." The uneducated murderer was a vociferous reader, obsessed with building up his vocabulary. He was also a guitar player and songwriter with absurd dreams of stardom. As he sat in his jail cell with little to contemplate but his dark fate ahead, a close and obsessive bond formed between Perry and Truman. Perry thought of Truman like a brother and a friend, the object of his obsession. For a time, anyway, the feeling was mutual.

Once the arraignment finished, Truman and Nelle got on a Santa Fe sleeper car for the trip back to Manhattan. They'd been in Kansas nearly two months, and enough was enough. They returned two months later for the trial. Both men had confessed, and the verdict was never in doubt—nor was the death sentence. Justice was swift in Kansas. Dick and Perry were scheduled to be hanged until dead at Kansas State Penitentiary a month and a half later, on May 13, 1960.

After hearing the verdict, Truman and Nelle once again took the Santa Fe back east. Truman had everything he felt he needed, and he had no intention of returning for the execution. It was clear he had enough material not just for a long *New Yorker* article but a book, and after signing a contract with Random House, Truman, Jack, twenty-five suitcases and trunks, two dogs, and one cat sailed to France. Not listed on the manifest was Nelle's thick folder of typed notes, which ran to more than 150 pages. Truman intended not to return to America until he had written his chef d'oeuvre. He and Jack ended up in a grand house on the sea in Costa Brava, Spain, with two maids, a cook, and a gardener.

Jack believed his lover needed solitude to write his book. But as soon as they got there, guests started showing up, including the Guinnesses, who dropped anchor in the harbor. As far as Jack was concerned, Truman's swans were so desperate for amusement that they showed up wherever he was, diverting Truman from the work he should be doing.

Jack exhibited what to him was good behavior, which meant he tried not to sulk. "All they ask is that you behave," Jack reflected. That wasn't an onerous request, but to Jack it was a stretch. Once the guests left, Jack berated them to Truman in savage soliloquys. He took special umbrage at the Paleys, who were forever praising Truman for his genius—while Truman lapped it up, insatiably.

Truman and Jack had hardly gotten settled in that summer when they heard the news that Nelle's little novel, *To Kill a Mockingbird*, was an enormous hit, selling half a million copies in its first year. Truman was envious that the sun stood so high in the heavens without his command, but he appeared genuinely pleased that his childhood friend had such a success.

But there was some other news about an old friend that was immensely troubling. The last time Truman had visited Newton Arvin at Smith, he was astounded at the sheer quantity of male nude images the professor had collected. Like everything else involving gay people, homosexual porn was in the closet, much of it masking itself as physique magazines. Truman may have been unsettled by the scholar's obsession, but he added to it by having sent his friend a rich load of porn from Greece.

Newton's collection did not go unnoticed. Massachusetts authorities raided his house and charged him with being a lewd person. To avoid going to prison, he turned in a number of other teachers at Smith who had similar interests, including twenty-nine-year-old Ned Spofford, a Greek instructor who Truman called "a gentle, charming gifted boy: much the nicest friend Newton ever had." Spofford and another colleague, forty-one-year-old English professor Joel Dorius, lost their positions at Smith and were given one-year suspended sentences. The Massachusetts Supreme Court acquitted Spofford and Dorius on all charges, saying they had been the victims of an illegal search.

It was a little unsettling though not unexpected when the Kansas Supreme Court gave Dick and Perry a stay of execution while the judges decided on the killers' request for a new trial. To make matters even more upsetting, the Menninger Clinic's Dr. Joseph Satten told Truman that Kansas governor George Docking was going to commute the sentence if reelected. That wasn't the ending Truman's masterpiece needed.

Of the seven deadly sins, jealousy is the only one that gives no pleasure to the sinner. And Marella was consumed with jealousy. It wasn't the mere acts of her husband's betrayal itself that troubled her—and the betrayals continued, at an almost dizzying pace—but something else. She was giving everything she had to this man, and he was finding something in these women he could not find in her. "I saw myself being so jealous for a long time," she said in 1991. "One realizes it was not worthwhile; the things were of very little consequence and always very short."

Despite what Marella said, some of her husband's affairs were of major consequence, and far from short. Gianni had a relationship with the voluptuous Swedish star Anita Ekberg for several years. With Fellini's classic 1960 film *La Dolce Vita*, in which she basically played herself, Ekberg became the sexual fantasy of almost every Italian male above the age of twelve, and Gianni had her. As painful as that was, his purported relationship with Marella's friend Princess Laudomia Hercolani was even worse. It wasn't just that he was seeing her while Marella was pregnant with their daughter, but that Laudomia was so much like Marella that he was sleeping with his wife's clone. A friend recalls, on New Year's Eve 1956, Marella throwing a tantrum as Gianni talked to his princess lady friend on the phone.

Gianni was what these days would be called a sex addict, never able to stop, never getting enough, always looking. It was a mark of his absorption in his own personal pleasure that he took some of these women to friends' homes for dinner parties, knowing that they would have to choose between him and his wife.

Some observers considered Marella the most beautiful woman in the world, but even that was not enough to keep her husband home. Marella didn't think she was beautiful. "That is why probably I give myself a lot of trouble to be elegant," she said. "I didn't like especially the image of myself, so I tried through elegance to project an image I liked more than the natural one."

That was precisely Truman's point about his swans. They created their beauty, and no one did it better than Marella. A professional-caliber photographer, she understood images and how they resonated. A talented textile designer, she appreciated colors. An astute interior

decorator, she sensed how clothes worked. When she went to the couturiers in Rome and Paris, she was their partner in choosing the outfits that would create this unique image that in 1960 for the first time
put her on the International Best-Dressed List.

That had been a long time building. In 1953, Richard Avedon took
a photo of Marella for *Harper's Bazaar* that is one of the most iconic
fashion photos of all time. Avedon did to Marella what Page did to
the gardens of Villar Perosa in transforming the foliage into the
shapes of his own making. Avedon had perfected a technique that
allowed him to bleach out imperfections, and that he did to extreme
effect with Marella's bare shoulders. Her neck was abnormally long,
but it wasn't long enough for Avedon, so in the dark room he length-
ened it beyond anything possibly human.

The resulting photo with Marella's face in half shadow is a stunning image of a person from some other time or place or realm. It is
no mere human but some other kind of splendid being. Marella had
no interest in the sordid business known as literal truth, and she was
perfectly fine being seen as an ethereal goddess. The couturier Christian Dior was so taken with Avedon's image that he used the photo as
inspiration for his "*ligne H*" of dresses with elongated torsos and
broad necklines.

Despite the problems with their marriage, when Gianni and Marella
went out together, they were a splendid couple. That was part of
Marella's obligations as a wife, and she performed this task to perfection. President John F. Kennedy and First Lady Jacqueline Kennedy
were the only other couple in the world equal to the Agnellis in sophistication and glamour. That comparison was in full view in November 1961, when Marella and Gianni attended a dinner party at
the White House. Marella sat next to the president, who was fittingly

mesmerized. There were any number of beautiful women in the room, but no one—not even Jackie—created the impact of Marella in her stunning green velvet gown and collar of diamonds.

Jackie sat next to Gianni at the dinner, and the following August, when she vacationed in the Italian resort of Ravello, he was there to shepherd her around on his eighty-two-foot yacht, the *Agneta*. A photo of him moving to apply suntan lotion to her back led to speculation that they were having a short-lived affair. Although judicious heads thought that even Gianni was not so rash as to sleep with the wife of the most powerful man in the world, there were others who said that was Gianni's way. His own sister Susanna, who was generally careful in what she said about her famous brother, later said, "I wouldn't be surprised."

Truman and Jack spent the next two years in Europe, dividing their time between Palamós, Spain, and Verbier, Switzerland, where Jack loved to go skiing. Truman led what he called a "monastery life," eschewing his frenetic social schedule for a routine of disciplined writing. By the end of 1962, he had finished almost all of his manuscript, and it had begun to irritate him beyond measure that Dick and Perry were still alive.

Truman had become close to KBI officer Alvin Dewey and his wife, Marie, and he was making Dewey a major character in his book. Truman corresponded often with the couple. Knowing the way things worked in Kansas, he wrote them that the two killers "would not have been executed before the [November 1962] elections (no such luck!)." Governor Docking had been defeated, and

Truman no longer had to worry about the politician commuting the sentence, but Dick's and Perry's lawyers were doing anything to keep them alive. When Dick filed a Supreme Court appeal on his own, Truman told the Deweys he was convinced it was "a trick to make the thing take twice as long."

Despite all the delays, the day of the executions was likely drawing near, and Truman was going to orchestrate that day so he would have the perfect ending. That meant having Alvin there to provide the "point-of-view." "Alvin, when the real time finally (pray God) comes, you must be there," he wrote the Deweys in October 1962.

Truman returned to the States in January 1963 long enough to interview Perry's sister and to travel once again out to Kansas to interview Perry and Dick on death row. Truman had done to Perry what he did to almost everyone he met either as friend or interviewee: he emotionally ingratiated himself with the killer until Perry opened up in a way he had to no one in his life. Sitting with him in his cell on death row, the author loved the tender, artistic, vulnerable side of Perry. But when he left him to go among his literary friends, he could be roundly dismissive of a man he knew would have killed again. Both of these feelings were true within Truman, and they pulled him apart.

In Manhattan, Babe gave an enormous party for Truman. In the past, he would have loved it, working the crowd like a presidential candidate. But his head was in Kansas, and even for one night he couldn't leave his obsession. When he wasn't writing, he was thinking about the murders and the murderers, as if in a trance that went on for hours. He worried that when he finally got out of it, he "should be good and nuts."

In March 1963, after having spent almost three years in Europe,

Truman and Jack returned to their apartment in Brooklyn. Truman appeared in some measure his old self. He headed to La Côte Basque or one of his other favorite restaurants for lunch with his adored swans and out to Kiluna Farm to spend the weekend with the Paleys. And he went to the White House to see the Kennedys.

But Truman's most important visit was to death row at the Kansas State Prison. He and Nelle drove out there together in his new Jaguar. Prisoners on death row were severely limited in their visitors. As for mail, they generally could send and receive letters only from close relatives and lawyers.

Truman needed to stay in intimate touch with the killers to write compellingly about their last months in prison. Truman said that he bribed an important official. It was a dangerous, daring thing to do, but Truman got the almost complete access he needed. Who did Dick and Perry have in their lives who cared about their thoughts and feelings other than Truman? They sent him hundreds of letters and spent many hours with the author in their cells on death row.

Did Truman and Perry consummate an affair? Truman's judicious biographer Gerald Clarke said Truman was "father, mentor, perhaps even surrogate lover." The KBI's Harold Nye was even more explicit. "They had become lovers in the penitentiary," he said. "I can't prove it, but they spent a lot of time up there in the cell, he spent a considerable amount of money bribing the guard to go around the corner." There is no way of knowing, and if it's true, Truman did not want anyone to know that the man on death row was his lover.

As consumed as he was with his book, Truman continued to resume some measure of his old life. When he was staying with the Guinnesses at their Florida estate in February 1964, he not only wrote a letter to the Deweys bragging about the twenty-two servants and his own personal butler, but he sent the couple a photo "of this place—or one small area of it." Immensely proud of his rich friends, one letter was not enough. When Truman was still at the estate two weeks later, he wrote to the Deweys to tell them that Rose and Jackie Kennedy had come for a quiet dinner.

Dick's and Perry's only hope to get off death row was to make a successful appeal that the murders had not been premeditated. When they learned that the title of Truman's book was *In Cold Blood*, it was like another death sentence. "I've been told that the book is to be coming off the press and to be sold after our executions," Perry wrote to Truman. "And that book IS entitled 'IN COLD BLOOD.' Whose fibbing?? Someone is, that's apparent." Truman lied to the condemned convict, saying there was no such title.

The killers' lawyers played out every appeal and every gambit until all that was left was a request to have the United States Supreme Court evaluate the case. If that failed, it would not be long before Dick and Perry ordered their last meal.

Truman had written everything but the ending, and he desperately wanted the business all over. He and Jack had gone to Switzerland for the winter, and he asked a *New Yorker* researcher, Sandy Campbell, to cable him what the court in Washington decided. On January 18, 1965, the court refused to hear the case, and Sandy cabled Truman.

"Just got the cable," Truman replied on a postcard. "Bless you! Now let's keep everything crossed—knees, eyes, hands, fingers!" Six days later, he wrote to Perry a different tale: "I've only heard about the court's denial. I'm very sorry about it. But remember, this isn't the first set-back."

Despite all his disavowals, as the execution day drew near, Truman sailed back to America and took the train out to Kansas City with his Random House editor, Joe Fox. Perry contacted Truman at the Muehlebach Hotel with a frantic request to have him hire a lawyer to fight for a stay of execution. It almost certainly would not have worked, but it would have given Perry solace that Truman truly cared for him and had not merely used him. Truman did not reply.

As the time of their deaths approached, Dick and Perry wanted to spend their last hours with Truman. Perry called again and again, but Truman did not reply. Truman felt so distressed that he could not imagine heading out to the Kansas State Penitentiary for the execution. When Perry could not reach Truman by phone, he sent a cable to his hotel. Truman cabled back that he could not come because it was not permitted. That was not true.

As strongly as he had vowed that he would not attend the execution, Truman arrived at the prison that evening. He had time to talk to Dick and Perry and say goodbye before he walked over to the warehouse where the gallows had been set up. At one o'clock in the morning on April 14, 1965, six guards brought Dick into the large room. There were straps binding his arms to his body, and it was not easy for him to walk, but he moved up the stairs beneath the scaffold. A noose was placed around his neck and a mask over his face, and he was gently pushed forward above the trapdoor. The executioner pulled a switch, and Dick fell to his death. The officials let him hang there for a good twenty minutes before they cut him down and removed the body to a black hearse.

An hour later, the guards brought Perry into the warehouse. One of the observers, Harold Nye, said that Truman could not watch Perry die and instead ran out of the building.

On the plane ride back to New York with his editor, Truman cried as if he would never stop crying. "When he came back from Kansas and the executions, he was just literally a basket case," said Slim. "One night he took Valium and drank vodka. Just crazy. He was really in love with Perry."

14

Princess from an Ancient Realm

THAT SUMMER OF 1965, Marella and Gianni invited Truman to join them on a monthlong cruise along the coast of Turkey and the Greek islands in their white sailing yacht, the *Sylvia*. Like everything around the Agnellis, the ship was lean, elegant, and perfectly attuned to its tasks.

"Truman, you must come with us at least once to see some of the amazing ruins," Marella implored him one day.

"Oh, forget it," Truman replied. "One old stone is just like another."

The other American guest the Agnellis invited was Katharine "Kay" Graham. She had taken over as publisher of *The Washington Post* after her husband, Philip Graham, committed suicide in 1963. Kay almost turned down the invitation, fearing in such company she would be exposed as boring. Rarely do boring people worry they are boring, and Kay was such good company that she and Marella became lifelong friends. Truman knew an opportunity when it appeared in

front of his eyes, and he read part of *In Cold Blood* to the most powerful woman in publishing.

In Cold Blood was a massive literary and commercial success when
it was published in January 1966, making Truman the most famous
author in America. Although the author had no professional training
in journalism, he had written a great work of narrative nonfiction.
Although Truman was not the first author to use fictional techniques
in a nonfiction work, in its sheer scope *In Cold Blood* was a groundbreaking piece of work. He told the tale in simple, evocative prose.
An astute observer, Truman peppered the pages with vivid details.
For readers of *In Cold Blood*, it was as if they were in that Kansas
farmhouse when Perry and Dick killed the Clutter family and there
when the murderers were hanged. When they finished, some readers
began locking their doors and no longer trusted strangers.

Truman had spent five years writing his masterpiece. He needed
time, lots of time, to decompress and to come to terms with what he
had been through, what he had seen, and how it had changed him.
But Truman was swept up onto the great train of celebrity from
which he never disembarked for the rest of his life.

Truman stood in the golden glow of the spotlight, believing this
was his rightful place. No way was he going to wait until he finished
Answered Prayers for his next grand moment of attention. Instead, he
decided at the end of the year to give the party of parties. The trium-
phant evening would signal his rightful place at the very pinnacle of
American life.

The idea was to have a spectacular ball at the Plaza Hotel. Everyone would dress in black and white, just as in the Ascot scene in *My
Fair Lady* as designed by his friend Cecil Beaton. And they would
wear masks, adding a soupçon of mystery to the whole business.

Truman took immense pleasure in creating a guest list of 540 names. In doing so, he brought together the glittery new crème de la crème of café society, doyens of the arts and the business world, with a few strays from politics and academia.

Capote was the true guest of honor for this event, but he could hardly name himself when he was paying for the ball. Thus, he decided to honor Kay Graham. When Truman called Kay to tell her she would be the guest of honor at "the nicest party, darling, you ever went to," she did not know quite what to make of it.

"Truman and I were good friends, but we were on a less intimate basis than he was with Babe or Marella, probably the two most famous beauties in the world," Kay wrote in her memoir. A few weeks later, when Kay had lunch with Truman at the 21 Club, she tried to figure out what the whole business was about. "I think he was tired from having written *In Cold Blood* and needed to be doing something to re-energize himself," she said. "I was a prop."

"I often thought that his famous Black and White Ball was a way of gathering together all the characters who were going to be part of his novel," Marella said. Not only did he invite all of his swans to his party but other people who might find their stories one day in the pages of *Answered Prayers*.

The Agnellis pretended they had no interest in personal publicity, but the public relations staff at Fiat worked diligently at creating an image of Gianni as this intrepid merchant prince with his beautiful princess by his side. Truman kept a diary of the sail on the *Sylvia* that was published in *Vogue*, further enhancing the Agnelli image.

One of the stories Truman told happened when the group was swimming in the clear waters of a Turkish bay. Out of the water appeared an enormous octopus. It was like some ancient monster rising from the deep, and everyone rushed to safety on shore except for nine-year-old Edoardo Agnelli, and a crew member, Giorgio. They killed the animal, and Giorgio cut it up for dinner.

It was an instinctive act of courage on Edoardo's part, and contrary to the way Gianni viewed his son, which was as a physical coward. As the eldest child and only Agnelli son, Edoardo was the heir apparent. As little time as Gianni spent with the boy, he wanted him to be his father's clone. He pressed him to jump off the deck into the sea and perform other daredevil acts that Gianni did as a matter of course, but the boy would not do them.

"They say that intelligent boys aren't that courageous," said Susanna Agnelli, Gianni's youngest sister. "That's something my brother didn't like." Gianni and his sister did not understand that it likely took more courage for this preternaturally sensitive boy to stand up to his father and refuse than to perform the acts. On those sun-flecked days, darkness was already descending on one young life.

In 1966, after two decades of being known as "the rake of the Riviera," forty-five-year-old Gianni assumed the chairmanship of Fiat. The company sold 75 percent of all Italian cars and had its tentacles throughout Italian life. In Turin, one likely read the Fiat-owned *La Stampa* in the morning, and when one went to a soccer match, it was to cheer on Juventus, another Fiat subsidiary. If one had fish for dinner, it might well have arrived in port on one of Fiat's fishing trawlers, and the chair one sat on could have been imported on a Fiat merchant ship. And if one wanted an aperitif, as likely as not it was by Cinzano, yet another Fiat company.

As burdensome as Gianni's duties were, he was not going to forsake his pleasures. Later that same summer, in August 1966, the Agnellis invited Truman on another cruise, this time a twenty-day journey through the islands off the coast of Yugoslavia. There were few more intriguing places to visit in Europe, and Truman should have had a fine time—but he didn't. Nothing was good enough for him on that interminable cruise.

The one blessing was that Lee and Stanislaw "Stas" Radziwill were among other guests. Truman knew Lee's older sister, Jackie, but as far as he was concerned, Lee was better in every way, and she was his newest swan. Truman simply loved her, and he could talk to her for hours.

The Agnellis were splendid hosts, starting from the point that they appreciated things as much as any of their guests. Gianni was amazingly energetic. Every day he was off to visit a village or an ancient site while Truman often stayed in his cabin. He may never have verbalized his discontent, but Marella and Gianni were highly observant people, and they surely guessed what Truman was feeling.

As the *Tritona* sailed along the magnificent coastline, all Truman saw was "the harsh and stony Montenegrin grayness, the subtropic pallor." He condemned the communist country for having nothing he wanted to buy and found the meals in the best restaurant a "so-so affair." The only food he found worthy of praise were melons that he was told were "flown in from Pittsburgh." If these were bottles of Heinz ketchup, that may have made some sense, but the western Pennsylvania city has never been known for its export of melons.

When Truman got back to New York, he had to deal with urgent entreaties from people begging him for an invitation to the Black and White Ball. He had many rich and famous acquaintances, but he did not have this many, and the ball had become a must-attend event. If you didn't go, you were a nobody. And nobody wanted to be a nobody.

Truman put together the Black and White Ball for surprisingly little money. For decorations, he settled on bunches of balloons. The event proved to be a watershed event in American social history, celebrating a new kind of social hierarchy—very different from traditional Society, with its reticence about publicity. Although Truman offered his guests a separate private entrance to avoid paparazzi and reporters, no one took advantage of that option.

When Marella walked into the grand ballroom of the Plaza Hotel that November evening, wearing a floor-length white Valentino gown, white gloves, and a white mask that swept around her eyes to attach to a plumage of feathers that rose far above her head, she looked like a princess from an ancient realm. For once Gianni did not outshine her, though he had been born to wear black tie.

Not only did Marella have an incredible sense of style, but she appreciated that quality in others. Her friend Gloria Guinness had flown in from her Paris home. No one would have imagined she was the oldest of the swans. In her white Castillo gown, elbow-length gloves, ruby and diamond necklaces, and black mask covering the upper half of her face, fifty-four-year-old Gloria could have been thirty.

Babe wore a white Castillo gown outlined in cardinal red. She had a magnificent collection of jewelry given to her by her husband, but she wore a startling necklace of rubies and diamonds made of paste. Only a woman with supreme social confidence would have worn such a necklace that evening.

Lee Radziwill had recently been on a cruise with the Agnellis where they had lazed around casually, but this evening Lee wore a white sheath by Mila Schön, white gloves, and a white mask that looked like designer goggles. Her appearance that evening was so important to Lee that Schön made several trips from Milan to fit the gown and mask.

Slim sauntered into the ballroom accompanied by her third husband, the mildly pompous British banker Kenneth Keith. Across the
floor, Pamela was dancing with the man Slim believed still should
have been her husband. While the other swans dressed in white, the
new Mrs. Hayward wore a black gown as dark as a subway tunnel.
Pamela had also been Gianni's lover, of course, and while Marella
had gotten used to attending social affairs where one or more of her
husband's mistresses (former or current) might be present, she had a
special aversion to Pamela.

C.Z. had chosen from her designer of choice, Mainbocher, one of
the least ostentatious gowns worn that evening, a lace number with a
white top and a black skirt. There was a casual quality to C.Z., and
her outfit fully exemplified that part of her.

Marella and Gianni sat at a table with other Italians and the Guinnesses. *The New York Times* described the ball "as spectacular a group
as has ever been assembled for a private party in New York . . . an international Who's Who of notables." The room contained everyone
from a visibly unhappy Frank Sinatra and his gamine-like wife, Mia
Farrow, to the author Norman Mailer in a rumpled trench coat (as if
trying out for a role in a detective movie). As Peter Duchin's band
played one danceable number after another, Truman walked among
the guests, spreading his beneficence on the multitudes, never alight-
ing for long. "I remember thinking it was Truman's one brief moment
of feeling power and recognition from the world that fascinated him
so much," said Lee.

The ball was a chance to meet people one had never met before
(and might never meet again), but there was little mixing among
the various groups. When the Italians got up to leave, Gianni announced that he was going off with a bunch of friends to play poker at

Elaine's, an East Side restaurant popular among celebrities. As the Italians walked out, a photographer heard them speaking in the Plaza lobby. "They were expecting something absolutely over the top," he said. "What they got were a bunch of balloons . . . hung off the chandeliers. And I heard them saying, 'Is this what we flew over for?'"

The following year, the Agnelli ball in Paris was decidedly different. The guests were overwhelmingly members of the European aristocracy. There was no need to garnish the evening with celebrities. The event took place on an island in the middle of one of the lakes in the Bois de Boulogne. Gondoliers ferried the formally dressed guests to the spectacular venue in brightly lit, covered boats.

As famous as Truman was, there came a day when the phone stopped ringing, and he was faced with the melancholy task of confronting an empty page. Jack recalled Truman boasting about how much he was writing when he was lying in bed paging through movie magazines. No matter. He talked so often and so well about *Answered Prayers* that it was as if the novel already existed. As if he didn't even have to go through the tedious process of writing it.

"It's a sort of *roman à clef*, drawn from some people I've known and places I've been," Truman told C. Robert Jennings, a writer for *New West*, in early 1968. "It is very strangely constructed, moving in time both past, present and future all at the same time, but it is a completely realistic novel—nothing experimental about it other than technique. I've been working on it for a year and a half and will finish by January of '69. . . . Four or five people in the book get precisely what they wanted and the result? I'm not tellin', baby."

Answered Prayers sounded so fantastic that 20th Century Fox sewed up the film rights for a phenomenal $350,000—$2.65 million in today's money. All Truman had to do was deliver to the studio a manuscript of at least sixty thousand words, in essence a novella.

With the deadline looming, Truman should have been writing as he always did, penning passages into a notebook. But he had become addicted to the easy pleasures of the rich, and in July 1968, he sailed off with the Guinnesses on their yacht for a cruise along the coast of Turkey. They were visiting some of the most fascinating archeological sites in the world. The Guinnesses had brought along an Italian professor to help everyone understand what they were seeing. As Truman had done when touring the coast of Yugoslavia with the Agnellis, he refused to get off the yacht to visit "dumb old rocks in the middle of nowhere."

"Truman, I really don't understand why you're not coming with us," Gloria said.

"Gloria, what you're doing is the single most boring thing I can conceive of," Truman fired back.

At the end of 1968, Truman drove out to Palm Springs with C.Z. and his cousin Joey Faulk. C.Z. was going because she wanted to spend time with Truman in the California resort town. It was one thing to sit in the back seat of a chauffeured car between the Hamptons and Manhattan, yet another to spend five days driving across the country. C.Z. had never traveled in such a plebian fashion in her life, but she was game. To make the journey a little easier, she arrived with a hamper full of fine wines and commandeered the front passenger seat.

The other passengers included not just Joey but Truman's two big bulldogs. There was hardly a restaurant across the wide expanses of

America that would admit the two dogs, so it was day after day of picnics along the highway. In so doing they discovered the joys of Stuckey's chili dogs. When eaten with frequent quaffs of Château Lafite Rothschild from the bottle, the meal was positively gourmet. There were all kinds of little adventures—from an Arizona snowstorm (a non sequitur if there ever was one) to running out of gas in Texas. Through it all C.Z. was a great sport, and she ended the journey better friends with Truman than before.

In Palm Springs, Truman discovered something that did not bore him. It was not the ancient temple of Apollo but the man who came to his rented house to service the air conditioner and ended up servicing Truman as well. Randy McKuen was his name, and he could talk rhapsodically about air conditioners, but beyond that his mind was a maze of emptiness. Randy had fought in the Korean War, but he was still the most provincial of men. Separated from his wife and the father of two children, Randy was a certified heterosexual, the kind of lover Truman found most appealing. Things had gotten tedious with Jack after two decades.

When Slim came to visit, Truman was delighted to introduce him to "this wonderful man who I know you'll adore." Truman had collected a group of formidable women around him full of authoritative opinions. Slim had seen some nondescript men among Truman's lovers, but nothing like this. She considered Randy "the nearest thing to nothing of anybody I'd ever met: a dim, mothlike creature who was nothing more than ordinary."

Truman was snottily superior to anyone he deemed stupid, so it was a mystery why he could be so intrigued with Randy. Truman's publisher, Bennett Cerf, came up with one answer when the author and his lover came for a weekend. When they put their luggage on the bed, it broke. Bennett told all who would listen that Randy and Truman had broken the bed having sex, a far more interesting story.

It was one thing for Truman to take Randy to the home of the Random House publisher, who was used to dealing with all kinds of quirky authors. It was a different matter to take him to the Agnelli home in Turin. Truman had been with Marella and Gianni so many times and understood them so well that he should have known you didn't bring someone like Randy into their home.

Truman and Randy happened to be there when Marella was giving one of her dinners. Behind every chair stood a footman. Marjorie Merriweather Post had done that at Mar-a-Lago in the twenties, but it was a custom that took so much staffing and planning that it had largely disappeared.

Randy sat next to the queen of Denmark. Endlessly adept at social patter, the queen asked Randy if he had been to Europe previously. "No, except for that time in Korea," he said. Truman found that funny. He thought "Marella liked him [Randy], but didn't know how dumb he was."

Marella understood perfectly well how dim Randy was and that he did not belong. But her face showed not a hint of what she truly thought. "I never understood it," she said. "He was not even very good-looking. Certainly not very interesting. Everybody tried to do their best with him, but nothing moved."

In December 1970, Truman invited Marella for lunch at the Colony restaurant on East Sixty-First Street. The fashionable establishment was a popular watering hole for café society, and Marella knew it well. When she arrived, she realized she was not eating alone. All of Truman's swans were there except Lee. Marella did not know C.Z. and Slim that well, but Babe was a good friend and Gloria she had known forever. As for Pamela, Marella did not know her and did not want to know her. The last thing she wanted to do was have lunch with her husband's former mistress.

The impish, easily bored Truman had set up the luncheon with the idea of sitting back and watching what happened. Slim had even more reason to be upset than Marella. She could not abide breaking bread with the British siren whom she believed had shoplifted her husband, and she hardly said a word to Pamela.

Truman had invited a *Women's Wear Daily* reporter and photographer to memorialize the occasion. Above the story the fashion daily ran a large photo of the group walking down the street together with Truman in the middle under the headline "LADIES MAN." Gianni had dropped by for a beer, and he was also in the photo.

Marella was upset about the luncheon. She felt that she had been used. She thought she had a unique relationship with Truman. And she was stunned and humiliated to see her dear friend with his head tilted toward Pamela or one of the others, giggling as he dropped yet another titillating revelation on them. As sophisticated a woman as she was, Marella thought such intimacies had only been for her.

"Strange, I thought I was the only swan," she told him afterward.

"Oh, well, darling . . . ," Truman said, and turned to another subject.

Truman treated Marella with this incredible intimacy. It was no wonder she thought she was the only swan. And in those moments, that was the truth.

Despite this little spat, Truman went off on yet another cruise with the Agnellis. He was already delayed on the delivery date for *Answered Prayers*. Random House wasn't upset. They had given him an extraordinary new three-book contract worth $750,000, $3.5 million in today's dollars. It included a new deadline for *Answered Prayers* of January 1, 1971, which he did not meet either. No matter, he had brought a few chapters of his putative masterpiece on the cruise to show to Marella.

Some authors show their manuscript to friends looking for criticism that will make the work better. Others only want to be praised. Truman was in the latter category. When he was working, he might spend an hour tinkering over one phrase, working and reworking it until he got what he thought was perfect. He showed the same minute concern for every last line. And when he was finally finished, he needed no kvetching asides from acquaintances who fancied themselves critics.

Although Marella spoke English fluently, she was a slow reader. Marella asked Truman if he would read to her chapters from *Answered Prayers*. She had read his major works and thought him one of the great writers of the age. And she felt that listening to his masterful words before the public heard them was a special privilege and honor.

As Truman read in that tiny voice of his, Marella began to sense that something was wrong. Where was the writer she admired so much? This was shallow, trivial, and just plain nasty. Some of these people she knew, some she didn't, but it was all the same. Everyone had seen Truman's dark, petty side, but now it had taken over and consumed his writing.

Truman had told her once, "You must realize that I am going to do to America what Proust did to France." If Truman had written that sort of book, Marella would likely have appreciated it even if it was a devastating portrait of her world. But these chapters weren't that at all.

Marella was angry at how Truman was betraying his best self. "Oh, Truman, this is a gossip column," she told him. "What are you getting yourself into?"

Marella was having a great awakening, and it was profoundly disturbing. Her husband found Truman the most diverting of guests, yet when the author was alone with Marella, he put Gianni down in the slyest of ways. Marella noticed Truman doing the same thing with Babe and Gloria and their husbands. "He would tell you about their little *défauts*, their *faiblesse*, trying to woo you away from them in a funny way," she said. It was as if Truman would only be happy if they left their husbands and he was indisputably the most important man in their lives.

In the past decade Marella had probably spent more time with Truman than anyone outside her immediate family. She was closer to him than to any man in her life other than her husband, and yet despite all that, she had this startling insight into the relationship. "For him I remained Mrs. Agnelli. The wife of a tycoon," Marella said.

Truman had picked up the manners and the language of Marella's world, but it took several generations to have the absolute confidence in one's place that was the essence of an aristocrat. He didn't have it. He was always the visitor. If Marella had told this to Truman's face, he probably would have been devastated. He thought he was as comfortable in the Agnellis' yachts and grand homes as if he had been born to that life.

The next time Marella saw Truman was when he was visiting in Turin. On a foggy winter day, they went to visit one of her favorite antique stores, an enormous, dusty trove full of secret treasures.

Truman saw a piece of English lacquer that he wanted, and he started bargaining with the aged proprietor. As he did so, he kept turning toward Marella to tell her the most vicious tales about one of her friends. He kicked at this woman mercilessly.

This was the kind of thing Marella had seen Truman do so often. In her way, she had indulged him, providing an audience for his savagery. Not this time. Something snapped within her. Truman no longer existed for her. When he left Turin a few days later, she vowed to end the friendship. Truman was so self-absorbed that it took him a long while to realize Marella had taken him out of her life.

Once Truman realized what had happened, the next time Marella came to New York, he had Lee set up a dinner for the three of them. When Marella arrived at Lee's apartment, she expected it would be a dinner party with all sorts of interesting guests, but it was only Truman and Lee. It was obvious she had put this together to manage some sort of rapprochement.

Sometimes when things are so important and so painful, no one dares to speak them. It was not until Truman was driving Marella back to her apartment late that night that he spoke the only words that mattered that evening.

"Why don't you want to see me?" he asked plaintively.

"But, Truman, it's not true. I want to see you. But you know how things are, you live over here. I live over there."

Marella never saw Truman again.

15

Fairy Tales

IN 1962, TRUMAN sat down with Lee Radziwill for an intimate chat over lunch in a Manhattan restaurant. As much as Truman enjoyed being the star at big parties, being one-on-one with a person was truly his thing. He liked boring into a person's life and exploring their most private secrets.

Lee had never talked with Truman like this before, and she had every reason to be suspicious. Her sister, Jackie, was the overwhelmingly popular First Lady, an iconic figure who was changing the way Americans thought about dress, décor, and culture. If Jackie had been lunching with them, there would probably have been a crowd in the street and a frisson of excitement inside this privileged sanctuary.

Lee had a gilded lifestyle. She was married to Stanislaw Radziwill, a Polish prince who had left his native land with a title that no longer had any meaning, and she lived in two grand homes in England— and later a major apartment in Manhattan too. With her sister in the White House, she had to be careful how she acted, what she said, and to whom she said it. She must have known that Truman was an infamous gossip.

It was a measure of the emotional pain Lee was suffering that, despite Truman's reputation, she told him the most painful secret of her life: she was wildly jealous of Jackie. It was natural that Lee would be somewhat covetous of a sister who was the First Lady and the most admired woman in the world, but her feelings went far beyond an understandable or controllable emotion. She was consumed with jealousy. It was all she could think about, all she could talk about. Her sister had done nothing wrong, but that did not matter. Jackie had transcended Lee in a manner that, in Lee's eyes, was destroying her life. She had what almost anyone would say was everything—more than everything—yet she was so dissatisfied, so empty, so lost.

After the lunch, Truman did what Lee should have expected him to do. He wrote his friend Cecil Beaton and told him all about it: "Had lunch one day with a new friend Princess Lee (My God, how jealous she is of Jackie: I never knew); understand her marriage is all but finito."

Caroline Lee Bouvier loved the summers she spent in the old clapboard house on the South Fork of Long Island in East Hampton. As far as she was concerned, there was nothing like the sea and the sand and the sun. Her mother was always telling her the right way to do things, and if she walked out too far in the surf, Janet Bouvier was sure to call out.

Every week, Lee looked forward to Friday evening, when she drove with her mother and her older sister, Jackie, to the train station to be there when her father stepped off the commuter train from Manhattan. There was no air-conditioning on the train, and on a torrid August day, the passengers staggered off with their coats in their hands, sweat pouring down their faces, desperate for the stiffest of gin and tonics. If Lee's father, John Vernou "Black Jack" Bouvier III, was in character, he strutted off as if he had just had a shave and a face massage in the number one chair at the Waldorf.

Jack had a seat on the New York Stock Exchange. His colleagues might set themselves apart with a boutonniere in their lapel, but beyond that they wanted to project a conservative, trustworthy image. Jack dressed like a Paris boulevardier. No woman was more concerned with her dress than Black Jack, who got his nickname because of his dark complexion. There was always something about the clothes he wore—the cut to his jacket, the colors of his two-toned shoes— that called attention to him and proclaimed that he was like no one else. Dashing and handsome, Jack was born for women to love, and love him they did.

Janet had pursued Jack as if he were the only prey in the forest. The twenty-year-old woman had gone to the right schools, made a proper debut, and had the socially acceptable kind of friends, but her father, James Thomas Lee, was a vulgar, cigar-chomping real estate magnate who had risen from nothing. It was an inspiring story in some circles, but that did not mean he was welcomed in the homes of the anointed.

By marrying properly, Janet would leave behind her Irish peasant past and her unrefined father and join the upper set. What the Lees wanted for their daughter was not unlike what Janet Cushing wanted for hers, but they did not have the savvy that it took to play this game. Janet Lee settled on a man sixteen years her senior who was a rake of no apparent morals. Up and down Fifth Avenue heads shook in bewilderment when Janet married Jack in July 1928.

Jack's detractors could say what they wanted, but he came from noble French roots, and that was one of the reasons Janet married him. There had even been a book published by the family in 1925 that traced the Bouviers back to a sixteenth-century aristocrat, François Bouvier. The only problem was that the gentleman in question had been an ironmonger and his wife a servant, but in America, anything was possible, including inventing noble ancestors. François's descendants had done extremely well in America, and Jack's father was a rich businessman. The Bouviers could have taken pride in how far they had come. Instead, they had taken the considerable trouble to spiffy up their past.

The day of the wedding, Mr. and Mrs. Lee, the devoted loving parents of the bride, sat side-by-side but alienated from each other. Good Catholics that they were, it would not have done for the Lees to divorce or even separate. They simply lived on different floors in one of Mr. Lee's buildings. To the world they appeared to be together, but they rarely had the unpleasant experience of seeing each other.

Jack was so wild in his financial dealings that even without the Great Depression, he likely would have encountered the shoals of financial despair. To help the newlyweds, Mr. Lee set up his daughter and son-in-law in an eleven-room apartment in a building he owned on Park Avenue. Jack never acknowledged that he was not paying for the place, instead strutting in and out of the building as if he owned it. His father-in-law also gave Jack money that allowed him to live in a proper manner, but not with the profligate style he thought his due.

Jack's daughters loved everything about their father—the way he smelled, the way he walked, the way he held their hands. He showed them endless charm and devotion, and they adored their father and thought him the model of what a man should be.

Lee was a chubby child. People looked at her pretty features and languid manner and assumed she had to be happy. They were not wrong until after that wonderful summer of 1936, when her parents separated for several months. Black Jack's endless philandering and boastful self-absorption had become too much for Janet, but soon the couple got back together before separating for good a year later.

All Lee wanted was a home with a mother and father, and she cried and cried and cried over her parents' divorce. When she set off for kindergarten, it was less like entering an exciting new world than leaving a broken one.

Mr. Lee had not become rich by squandering resources. As soon as Jack left for good, he did not think his daughter needed that massive Park Avenue apartment any longer and moved them into more modest quarters at 1 Gracie Square. Lee and her sister, Jackie, headed off with their governess each morning in their linen jumpers to the Chapin School for Girls.

There was just enough space in age between the two girls that they played in the same set and attended the same schools, but Lee looked out upon an older sister who went places and did things she could not. Lee was jealous, though that word hardly captured all the complexities of what she felt. The sisters were exceedingly close and, when challenged, stood together like an impregnable fortress. Yet they fought incessantly. Once Jackie knocked her little sister out with a croquet mallet. There came a day when Lee was big enough and bold enough to toss her big sister down the stairs. "From that moment on, she realized I could stand up to her, and the childhood fights were over," Lee said.

Now that Lee's father was gone, her mother was even more important to her. Yet Janet often went off in the evenings with strange men, returning only after Lee and Jackie were asleep. That made for more anxieties. Lee was clearly her mother's favorite, but what good did that do when it only meant Janet lectured her even more, telling her how she must sit and dress and enunciate her words, always striving for perfection?

Their father was around on weekends, an overwhelmingly exuberant presence who took his daughters to racetracks, casinos, and all kinds of exotic places, worlds where their classmates never ventured. As exciting as that was, it was painfully clear to Lee that their father preferred Jackie. She had abrupt, angular features that looked like Black Jack's, and he adored holding Jackie's hand and telling her about a world where men were out to betray her, a subject about which he qualified as an expert witness.

It was all too much for the slight, sensitive Lee, who took refuge in a series of imaginary characters that were as real as anything in her life. Their names were Shahday, Dahday, and Jamelle, and these ethereal spirits lived with Lee.

Lee's mother had been brought up to think that nothing mattered more in her life than marrying a rich and proper man. She had come up woefully short the first time, but only a fool makes the same mistake twice, and Janet was decidedly not a fool. Unlike Black Jack, who pretended to wealth he did not have, her second husband, Hugh D. Auchincloss, was truly rich. The scent of Standard Oil money went so far back that one could hardly smell it on him. A dour, unexciting man, though one who was loyal and true, he had a total lack of imagination. Janet decided he'd do just fine.

When Lee went to Hammersmith Farm, the Auchincloss estate in Newport, Rhode Island, for the first time, she was enchanted. "To arrive there, as a child of eight, was just a fairy tale," Lee said. There, once again, was that theme of a fairy tale, like the one with her imaginary friends, but this new fairy tale did not last very long. Hugh had three children from previous marriages, and he and Janet would have two more on their own. Janet did not purposely shuttle Lee and Jackie aside, but she had a new family to take care of and a new marriage to make work, and her two daughters were no longer her primary concern. It was just another reason for Lee to think she was an unwanted guest at the table.

When Jackie went off to Miss Porter's School in Farmington, Connecticut, Lee had a respite from her older sister, and yet Jackie still overshadowed her life. Like her mother, Jackie was an expert rider, taking home blue ribbons in horse shows. Horses were one of the key elements in the family's identity, and Lee took part as best she could until one day a pony rolled over on her. That was the end of horses for Lee, just another arena in which she could not compete.

Lee's mother sent her to Miss Porter's for her sophomore year, in the fall of 1947. Although Jackie was now off at college, she had left her mark on the school, and her sister could not avoid hearing about her. It was Jackie this, Jackie that, enough to drive one crazy. Jackie had kept a horse in Farmington, and that was only one of the things that set her apart. With her fierce intellectual spirit, she had done well in her classes. "All I ever heard was how *Jackie* had been a better student than I," Lee bemoaned. "It does tend to wear one down."

Sometimes on weekends, Jackie would come dashing in from

Vassar, her lips bright with lipstick, her dress sophisticated, her manner assured. Beside her, Lee appeared dim and washed out. That wore one down too.

As Lee saw it, her big problem was her weight. Her cheeks were so plump that people liked to tweak them as if on a Kewpie doll. For the first time in her life, Lee focused with profound attention on an issue that mattered to her. She dropped weight until she was so thin her features stood out in bas-relief. The infirmary was worried enough about her that they insisted on her regularly coming in to be weighed. Anorexia was the swans' occupational disease, and Lee was obsessed with her weight all her life.

Whereas the school and her mother worried that if Lee lost any more weight she would have serious health problems, she thought she wasn't thin enough. She had lost enough weight to present her new stylish, svelte image to the world. At Jackie's debutante party at the Newport Clambake Club in August 1947, Lee arrived in a stunning strapless pink gown of her own design that few fourteen-year-olds would have dreamed of wearing. In doing so, she upstaged Jackie on her night of nights, which was clearly the point. Jackie wore a lovely dress too, but Lee's older sister had no great interest in clothes. She projected a natural beauty and wore little makeup.

Jackie appropriated whatever she wanted, including her sister's clothes, and she wore Lee's gown to the grand debutante ball in New York. She was such a hit that Cholly Knickerbocker named her Debutante of the Year, and *Life* featured her in a picture story. Jackie said she did not care about such things, but there she was.

Like her mother, who never went out without gloves and was always impeccably dressed, Lee fretted over style. She was endlessly concerned with her clothes and the image she projected. Smaller, more delicate, and with far more curves than her older sister, Lee had become as much a beauty as Jackie.

Like the rest of the swans, Lee's great goal in life was to find a rich and proper husband, a quest that began when she was scarcely a teenager. That did not mean she was going to be carried off as a child bride, but that she lived within the ambience where she would come upon the man who would take her off into a fairy-tale ending. The beginnings of this were the Ivy League men who drove over to Farmington on Saturdays. One of them was Michael Canfield. The Harvard sophomore was tall and startlingly handsome. He had served as a marine in the war and had been part of the bloody invasion of Iwo Jima. His persona was not that of a tough ex-marine but of a twenty-two-year-old gentleman. It was unthinkable that he would attempt to push himself on fifteen-year-old Lee. No problem: Lee ended up in the bunk bed of another Harvard man.

When it came time for Lee to make her debut, it was ridiculous to think that she could come close to Jackie's triumph, but she proved to be an even grander success. Not only was she named Debutante of the Year, but *Life* ran a full-page picture of her. The title was no trifle. It was one of the few places where Old Society and the new celebrity-obsessed world came together. It bestowed on the young recipient a measure of celebrity that was not looked down upon by the old guard.

In June 1951, eighteen-year-old Lee and twenty-one-year-old Jackie sailed to Europe for a summer of adventure. It wasn't the classic Grand Tour of old, burdened with trunks and endless letters of introductions, but something more modern. Away from all the competition and strife of their relationship back home, they discovered that they were in fact wonderful traveling companions, finding wit and joy even in the most trying of circumstances—like the time in Paris when Lee's underwear fell to the ground during a fancy cocktail party, or the day they drove their little car into the midst of the French army summer maneuvers and had to get down on the floor when they were caught "in a cross-fire of flame belching anti-tank guns."

The sisters memorialized the trip in a pamphlet written for their mother, full of Jackie's charming caricatures and saucy prose primarily by Lee. She had written the great art historian Bernard Berenson before the trip, and they went to see him at his villa outside Florence. That led to the most serious moment of reflection of the summer. "He set a spark burning," Lee wrote. "It was the difference between living and existing that he had spoken of, and both of us had simply been existing in our selfish ways far too long."

After their splendid summer together, Jackie went to visit Lee at Sarah Lawrence College, where she was studying, and the bile of jealousy arose once again. Jackie was proud of her artwork, and she showed some of it to Lee's favorite art professor. He spent a good amount of time going over the work, treating it and the young would-be artist seriously. Lee felt it was a betrayal. "I wish you would someday spend half as much time on me!" she said.

Lee had no portfolio of art. That was emblematic of her problem. She had an heiress's curse—a lack of focus and drive—without an heiress's money. At college she had few friends because she gave little friendship. Sarah Lawrence was a casual kind of place where students dressed in jeans and shorts. Lee set out to class in designer skirts and cashmere sweaters. She was a snob of a particularly virulent sort, referring to lower classes as "the little people."

Whatever Lee took up, she soon grew bored or distracted and then moved on to something else. She decided she wanted to be a singer and, in the spring of 1962, dropped out of college to go to Rome to study voice. That lasted no more than a few weeks before she was off cavorting with her social friends in Paris and London. Most women considered a college degree worthy and important, but Lee wasn't going to squander her time in something so tedious, and she never went back to Sarah Lawrence.

That fall Lee went to work at *Harper's Bazaar* as one of Diana Vreeland's assistants. The fashion editor liked to surround herself with beautiful, well-born young women, and Lee fit in as if the role had been designed for her. With her interest in style and couture, this was the perfect job for her. Diana was a difficult taskmaster, but Lee was more than up to it and likely could have had a notable career in fashion journalism. But as usual, it was too much, especially when marriage beckoned.

Lee's mother had given her only one task, which was to marry well and properly. Her choice was Michael Canfield, the ex-marine she had known when she was a student at Miss Porter's and he at Harvard. Michael did not have the wealth of a Rockefeller, but he was far from impoverished. Moreover, he had a masculine, aristocratic beauty she found irresistible.

Michael was the adopted son of Cass Canfield, one of the most successful book publishers in America. When Michael learned that his biological father may have been a British prince and his mother a sexually adventurous American, he began to effect his putative father's attributes. He dressed like British nobility and took on a perfect upper-class British accent. To finish his new persona, he effected a subtle stutter, gently interspersing it in his speech. That was the mating call of the British upper class and was the perfect last touch.

Michael drank too much, but so did almost everybody in his set. Just before the April 1953 wedding, Michael's adoptive father hosted an ushers' dinner at his Manhattan town house. The guests got a little drunk, and well on into the evening, Michael's soon-to-be father-in-law, Hugh Auchincloss, mumbled, "He will never be able to afford her. He will never be able to afford her." Hugh had every reason to know, since he had not made Lee part of his will and her entire fortune consisted of the $3,000 her father would leave her.

Michael looked like the kind of man Lee wanted, but soon after their grand wedding, she realized he did not have enough of the other traits she insisted upon. Michel was working at his father's publishing company, Harper & Brothers, in Manhattan, and the newlyweds were living in a two-bedroom apartment that would have pleased most young married couples. But Lee thought the life Michael was providing for her was barely acceptable. As part of his editorial duties, he hauled her off to parties up dank staircases to grubby apartments where poorly dressed writers drank cheap wine. Jackie would have found such excursions a worthy adventure. Lee found them disgusting and far beneath her standards.

To placate his increasingly unhappy bride, Michael agreed to go to London, where he would run Harper & Brothers' British office. Once the couple got there, Lee realized her husband's position did not have quite the social cache she felt to be appropriate. She pushed Michael to become social secretary to her family friend, American ambassador Winthrop Aldrich. Taking that position meant getting an open invitation to every grand party and estate in Britain.

There is nothing like a frenetic social life to hide the fissures of a broken marriage, and Lee and Michael went to endless events. Lee was obsessed with royalty, celebrity, noble lineage, and money. With the entry her husband's new position gave her, she was like a child in a candy shop with a full purse. Of course, there was the queen's Garden Party; and what was the season without Wimbledon, properly dressed, of course; and then there was dinner with such notables as David Niven and Prince Aga Khan and whatever celebrity she could attract with her youth, looks, and studious charm.

Upper-class Brits are a randy lot, though it is considered good form for a wife to bring forth an heir before she starts having affairs. Lee had no use for such formalities. She began taking on lovers at the drop of an invitation.

Nothing was more intriguing than weekend parties at England's premier estates. In the fall of 1956, Lord and Lady Lambton invited Lee and Michael for a shooting weekend at Fenton, their country house near the border of Scotland. One of the other guests, and an avid hunter, was Stanislaw "Stas" Radziwill and his wife, Grace Radziwill. Born a Polish prince, when he took British citizenship, Stas gave up rights to his hereditary title.

In Britain, people take titles seriously, and some found it appalling that Stas continued running around insisting that people call him "Prince." Lee knew nothing about this, and with her fairy-tale view of the world still partially intact, what could be more exciting than spending the weekend with a prince?

Almost twenty years older than Lee, Stas was a bit long in the tooth for a prince charming who would sweep her away to the castle he did not have, but he surely looked the part. Handsome in a debonair, European way, his thin mustache was positively rakish, and he had the kind of charm and self-confidence that comes from generations of being told the world is yours. He had arrived penniless in London, but with his connections he got into the real estate business and made himself a considerable fortune. Looking at Stas, Lee checked off every attribute she sought in a man, and they began an affair.

The Radziwills became the Canfields' closest friends, and everyone knew what was going on. Michael could not drink himself into blessed oblivion (though sometimes he surely tried); reality still had a way of confronting him. "In those days I never knew when I got home after work whose hat I was going to find hanging on the peg downstairs," he said.

It was Stas's hat more than anyone else's, and after he and Lee divorced their spouses, the pregnant Lee and the fallen prince married in March 1959 in a civil ceremony. Stas treated his young wife like a child bride to be indulged in everything. As a newlywed, she lived in a terraced house in Victoria in London. The couple later purchased Turville Grange, a stately seventeenth-century Queen Anne seven-bedroom brick mansion surrounded by forty-nine acres of countryside an hour from London. Stas gave his bride free rein and ample funds to redecorate the homes as she desired.

Lee had exquisite, expensive taste and an obsession with décor. In this quality and at this point in her life, she clearly outshone her elder sister, who had married a philandering Massachusetts politician whose family estates in Hyannis Port and Palm Beach looked downright primitive in comparison.

16

Everything

W ITH HER SPLENDID homes; her son, Anthony, born four and a
half months after the marriage; her daughter, Anna Christina,
or Tina, born three months premature in 1960; and her loving husband, Lee had what appeared to be everything. But she had grown
tired of Stas and, starting in 1961, she began spending more time in
the United States.

There is a clause in the U.S. Constitution banning inherited titles.
Yet Americans are obsessed with royalty, even when it is patently
false. As Lee moved around New York City and Washington, D.C.,
she was known as Princess Radziwill. Even *The New York Times*
bought into it. In November 1961, America's paper of record did a
story on Lee headlined "Princess Lee Radziwill Adds Charm to Any
Setting." The story referred to her as a princess again and again, and
in that way, it was a pure delight. But the story was there for only one
reason: Lee's brother-in-law was now president of the United States
and her sister First Lady.

Lee loved attention and publicity that sanctified her worth, but for the rest of her life, Jackie would always be lurking there somewhere. During a dinner party at Buckingham Palace that Queen Elizabeth gave for the President and Mrs. Kennedy, Prince Philip said to Lee, "You're just like me—you have to walk three steps behind."

Nobody had much fun at the staid dinners of the Eisenhower administration, but there was a new energy and excitement in Kennedy's White House. That reached a pinnacle of sorts in November 1961, when the Kennedys had a dinner with Lee and Stas as the honored guests. Some of the invitees in the Blue Room danced the sensation of the moment, the twist, an inelegant dance in which the partners gyrated in place. It would not do to project a frivolous image for the young administration, and the White House press office denied that anyone had danced the provocative twist.

Toward the end of the dinner, JFK made a toast to his sister-in-law. The president called Lee an enchanting woman and noted that whenever he chanced into a room "when she and Jackie are talking, they always stop." He said he assumed these were nice things "they are saying about Stas and me," though if that was the case, why would they go quiet? The room was full of knowledgeable Washingtonians, and they laughed as if they had heard an insider's joke; if the sisters were talking about their husbands, they were as likely pillorying as praising.

It was rare to see drunks at a White House party, but few events there went on until 4:00 a.m., as this one did. By the early-morning hours, things got sloppy. One of the inebriated guests was the author Gore Vidal. His mother had been married to Hugh Auchincloss before Lee's mother, Janet, and Gore was a relative of sorts. Gore moved unsteadily around the floor like a ship without a rudder until he came upon Jackie. To prevent himself from stumbling to the ground, he reached out and touched her back. His sexual predilections were such that he was not grabbing at the First Lady for sexual pleasure, but still, it did not look right.

Bobby Kennedy pulled Vidal's arm away. The attorney general was his brother's main protector, and he would not have this intruder touching the First Lady. "Never do that again," Vidal said. When the outraged author came upon the president, he said, "I'd like to wring your brother's neck." Vidal was ushered out and never again brought back into the inner circles of the Kennedys.

Lee and Stas returned for the Christmas holidays, and she saw her sister often. In March 1962, Lee joined Jackie on what was called a "private" visit to India and Pakistan. Rarely had "private" had such a meaning. Even before the sisters set out, *The New York Times* reported that the "tour has turned into an Asian caravan of some proportions." And through it all, Lee was in the giant shadow of her sister.

Lee's marriage to Stas had been like Fourth of July fireworks, flashes in the night and then nothing but darkness. Painfully, it had turned out that Stas was not the prince charming of Lee's childhood dreams but rather an aging, quirky man who took far more than he gave. Although Lee still bore his name, she had moved on and found a new lover, Aristotle Onassis, a man with animal vitality and a great fortune. Not so much self-educated as uneducated, there was a raw immediacy to the man that was exciting and dangerous.

When Aristotle wanted a woman, he devoured her with his attention, and he wanted Lee. The shipping magnate had a long-term relationship with the opera singer Maria Callas, but that did not prevent Lee from going off on Onassis's magnificent 325-foot yacht, the *Christina O.* The shipping magnate had the barstools made of the scrotums of whales, but the bar was not the only place on the ship where sexual games were played. Stas was understanding. Having little choice, he took some measure of solace in the steady downing of vodka and his own affairs.

When the Kennedys' newborn son Patrick died in August 1963, Lee flew to the States to console her sister. Then she flew back to Greece to be with Ari. Lee's brother-in-law was the president of the United States, a fact that she could hardly escape. Americans were for the most part socially conservative, and it would hurt Jack politically to have it known that his married sister-in-law was sleeping with the controversial Greek magnate.

Discretion was crucial, but neither Lee nor Ari seemed to care. As a couple they attended the spectacular opening party for the new Athens Hilton, an event so important to the company that the founder's son, Nicky Hilton, had flown in for the evening. "She's a real looker, that one," Nicky said to Ari as he eyed Lee. "You're a lucky man."

"I am lucky. She's magnificent, isn't she?" Ari said. Not even waiting for a reply, he continued. "You know she's Jackie Kennedy's sister, don't you?" That was the pedigree Ari cared about.

Jackie was having a terrible time getting over the death of Patrick, and that October, Lee asked Ari to invite the First Lady to join them on the *Christina O*. It was an appropriate sisterly gesture, but as soon as Jackie walked up the gangplank, Lee knew she had made a horrendous mistake. Ari was mesmerized by Jackie and could not keep away from her. Lee had never faced such an immediate and painful comparison to her sister, and her nightmare of a life lived as Jackie's coat holder returned in vivid form.

Ari made little attempt to hide his feelings and compounded them with the gifts he gave the sisters when they left the yacht. Jackie received a superb necklace of diamonds and rubies. Ari gave Lee three bracelets so dinky that she believed even Jackie's five-year-old daughter, Caroline, wouldn't have worn them to her own birthday party.

Lee flew back to Washington a month later to aid and comfort Jackie once again, after the assassination of President Kennedy. As bereft as she was, Jackie was not going to wear widow's weeds all her life, and she moved with her two children to New York to start a new life. Lee needed something new in her life too, and in 1964, she and Stas also purchased an apartment in Manhattan on Fifth Avenue and Seventy-Eighth Street, near the Metropolitan Museum, nine blocks south of her sister's apartment. Lee took the large bedroom as her own and shuttled her husband off into the antechamber, no bigger than a maid's room.

Lee had creative instincts that she never seemed able to focus. She dressed well and lived well, but that was largely it. In New York, she started writing again about fashion for women's magazines, but the disciplined routine of a magazine writer was not for her, and she soon sought other diversions that her friend Truman was happy to provide.

Truman had vowed his love and eternal devotion to Babe and Marella, but that was nothing compared to the passionate vows he made to Lee. They had a special kinship. Whatever Lee did, wherever she went, she felt she was second best, always standing in the gigantic shadow of her sister. As for Truman, as a gay man he felt that when he went into the salons of the powerful and elegant, he could always be spurned. That was the shadow that hung over him.

In those days, one could hardly go into the most prestigious restaurants for lunch without seeing Truman there in tête-à-tête with Lee.

Their meetings were so numerous that Suzy Knickerbocker took due note: "Somebody has to tell Truman that Lee Radziwill can't have him all the time. There's only one Truman and we saw him first."

In January 1967, Truman flew off with Lee for a vacation in Morocco. He had long since ditched the bohemian lifestyle of his Tangier days. They traveled in ultra-luxury from Rabat to Marrakech. On those long days, they had plenty of time to discuss Lee's favorite subject, her star-crossed life, almost certainly focusing on her newest dream. She had the idea of going onstage and from there possibly to Hollywood stardom.

There was no reason to think this was any different from any of her other pursuits, which had been dropped as soon as there was heavy lifting she could not foist off on others. But she appeared determined this time. She was taking acting lessons in London. Her advisors suggested that once she was ready, she should take a small part in a provincial theater production and build from there.

As Truman heard Lee talk about her dreams, he was not going to have his beloved friend accept some humiliatingly modest role. He knew she was a star, and as a star she should begin her theatrical career. He got her a top agent who booked her into the Ivanhoe restaurant, a dinner theater in Chicago. The Ivanhoe was located in a downscale North Side immigrant neighborhood where, if the Kennedys came at all, it was to look for votes.

Lee wanted to play Chekhov. The beautiful Helena Andreyevna Serebryakova in *Uncle Vanya* sounded about right, but that role required the most sensitive of acting skills. They settled instead on the romantic comedy *The Philadelphia Story*, where Lee would play Tracy Lord, a spoiled, rich heiress. Lee had hardly signed on to play the role before she was putting it down as unworthy of her talents. "*The*

Philadelphia Story is nice, but it's really just frivolous, charming non-sense," she said. Lee thought she had nothing in common with her character. "She has none of the feelings I understand of sadness, de-spair or of knowing loss," she said, berating those who suggested some similarity.

Lee insisted that they place her maiden name, Lee Bouvier, on the marquee. No matter what she called herself, the only reason there was a full house of prominent Chicagoans on opening night in June 1967 was that she was the sister of the most beloved woman in Amer-ica. Truman was out there at a table, but the president's widow was not.

The audience was prepared to enjoy Lee's performance, but from her first line, she was beyond dreadful. Speaking in an affectless monotone, she wasn't so much acting as reading memorized lines, and reading them terribly. But she looked fabulous. "Miss Bouvier had her clothes designed by Yves St. Laurent," wrote the *Los Angeles Times*. "George Masters flew in in a big jet with his bag of tricks to do her hair." Searching for something kind to say, the *Chicago Daily News* wrote that she had "at least laid a golden egg." She laid no other kind.

Any other thirty-four-year-old wife and mother would have given up her dreams of stardom after the dispiriting run of *The Philadelphia Story*. But because her sister had brought her such celebrity, she still had her illusions. As Lee continued her nightly performances, Tru-man talked with David Susskind, one of the most aggressive, publicity-conscious television producers. Lee was hardly a week into the Chicago run when Susskind announced that Lee would be play-ing Sally Middleton in *The Voice of the Turtle* in a two-hour adaptation on ABC written by none other than Truman Capote.

"Just imagine the rating!" Susskind enthused to his associate Alan Shayne. "The whole country will tune in to see Jackie Kennedy's sister." Whatever the producer told Truman and Lee, this was stunt programming, and it was all about Jackie.

Alan understood that Susskind might be right, but not when he heard the name of the play they would stage for television. "*The Voice of the Turtle!*" Alan exclaimed. "That's virtually a two-character play, the third character just comes in for a few scenes." Alan knew he had to talk Susskind out of this, or it would be a disaster for all parties.

It did not take Alan very long to come up with a wonderfully cynical solution. "I've got it!" he yelled in his eureka moment. "*Laura*, you know, the movie where they all think she's dead. They talk about her all the time, but she doesn't appear until a third of the way into the picture, then all she has to do is just stand there and look enigmatic."

The other part of the solution was to surround Lee with first-rate actors, and so they did, including George Sanders, Robert Stack, Farley Granger, and Arlene Francis. To make Lee even more comfortable, the producers agreed to film *Laura* in London. Truman's script was a disaster, probably because he foisted the project off on a friend. "Truman didn't write any of the script, I don't think," said Alan, who called in another writer to turn the material into a script that was merely bad.

If Lee had come into the rehearsal the first day as a novice who had much to learn, she might have made the project tolerable. But she came floating in as a princess living an illustrious life. Actors are used to treating one another as equals, not this royal presence descending into their lives. "Lee thought she was a great actress and would be a sensation," said Alan. "Most of the time she was haughty and knew it all. She was impossible."

The first time the cast read through the script, Lee spoke in the same denatured voice she had used in Chicago. By the time the actors reached the last scene, the director, John Moxey, realized he had a lead actress who could not act. Moxey had only two weeks to change this, and he was abrupt in the way he challenged Lee. It was unlikely anybody in her life had ever talked to Lee the way the director did. Lee got so angry that she tried unsuccessfully to get Moxey fired. Robert Stack was so distressed to be working with such a pathetic amateur that he implored Alan to bring in Elizabeth Taylor to play the role.

Lee was even inept in taking simple stage directions. In one scene, the phone rings, and Lee's character picks up the phone to speak to the caller—only Lee would start talking before she had raised the phone to her ear. No matter how many times she was told that was wrong, she couldn't get it right.

When the two-hour film ran in January 1968, the reviews were universally negative. In the avalanche of criticism, Lee's performance received most of the blame. "There was no question of who murdered 'Laura' on the nation's television screens last night," wrote the *Chicago Tribune*. "It was Lee Bouvier, also known as the Princess Radziwill."

As much as Truman pretended otherwise, Lee's career as an actress was over. Soon after the debacle on ABC, she came out to visit Truman in Palm Springs, where he was spending the winter and telling everyone he was working so hard on *Answered Prayers* that it would be finished in a year. Truman had warned her that the winter nights in the California desert could get cold, and she had brought the sable coat Stas had given her for Christmas. The first thing she did was to hang the coat in the closet. Truman's bulldog Maggie took one look at the sable and, likely thinking there hung her next meal, rushed in and tore the coat into chewable pieces. Truman thought it was funny. That was Lee's leading memory of her visit.

Back in London that June, Lee was so upset to hear that Bobby Kennedy had been assassinated, she could not even drive straight and crashed into another vehicle. Her sister was even more devastated, fearing that America had turned into a land of uncontrolled violence where if your name was Kennedy, you were not safe. There was only one reasonable solution: to get out.

That autumn, a distraught Lee called Truman. She had just heard what she considered a betrayal beyond imagination. Jackie had agreed to marry Onassis. The Greek shipping magnate should have been hers. As far as Lee was concerned, for her sister, it was nothing but a business deal. "How could she do this to me!" Lee screamed to Truman on the phone. "How could she! How could this happen!" Despite her rage, to the world Lee displayed only sisterly devotion and delight in Jackie's soon-to-be husband.

In the summer of 1971, Lee visited Jackie on Ari's island of Skorpios. There Jackie introduced her sister to Peter Beard, who was spending most of his summer on the island. The Yale graduate had become a wildlife photographer and conservationist. In 1965, he had published *The End of the Game*, a book of text and photos documenting the destruction of African wildlife and wilderness.

When Beard needed money, the photographer returned from his life in the African bush to shoot models for money, enjoying their pleasures as he did. He dressed in a disheveled sixties-chic that worked only if you were as stunningly handsome as Peter.

Stas had gone off on safari with Peter and considered him a friend, but that was no matter to Lee and Peter, who began an affair on the

island. Lee might have asked herself that if her new lover would betray his friendship with her husband so easily, would he not just as
easily betray her? But that was not a question to be broached in the
throes of passion with a man almost five years younger than thirty-
eight-year-old Lee.

Stas had tried to play the sophisticated husband understanding of
his wife's dalliances. Maybe he didn't know what was going on each
night in Peter's bedroom in the villa near his, but he knew his wife
was dismissing him. The pain was there, and his drinking grew worse.

Obsessed with Peter, Lee arranged it so she and Stas could go on
an African safari, where she snuck off to have her ecstatic moments
with her lover. Then Lee invited Peter to come and stay with her and
Stas in London and join them on a Caribbean vacation. Fifty-seven-
year-old Stas accepted his diminished circumstances. At his age, he
had no grand vision for the future except hanging on to the remnants
of his marriage. But Lee had a dream, and that was to divorce Stas
and start a new life in America with Peter beside her. She would keep
the title "princess."

By January 1971, Truman was so late in delivering *Answered Prayers*
that not only was it becoming an inside joke, but the delay was creating financial consequences. Twentieth Century Fox insisted he repay
the $200,000 the studio had given him as a down payment for the
film rights. That he did, and whenever people asked him about the
manuscript, he said it was two-thirds done and changed the subject.

Lee knew her friend was having a torturous time writing his self-
described masterpiece. She sensed that he needed a break. What

could be better than to go off with her and Peter on the Rolling Stones' 1972 American tour, writing a story about the greatest rock band in the world for the hip weekly *Rolling Stone* while Peter took the pictures? It would be a rock 'n' roll version of "The Muses Are Heard," Truman's classic *New Yorker* piece about the theater company of *Porgy and Bess* touring the Soviet Union, and like that story, it also would be published as a book. The novelist Terry Southern was the only other writer allowed on the Stones' plane, bus, and hotel floor. For a writer, it was like having a feast laid out before him that only he could eat.

Soon after Truman arrived to start his reporting in Kansas City, where the band was halfway through their two-month-long tour, the problems began. Backstage he complained about the noise. The band was about blasting walls of sound, and to suggest that it was all a bit too loud was heresy. The Stones felt Truman was out of it, a hapless relic of an old generation. They nicknamed him "Truby" and Lee "Radish," a rollicking dismissal of them.

The Stones' Keith Richards was not about to just sit there and take what he considered to be Truby's "snide, queenie remarks." The evening after the show in Dallas–Fort Worth, he noticed a ketchup bottle on a trolley in the hotel corridor. Opening the bottle, he spattered it all over Truman's door and tried to kick it in. "Come out, you old queen," Keith shouted. "What are you doing round here? You want cold blood? You're on the road now, Truby! Come and say it out here in the corridor."

Keith was stoned much of the time, and he must have thought he was being funny. But for Truman, it surely was unsettling, even frightening. He was used to being treated with a measure of respect, never anything like this.

Truman shared a hotel room with Peter. In bed at night in his underwear, Truman laid out a bunch of pills on his stomach with a bottle of Jack Daniel's beside him. As Truman washed the pills down with the whiskey, Peter worried about the road his companion was traveling.

The other journalists covering the tour did not have the access Truman had, but some of them wrote vivid, compelling stories that burst with color and life. Truman read the pieces and understood he was the king these other writers wanted to dethrone. "They'll be nothing when mine appears," Truman told Peter. "No one'll even remember them."

Truman had written *The Muses Are Heard* when he was thirty-one years old and life was fresh and new. He'd observed that moment with passionate concern and recorded a mosaic of detail that allowed him to create a compelling piece of nonfiction. But now, at fifty-seven and facing a whole new generation of music and culture he didn't really understand (and certainly didn't enjoy), he had neither the ambition nor the discipline to produce what was expected of him. He wrote a few hundred words that he proudly read to Peter, but that was about it, and he never turned in his piece.

Maybe Truman was having trouble with his writing, but Lee decided she would write her memoirs. Interest was high, and *Ladies' Home Journal* published a thousand-word excerpt of the book when Lee was just beginning to write it. Most authors are fortunate to get a book party with cheap wine and cheese on publication day. With one measly chapter, Lee got hers at the Four Seasons, one of the most exclusive restaurants in Manhattan. Truman was there with a raft of other celebrities to drink champagne and eat a piece of the cake in the shape of a book.

Few first-time authors receive a $250,000 advance, equivalent to $1,462,000 in today's dollars. As she did with all her projects, Lee began with due diligence, researching her family's past. Then the melancholy day came when she had to sit down and write. Her life was messy and complicated, and that was a story she was unprepared to tell. Lee paid back the advance and moved on.

Whatever Lee did brought attention to her or there was no point. She went to Bill Paley at CBS and suggested a half-hour show in which she would interview celebrities. Lee was not bad at tossing easy questions at the likes of her friend the ballet dancer Nureyev and the designer Halston, but she was no Barbara Walters. The interviews ran on local television stations, and that was the end of Lee's latest career.

"My deep regret is that I wasn't brought up or educated to have a métier," Lee told *Interview*. "I am mainly interested in the arts, but because of my kind of education, my interests were never channeled in any particular field until it was too late to make use of them except in a dilettante way."

Lee seemed not to realize that there are few things less appealing than listening to the whining rich. Her life of privilege had given her almost everything. She dropped out of college because she did not have the focus and discipline to follow through and found it boring. That was the pattern of her life, never doing the hard work required in almost anything of consequence, and then moving on when things got difficult.

While trying to sound candid, Lee was not about to tell Andy Warhol's magazine or any other journalist what truly bothered her. She had tolerated Peter's other lovers, but he had moved on from her for good to a young model. She had loved the photographer. The affair had been the most daring act in her life, and it was painful to be a cast-aside forty-year-old woman. "It was the first time that anybody had ever dumped her, because she had always done the dumping, and she was really devastated by it," said Truman.

Lee had other problems. Jackie had returned to New York a rich widow with a fortune that dwarfed anything Lee had. If that was not difficult enough to face, Jackie took an editor's position at Viking Press without telling her. Maybe that was not as outrageous as Jackie marrying Ari, but it came close, and Lee was infuriated.

Then there was another problem with Jackie that Lee could hardly talk about. Lee's daughter, Tina, was overweight and insecure, and her thin, elegant mother made the teenager feel even worse. Although Lee loved her two children, she was far from a hands-on mother, and Tina had reached the point where she could hardly tolerate being around Lee. She loved her aunt Jackie, who was so much more under-standing. Tina packed up and moved a few blocks north to live with Jackie.

With all the parties Lee attended, she always seemed to have a drink in her hand. Vodka was her drink. It was perfect. She was used to disguising things, and nobody smelled liquor on Lee's breath. She never slurred her words or wobbled across a restaurant floor. She was as impeccably dressed and well-mannered as ever, but vodka had be-come her closest friend.

Knowing how much Lee loved publicity, Truman gave her the greatest gift he could give her, a one-page celebration in *Vogue* in June 1976. He called it "Lee: A Fan Letter from Truman Capote," and it was a sea of hyperbole. There was one assertion after another about how great Lee was with her "first-class intelligence," her "beautiful eyes wide-apart, gold-brown like a glass of brandy resting on a table in front of a firelight." That was heavy-duty work for a jigger of brandy.

Truman was not through giving. Later that year, in a cover story on Lee in *People*, he gave a gushy tribute that opened the piece: "She's a remarkable girl. She's all the things people give Jackie credit for. All the looks, style, taste—Jackie never had them at all, and yet it was Lee who lived in the shadow of this super-something person." It was not enough to praise Lee. Jackie must be denigrated. The sisters were on a teeter-totter. If one rose up, the other must go down.

17

"Naaaah,
They're Too Dumb"

Truman received all kinds of warnings about publishing "La Côte Basque 1965," the eleven-thousand-word excerpt from *Answered Prayers*, scheduled for inclusion in the November 1975 edition of *Esquire*.

When his biographer, Gerald Clarke, read the pages, he was aghast. He knew that Truman's swans—women who considered him one of their dearest friends—would be upset about the stories he told. No, more than upset: *furious*. Some of these were secrets, after all, that had been told to him in the deepest confidence. (Never mind that Truman had been telling those tales around town at lunches for years. This was different.) This public airing of their dirty lingerie was nothing less than a betrayal.

"You can't publish this," Clarke told Truman flatly. "The characters are barely cloaked. Everyone you're writing about will recognize themselves," he explained to Truman—and worse, others would recognize them too.

But Truman dismissed his concerns: "They won't know who they are," he said with a wave of his hand. "They're too dumb."

They'd have to be pretty dumb, indeed, not to recognize themselves in Truman's pages. The novella takes place over a lunch at the (very real) esteemed French restaurant on Manhattan's East Fifty-Fifth Street frequented by the New York elite. The action flits from one table to the next, exposing the secrets and intrigues among Manhattan café society. While Truman invented pseudonyms for many of the rich, unhappy women on his pages, anyone knowledgeable about New York's haute social world would guess the unfortunate real people (and stories) chronicled in this nasty epic.

Others who saw early versions of the pages were similarly alarmed. Truman's lover John O'Shea, scarcely a man of literary discernment, was nonetheless also appalled when he saw what Truman was going to write. "That's gossip! That's bullshit!" he exclaimed.

Truman dismissed these concerns with studied disdain. No stranger to controversy, he was not afraid of ignorant critics. "La Côte Basque 1965" was a delicious tranche of his masterpiece, and it would turn him once again into the most talked-about author in America.

As "La Côte Basque 1965" opens, Lady Ina Coolbirth—based on Slim Keith—is seated at a privileged table swilling Cristal champagne and spouting outrageous tales about those in the grand dining room and beyond. This big, brassy daughter of the American West opines that Princess Margaret is a "drone" who doesn't like "'poufs.'" That judgment could not have set well with Lady Ina's guest, P. B. Jones, a bisexual hustler.

Lady Ina goes on to reminisce about a weekend she spent at the Kennedys' when she was only eighteen years old; late at night, randy old Joe entered her bedroom to assault her. The most painful tale was not about royalty domestic or otherwise but about Lady Ina's recent husband, Lord Coolbirth. This dour, uninteresting Brit had the considerable audaciousness to leave her for another woman.

After taking another flute of champagne, Lady Ina mused on her lonely fate, approaching an age when only gay men would treat her with kindness. "I adore them, I always have," she said, "but I really am not ready to become a full-time fag's moll; I'd rather go dyke."

Truman's friends Gloria Vanderbilt and Carol Saroyan made appearances in "La Côte Basque 1965" under their own names—several of their names, in fact. In doing so, Truman took a deliciously bitchy dig at a weak spot in each woman's armor: their serial divorces. He referred directly to each woman's multiple marriages, calling Gloria "Gloria Vanderbilt di Cicco Stokowski Lumet Cooper" and Carol "Carol Marcus Saroyan Saroyan (she married *him* twice) Matthau."

Truman didn't stop there in savaging his lifelong friends. His fictionalized dialogue had both of them gossiping relentlessly about others in their circle, some cloaked and some clearly identified, like their friend Oona Chaplin (married to Charlie). He summed them up with a devastating kiss-off: "charmingly incompetent adventuresses."

But the woman most hurt by Truman's betrayal in the story's pages was the one whose approval and attention he actually desired the most: Babe.

In the published story, Truman included a character named Dillon, a successful businessman clearly based on Bill Paley, and laid out the tawdry details of his supposed one-night stand with what was obviously the very real Marie Harriman. The story is told by Lady Ina, who had an affair with Dillon when she was young. He had asked her never to repeat the story, but oh well. . . .

The event in question had happened back in the late fifties, when Marie's husband, Averell, was governor of New York. Lady Ina set the question out bold and straight: "Why would an educated, dynamic, very rich and well-hung Jew go bonkers for a cretinous Protestant size forty who wears low-heeled shoes and lavender water? Especially when he's married to Cleo Dillon, to my mind the most beautiful creature alive."

"Cleo Dillon" was, of course, a thinly veiled Babe Paley. And why Bill (or Dillon) would cheat on her with the governor's wife was simple and direct: the Harrimans were the center of power and the epitome of the Protestant Establishment that had barred the Jewish businessman from its clubs and his sons from its schools. As successful as Dillon was and as much as he had assumed a WASP identity, he was still a Jew banned from the Racquet Club, an exclusion that rankled him profoundly. If Dillon could just sleep with the governor's wife, he would get even for all these brutal slights. "Whether he confesses to it or not, that's why he wanted to fuck the governor's wife," wrote Truman, "revenge himself on that smug hog-bottom, make her sweat and squeal and call him daddy."

The businessman and his wife had a pied-à-terre at the Pierre. As relayed in "La Côte Basque 1965," that was where Dillon brought the governor's wife. There was only the marital bed in the small apartment. She insisted that he leave the lights off. It did not go well, and she was already dressed and leaving when he turned on the lights. As he looked down on the bed, it could have been the severed horse head scene in *The Godfather*—that was how bloody the sheets were. The governor's wife was having her period.

Dillon thought the governor's wife had done this to get even with him. He had no time to worry about that. He had to get the sheets clean before his wife returned from out of town. The businessman did not finish until eight in the morning, when he fell asleep on the soggy sheets.

By the time the November *Esquire* started showing up in subscribers' mailboxes, Truman was out in Hollywood playing a starring role in *Murder by Death*, a manic comedy scripted by Neil Simon. Truman played Lionel Twain, an eccentric millionaire hosting a dinner party for a group of the most famous detectives in the world. Thanks to the massive celebrity he had cultivated over the last two decades, Truman was probably the only author in America who would have been considered for a headliner's role in a Hollywood film. It did not matter what name his character had, though—Truman only played himself, and he did not do it that well, lisping along and mouthing his lines as if reading them off a teleprompter. Overweight and pallid, he cast a troubling image onto the screen.

The life of a Hollywood star was not what it was made out to be in the movie magazines. Up before dawn, into makeup, and then sitting around for hours: it was hardly Truman's thing. The work was tedious enough, but what made it even more enervating was the devastating response to "La Côte Basque 1965."

Truman was staying with his friend Joanne Carson, the ex-wife of the *Tonight Show* host Johnny Carson, in her home above Sunset Boulevard. While not a swan, Joanne did make an appearance in "La Côte Basque 1965"—in it, Joanne is portrayed as Jane Baxter, married to Bobby Baxter, the night talk show king. Bobby goes down to Miami, where he calls his wife back in their home in New York while he is in bed with another woman. Jane tells the woman, "I've got a double dose of syph and the old clap-clap, all courtesy of that great comic, my husband—Bobby Baxter." Truman's narrator gives two reasons why Jane does not leave Bobby: "One: dough. And two: identity." It was a devastating depiction, and immediately recognizable to anyone who knew anything about Johnny Carson's famously roving eye. But Joanne was so insecure (and so desirous of having Truman as her friend) that she did not let the shattering portrayal bother her.

At first, Truman was giddy with anticipation about the reception his brilliant work would receive. But as news started trickling in about how upset his friends back east were with their portrayal, Truman's excitement curdled.

Joanne said that week Truman "looked like a baby who had been slapped." As close as he was to Joanne, he did not talk to her about the pain he felt. Instead, he went into his bedroom and lay there reading and rereading the passages that had so offended.

If only Truman could talk to his swans, he believed he could soothe their rumpled feathers, but almost no one was willing to deal with him.

Slim was in her suite at the Pierre Hotel when Babe called. "Have you read Truman's piece in *Esquire*?" Babe asked in a voice charged with nervous anxiety unlike the impenetrably cool self she showed to the world.

"No," Slim said.

"Well, get it and read it and call me back," Babe said.

Slim sent her maid down to the lobby, and the young woman returned clutching the magazine to her chest. On its cover was Truman, dressed in a black turtleneck, a black fedora, and dark glasses, holding a stiletto in his pudgy little hands. Slim read scarcely a page of "La Côte Basque 1965" before she realized Truman had based the narrator on *her*. This so-called "Lady Ina Coolbirth" spewed grotesque gossip about women who were Slim's friends. Beyond that, Lady Ina mused about how terrible it was to be single again after her husband left her for someone else. It hadn't taken an affair for Slim to leave Lord Keith, but other than that, the British royal was a tintype of Slim's ex. Like Lady Ina, Slim felt dispirited and lonely without a husband. But these were not matters to be decanted in public, and from beginning to end, the whole story was a shameful business.

Slim saw that Truman did not trash all the swans. Truman's story had Lee (using her real name, not a pseudonym) sitting in the restaurant at a prominent table with her sister, Jackie. Truman had picked up on Lee's attitude toward her sister and put it front and center in the story. In "La Côte Basque 1965," the author described *la grande Jacqueline* as "unrefined, exaggerated" looking, "an artful female impersonator impersonating Mrs. Kennedy." As for Lee, she was "marvelously made, like a Tanagra figurine; she's feminine without being effeminate."

Truman did not even mention all the swans. There was nothing about Marella, veiled or not, in the pages. She had already dismissed Truman as a friend, and the scandalous story affected her the least of any of the swans. C.Z. was not a character in "La Côte Basque 1965" either, and in the following years she became even closer to Truman.

As badly as Slim believed she had been treated, it was nothing compared to what Truman did to Babe in pillorying her husband. The Paleys had been so generous to Truman. They had given him myriad gifts. They had invited him to fly with them around the world. They had introduced him into the most elite and rarefied circles, vouching for him. And now this.

As soon as she finished reading, Slim called Babe. "I feel absolutely . . . as though I've been hit," Slim said. "All the breath is out of me." That was how terrible and inexplicable a blow it was.

"So, who do you think it is?" Babe asked. Of course, Slim knew what Babe was talking about—who was the businessman "Dillon" sleeping with the governor's wife? Slim had absolutely no doubt the story was about Babe's husband. Bill, after all, was a serial philanderer—and this was exactly the sort of thing he'd do. Whether the story was true or not, it was a betrayal of the worst kind to write that anecdote. Only Slim could not say that to her friend. Maybe it was cowardly, but the only thing to do was to say nothing.

"No idea in the world who it is," Slim said. "It could be anyone."

Babe never spoke with Truman again.

The story of Dillon and the governor's wife left a stain on Babe's life larger than the one in Dillon's marital bed. Had Truman ever really cared for her? Was any of his friendship real if he could do such a thing?

Truman tried calling Babe for days, but for the first time in their long friendship, he could not get through to her. Finally, he reached Bill, who took the call. Bill had an out-of-control temper, raging at the smallest disturbance to his equilibrium. But his anger was so extreme that day that he was beyond rage.

"Have you read my *Esquire* piece?" Truman asked. It was a measure of how self-absorbed and obsessed with attention Truman was that he could even ask Bill that question. The executive replied with the most devastating response of all.

"I started, Truman, but I fell asleep," Bill said. "Then a terrible thing happened: the magazine was thrown away."

"I'll send you another copy," Truman said.

"Don't bother, Truman," Bill said. "I'm preoccupied. My wife is very ill."

Babe was in fact dying of lung cancer, a slow and excruciating death. She had always been terribly svelte, but now with her illness she was by any standard far too thin, and she wore thick makeup to cover up the darkness that had fallen across her countenance. A third of her right lung had already been removed, but the cancer had come back, and in May 1975, surgeons removed the rest of her lung.

For most of their marriage, Bill had been dismissive of Babe. In the last months of her life, Bill decided he wanted to succor his wife as he had never done before and show her how much he cared. But Babe wanted none of him, and in these fateful final days, she pushed him away and faced her death without the two most important men in her life—her husband and Truman.

When Truman flew back to New York City, he had lunch with Gerald Clarke at La Grenouille. The biographer operated by one of the fundamental rules of good journalism: always be the first to arrive. Clarke was sitting in one of the most desired banquettes at the front of the upscale restaurant when Truman walked in the door. He could see the maître d' had not taken his place away, though the damage from the *Esquire* piece kept compounding, offending those who, as Truman saw it, had no business being offended.

Jerry Zipkin was also at lunch that day, seated at a banquette a few tables away with a female guest. Zipkin was the most celebrated walker of the era, going nowhere without a woman of a certain age and bankroll on his arm. A man of studied obsequiousness, a month earlier, Zipkin would have jumped up and come running to fawn over Truman. The two tiny men could have been brothers, though Zipkin was Truman without the talent or wit.

Zipkin sniffed the social air at regular intervals. Truman had hardly sat down when Zipkin called for the captain and asked for his table to be moved a distance away. It was clear he found the stench overwhelming.

Truman laughed.

Despite the initial fallout, Truman was convinced that once the swans realized how much they needed him, they would all come fluttering back. It did not happen. Truman's defenders dismissed the women whose stories appeared in *Answered Prayers* as spoiled socialites who had finally gotten what they deserved. But these women were profoundly hurt. As they saw it, he had abused their friendship and betrayed them in a display of appallingly bad manners. He never should have been invited into their set in the first place. Babe was a gentle sort, and even if she had been healthy, she would not have spoken openly about Truman's betrayal. Slim had no such qualms. She raged against him for the rest of her life.

As painful as it was for the swans, they had husbands, lovers, other friends, and extensive social lives. They could move on.

Truman could not. He needed these women more than he had ever imagined.

Although most of the swans no longer talked to Truman, they and other friends puzzled over why he had not written the kind of intimate, inside look at the world of wealth and privilege that he said he was writing. Some blamed the failure on the emotional overload of *In Cold Blood*. As sensitive as he was, he had been devastated by Perry's death and never quite recovered. But that was a decade earlier, and he had written other short works that showed his talent was intact.

Others said he had been sucked so deep into these spoiled lives that he could not extricate himself to write truthfully about his friends. But from the evidence of what he had written so far, he had no problem betraying his closest friends in the name of his art.

In vivisecting the playwright Tennessee Williams in another section of *Answered Prayers*, Truman could have been writing about aspects of himself: "Here's a dumpy little guy with a dramatic mind who, like one of his own adrift heroines, seeks attention and sympathy by serving up half-believed lies to total strangers. Strangers because he has no friends, and he has no friends because the only people he pities are his own characters and himself—everyone else is an audience."

18

The Good Pocket

TRUMAN HAD NO real family, and he needed friends around him. Jack Dunphy had always been there for him, his constant companion. Jack made almost no money as a writer, and Truman had been generous, giving him a house on Long Island and access to a home in Switzerland where he went skiing each winter. But the two lovers had grown apart, and Jack was not there for him the way he once would have been.

For years, the best of Truman's friends had been his swans, but most of them were gone now, and with it those splendid times and rich ambiences that he adored. It meant even more to him that Lee and C.Z. were staying by his side, but so many others had left.

For most of his adult life, Truman had a shimmer of celebrity around him. Wherever he went, people looked at him and wanted to be near him. He could still get his favorite table at the Colony, but it was no longer the same. Celebrity was the ocean he swam in, but it was slowly drying up as times were changing and the culture moved on without him. He started drinking so much and taking so many drugs that he attracted a new breed of acquaintance.

Although Truman was no longer the crown prince of café society, there was a new faux royalty ready to embrace him. Their hangout was Studio 54, an enormous, wildly trendy disco that opened in the spring of 1977 on West Fifty-Fourth Street. To Truman, it was the Agnelli yacht, the Paley estate, and the Guinness plane all rolled into one dark, raunchy package. And he was welcome there: no matter how many hundreds pushed to get in, a way always opened for Truman. Admired in this set as much for being one of the first publicly open gay men as for his writing, he could go whenever and wherever he wanted in the club and do whatever he wanted to do.

Much of the time, Truman headed down to the basement. About all Studio 54 co-owner Steve Rubell did to fix up the grungy space was to throw down a few mattresses. Other than that, it was dirty little cubicles, puddles of water, unwanted props, assorted junk, and lots of naked and half-naked bodies, everything in the shadows. The unenlightened could dance their hearts out above, the sounds of the music and their feet hitting the dance floor reverberating into the cellar, but this was the place to be, and Truman was there.

One of the other regulars in the basement was the designer Halston. Like Truman, he was descending into a netherworld of drugs and dissipation, but unlike Truman so far, he had kept a measure of his good looks. Halston wore a sports jacket. In one pocket he had the good coke, in the other the cheap stuff. "Truman always got it out of the good pocket," said the publicist R. Couri Hay, who in those years was close to Halston.

Truman was a voyeur. Sometimes he preferred to hide himself in a corner upstairs and simply watch. One evening he saw a beautiful boy standing at the bar. He walked over to him and grabbed his crotch. The teenager's name was Richard DuPont. He had taken the train in from Connecticut to see what life was all about, and it wasn't this. "You're nothing but a tired old queen," Richard told him.

Maybe Truman was no longer celebrated as a number one bestselling author, but he was still such good copy that journalists hectored him for interviews. In July 1978, it was Anne Taylor Fleming's turn, in a two-part series in *The New York Times Magazine*. Reporters were constantly bugging Truman about *Answered Prayers*. He got that behind him by telling Anne it was two-thirds finished and would be completed by the following August.

Truman kept telling the reporter he was on the wagon, but the more time Anne spent with him, the more she was sure that was not true. "He was a mass of confusion at that point," she said. Anne knew that Truman was playing her, but it was so fascinating, she let him roll.

Truman was full of such vivid fantasies about his life that Anne could do little but record them. He said there was no way he was going to wait until *Answered Prayers* was published to have a bash to outdo the Black and White Ball in its creativity and daring. He was going to do it that December for 540 of his closest friends in a warehouse. Inside the giant structure he would place blue and khaki tents that he was already having made. The male guests would arrive that evening in black caftans, the female guests with mysterious veils that they would take off at midnight, and Truman would be at the center of it all: "I will be all in white, a white galabia with appliqued butterflies and a white turban, on the side of which will be one large emerald. I will be barefoot and will carry a fabulous Faberge walking cane. I will be the prince of all Araby and you will all kiss my hand when you come in."

That story had hardly appeared with its assertions of Truman's glorious future and the party that was never to be when he felt so depressed and apparently suicidal that he was checked into a hospital. Of the old friends, C.Z. was always there for him, and he for her. When she wanted to write a book about gardening, he had helped her get a publisher by agreeing to write the introduction and getting his friend Cecil Beaton to do the drawings. In *First Garden*, C.Z. detailed all that had to be done to maintain a garden over the seasons. She had been there and done it, and it showed on every page. The book led to *Ladies' Home Journal* asking C.Z. to do a monthly gardening column, and from there to a business selling gardening supplies.

When C.Z. and her husband, Winston, heard about Truman, they rushed in to help. It wasn't a question of quid pro quo. It was simply what friends did. Winston was an alcoholic himself. He would sometimes disappear for days. Understanding as well as anyone what Truman was going through, Winston helped bundle him up and drove him out to the Guests' estate at Templeton. Winston thought the only answer was for Truman to go to Hazelden, the famed rehabilitation center in the woods of Minnesota. Winston and C.Z. would not listen to Truman's doubts. When the day came, they drove him to the airport and flew with him to Minnesota.

Soon after Truman got out after his month at Hazelden, C.Z. joined him for an evening at Studio 54. Still a handsome woman, C.Z. wore a black suit, a pearl necklace, and heels, and on the dance floor she looked distressingly out of place. Truman had lost considerable weight. He wore a white sports coat with sleeves so long that they covered all but the nubs of his fingers, and a white fedora, and eyes that appeared blank. *Women's Wear Daily* put a picture of the couple dancing on the front page.

Truman had an addict's cunning. Although he said he was sober, it is likely he did not give up all his liquor, pills, and coke. He had been doing them for so long that he could cruise, never getting so high that he could not write. For a few months, it worked well. Despite his one big book, *In Cold Blood*, Truman was a miniaturist. The rest of his work was relatively short: small novels, novellas, reportage, short stories, and essays. And that was what he did now, not even pretending to go back to *Answered Prayers*. The longest piece he wrote was a novella, *Handcarved Coffins*, published in *Interview*, that he called a "Nonfiction Account of an American Crime." It was clearly fiction, cobbled together from any number of stories he had heard. Whatever it was, *Handcarved Coffins* was wildly entertaining, and Lester Persky, who had produced such edgy hits as *Shampoo* and *Taxi*, purchased the movie rights for $300,000.

As Truman tried to focus on his writing, he was faced with a pestering legal problem that would not go away. It all had to do with Gore Vidal. Truman thought that Vidal was a mediocre writer and a miserable human being, feelings that Gore richly reciprocated. Whenever the opportunity arose, Truman took out his carving knife and slashed away. One such occasion was in 1975, when he gave a drunken interview to *Playgirl*, a monthly whose main contributions to American culture were nude or seminude male centerfolds.

With the tape recorder rolling, Truman talked about the party at the White House in 1961 that Gore attended. Lee had been there too, and Truman knew that Gore had inadvertently touched Jackie's back and had an altercation with Bobby that ended with his exiting the event. That was startling enough, but Truman used those facts as his takeoff point for an elaborate reverie about what happened. "It was the only time he [Gore] had ever been invited to the White House and he got drunk," Truman said. That much was true.

"*Annnnnd* . . . he insulted Jackie's mother, whom he had never met before in his *life!*" Truman continued. "But I mean insulted her. . . . And Bobby and Arthur Schlesinger, I believe it was, and one of the guards just picked Gore up and carried him to the door and threw him out into Pennsylvania Avenue."

Gore sued Truman for $1 million, almost $5 million in today's money. In most lawsuits, the lawyers do the battling while their clients keep studiously silent. But both authors were full of savage wit and would not be quiet.

"Capote has spent most of his life with some success trying to get into a world I have spent most of my life with some success trying to get out of," Gore said.

"You see, behind his facade he's [Gore] really just a bowl of not-quite-congealed jello," Truman said.

The public spectacle was amusing to those who liked such things, but it was emotionally debilitating for the fragile Truman to be in such a battle. There were depositions and court filings as the case marched ominously forward toward trial. He had pointedly named Lee as his source for the story. Truman said that originally Lee promised to give an affidavit in his defense, but she backed off.

Lee's lawyers warned her if she came forward as the person who told Truman the story, she might be added to the suit and would have her own legal bills. When Gore's lawyers came to Lee toward the end of 1977, she gave them an affidavit saying she did "not recall ever discussing with Truman Capote the incident or the evening which I understand is the subject of his lawsuit." The sworn statement was written in the slick legalese lawyers use when a client does not want to say certain things.

Lee did not tell her closest friend what she had done. It was not until the spring of 1979 that Truman learned about Lee's statement. Despite her affidavit, he needed her to testify for him. When he tried to call her, she did not pick up. In a desperate attempt to reach her, he asked Liz Smith to try. Ever sniffing the possibility of publicity, Lee took the gossip columnist's call.

No way was Lee going to testify. "The notoriety of it is too much," Lee said. "I am tired of Truman riding on my coattails to fame. And Liz, what difference does it make? They are just a couple of fags."

Truman was beyond devastated when Liz told him what Lee had said. Other than Jack he had done more for Lee than he had anyone in his life—not just helping with her failed acting career but listening to her endlessly and saying and doing things that would make her happy—and he considered her his closest friend.

Lee was suffering in her own way too. She was supposed to marry San Francisco hotelier Newton Cope. Unwilling to sign an agreement promising her $15,000 a month, Newton called off the wedding two hours before the ceremony. That was an embarrassing spectacle by itself. Lee was drinking heavily, and Andy Warhol thought she might kill herself.

Truman did not care. He was going to have her "shitting razor blades." There was no one to tell him it was a terrible idea to go on *The Stanley Siegel Show*, a live New York talk show, to talk about Lee. No one to tell him he was a great writer, and this was beneath him.

Lee had said he was a fag—well, he would play the fag, not just any fag but a Southern fag, and that was a category all by itself. He would take over little Stanley's show and, in a monologue of devastating truth, expose everything about Lee and the Kennedys.

New Yorkers who tuned in that June 1979 morning were greeted with the best show in the city. Truman had planned his performance out to the last detail, and he was beyond bitchy, trashing Lee with unmitigated pleasure. "I'll tell you something about fags, especially Southern fags," he said. "We is mean. A Southern fag is meaner than the meanest rattler you ever met. . . . I know that Lee wouldn't want me to be tellin' none of this. But you know us Southern fags—we just can't keep our mouths shut." And then he took off in a manic rant exposing Lee's secrets, her jealousy of Jackie, her hopes to marry Onassis, the pain of Peter leaving her, her thanklessness for all he had done for her. Nothing like this had ever happened on Siegel's program, and as much as the host wanted a little controversy, it was all too much, too outrageous, too flamingly gay, and the host called a break. When Truman began again, the crazed energy was gone— leaving behind only scorched earth.

No one felt sadder about this than Liz Smith. She blamed herself for setting off this whole terrible business by telling Truman what Lee had said. "From that day until he died, Truman never got over it," Liz said. "And I never saw him again when he appeared to be happy. Naturally, his bad-mouthing of Lee only worked against himself. She ignored it all and rose above it. She dispensed with her lifelong admirer as if he were a used Kleenex. I suppose she never knew, realized, or cared that she and I, between us, had broken the heart and spirit of a great American talent."

Truman flew into Los Angeles in September 1980 to spend a few days working on *Handcarved Coffins* with producer Lester Persky. Waiting for him at LAX on Friday afternoon was David Patrick Columbia, a young writer who had recently signed on to be Lester's assistant. All the passengers appeared to have gotten off, and David was disappointed that Truman was not on the plane. Then he saw him. "He seemed to be almost clinging to the wall, moving with a slight tentativeness like a brave but lost child traveling without chaperone in a strange city," David wrote. "Most of the crowd had swept by him, leaving him behind, like dust in the road."

Even before David shepherded his passenger into a car for the drive to the Beverly Wilshire hotel, he could tell Truman was drunk. The author was still a major celebrity, and when they arrived at the hotel, an assistant manager waited to take them up to Truman's room. The first thing Truman said when the assistant manager opened the door was "Stolichnaya?" When he was told the vodka was on its way, he went to the bathroom and with the door half-open did a few lines of cocaine.

Truman spent most of the weekend by himself in the room. On Monday afternoon, when he did not answer phone calls, Lester entered the room and found him lying disheveled in a soiled bed, his only company empty bottles of vodka. The producer was a blustery, arrogant man, but he had a measure of humanity. He and a friend cleaned Truman up and carried him over to Lester's home in Bel Air.

While a bedroom was being prepared upstairs for Truman, he sat in the living room looking out with eyes that would have been brighter on a blind man. "Don't you realize you have this great talent and that you have to finish *Answered Prayers*?" Lester said. It was something Truman had heard a thousand times before, and it did no more good this time than it ever did.

Truman was helped upstairs. He spent several days recuperating. When it was time for Truman to fly back to New York, Lester went with him in a limousine to LAX. As he left, the question that hung out there was: What would happen now? Would he relapse? Was there anyone in Manhattan to truly help him?

When Truman got back to New York, he had a problem that had nothing to do with drugs or his writing. It was about his relationship with John O'Shea, his longtime Irish American lover. In 1973, Truman met him in a bathhouse in Manhattan and fell in love. As perceptive as Truman was and as astute a judge of character as he usually was, when he loved someone, be it Lee or John, he built them into gigantic figures beyond reproach.

John was a nondescript middle-class suburban father of four, ensconced in a boring marriage and a dreary banking job. When he drank, he became foulmouthed and sometimes violent. To Truman, he was as handsome as any man he had ever met, graced with a personality that bubbled like Roederer's Cristal. That no one else saw any of this did not make it less true to Truman.

To keep John near him, Truman hired him as his business manager. Almost from the beginning, it was the most troubled relationship of Truman's life, an endless soap opera of recriminations, spats, dramatic exits, and equally dramatic returns. Drink brought out the worst of both men, and they drank all the time. Truman desperately needed to get sober, but as long as he was with John, there was little chance of that happening. The doomed relationship was as bad for one man as it was for the other. When John found another lover, a *woman* at that, Truman became so angry that he sent associates out to break John's bones. They settled for pouring sugar into his gas tank.

But nothing could end the sick obsession that drew the two men together. Truman was more alone than ever. Babe had passed on. So had Gloria and Cecil. And Lee was dead to Truman. But John was still there, and they were back together in Miami in January 1981 when Truman said he wanted to end the affair and John flipped out. He pummeled Truman, breaking his nose, fracturing his rib, cracking his finger, and putting his mark over much of the rest of his body. Truman spent almost two weeks at Miami's Larkin General Hospital before flying back to New York.

Not only did Truman not press charges against his lover, but he invited John to join him for Easter dinner at La Petite Marmite, a favorite restaurant near his apartment at the UN Plaza. The meal had hardly begun when Truman lashed out, saying he never wanted to see John again. After eating, when they walked back to the UN Plaza, Truman told the desk clerk to evict John from his apartment. Truman's lover grabbed his bags and took a cab to the airport.

John returned to stay with Truman in June. In the interim, Truman had been in and out of several rehabilitation centers. It had not done much apparent good. He was drinking and doing so many drugs that he was hallucinating, bouncing in and out of paranoia. At one point, Truman was convinced that John was an intruder and called the police. He did the same thing a few nights later. It was so crazy, excessive, and dangerous that John packed up and left, vowing to rejoin AA and to never take a drink again.

Lee was as jealous as ever of Jackie, but in times of need, it was your sister to whom you went, and if she was a good sister, she would be there for you. On a summer evening in 1981, the sisters drove to St.

Luke's Episcopal Church in East Hampton, not far from where they had spent such wonderful summers as girls. Behind the stately stone church sat a meetinghouse that seemed almost hidden away.

After parking the car, the sisters entered the modest building and sat down. At the height of the summer, it was full of a staggering diversity of people, from locals to Manhattanites and working-class types to the rich. As happened wherever Jackie went, the people turned with a murmur of excitement when they saw the former First Lady, but soon after they spied her, she got up and left Lee there to go out and sit in the car.

Lee had been brought up to think she was better than just about anyone. But at Alcoholics Anonymous, everyone is the same. It took a measure of courage and likely an equal measure of desperation to walk into that roomful of strangers and, simply by doing so, admit that she was an alcoholic. And, in that regard, that she was the same as everyone else in the room.

At AA meetings, no one forces a person to talk, and Lee said nothing that first meeting, preferring to listen. Lee returned and, at later meetings, stood up to tell her story. She said she had always felt second-rate and covered it up with grandiosity. She talked about the imaginary friends she had as a child, Shahday, Dahday, and Jamelle, who were more real to her than anything out there in tawdry life. "I created a realm of fantasy and lived in it," she said. "I only remember that we flew and danced, and everything was beautiful. They took me out of reality."

Lee had been doing that her whole life, flying off with friends, imaginary and otherwise, to lift her out of reality. Everything had to be beautiful. Everything had to be perfect. She had truly loved Truman, but when that relationship risked leading her into complicated, unpleasant consequences, she jettisoned him as if he had never existed.

However she tried, Lee could not jettison Jackie. She was tied to her sister forever. When sixty-four-year-old Jackie died of non-Hodgkin's lymphoma in May 1994, she left nothing, not even a vase or a rug, to Lee. It was the purest statement possible of what Jackie thought of her only sister. For Lee, it was a devastating public rebuke.

In 2014, Sam Kashner and Nancy Schoenberger interviewed Lee in her apartment for a dual biography they were writing of the two sisters. They noticed "that when talking about Jackie, Lee always refers to her as 'my sister,' never by name." That was a measure of how painful the memories were.

In December 1983, Truman attended a party in Manhattan honoring Liza Minnelli. In the old days, as soon as the guests greeted Minnelli, many of them would have crowded around Truman hoping to hear a memorable bon mot. This evening, it was as if Truman had a contagious disease. People did anything to avoid him, and he ended up sitting by himself.

When Liz Smith arrived and saw this, she was upset. One of her weaknesses as a gossip columnist was that she was a mite too kind. In this instance, she felt overwhelming guilt that she and Lee had led Truman to this sad predicament. Liz knew everyone who mattered, and she arranged a team of people to take turns sitting with Truman a half hour at a time.

Even the strongest body can take only so much abuse. Truman's was slowly and painfully shutting down. He was only fifty-nine years old, but he began having painful falls like an old man who could not keep his balance. His left leg swelled with phlebitis. He had blood clots in his lungs. Truman knew he must stop drinking, but alcohol was this monstrous force that controlled him. And through it all *Answered Prayers* stood out there beyond the horizon, dreamlike yet real. "I dream about it, and my dream is as real as stubbing your toe," he told a friend. "All the characters I've lived with are in it, so brilliant, so real."

On Thursday, August 23, 1984, Truman flew out to California on a one-way ticket. While he was there, he met up with his longtime friend Joanne Carson, who watched over him as she always did. He had taken to visiting her frequently over the past few years, and she had set up diminutive rooms for him behind her kitchen. There was a certain kitschy feeling about the homey, modest arrangement, but Truman probably liked that it was so different from most of the places he stayed. Two grand piñatas hung from the ceiling above his canopied bed. Beside it on a small table sat a Snickers bar, caramels, and licorice comfits.

Truman referred to Joanne's décor as "Tibetan eclectic," a new age setting with an emphasis on wicker. She had a large assortment of votive candles that she lit for her parties. When he was there, she lit them and the home looked like a Buddhist temple or the scene of an elaborate wake.

Joanne was endlessly solicitous and caring—and by this point there was nobody else in Truman's life like her. That evening she gave him the healthy dinner he wanted: scrambled eggs, tomatoes, cottage cheese, and bread pudding. By the following evening, he was revived enough that he asked Joanne for two pens and began work on

Answered Prayers. Saturday morning, he was so weak that Joanne wanted to call the paramedics.

"No," Truman said, holding Joanne tightly to him. "No paramedics, no doctors. If you truly love me, you will let me go."

"What do you mean, let you go?" Joanne asked.

"Just let whatever is going to happen, happen. I'm tired. I don't want any more hospitals, any more doctors, any more IVs . . . I'm very, very tired. I just want to go in peace."

And so, Truman did.

19

Afterword

JOANNE HAD TRUMAN'S remains taken to the Grand View Memorial Park in Glendale for cremation. She said he had given her written instructions to divide his ashes in two, half to remain in Los Angeles, half to be in New York. It was an unlikely story. She told no one but had the funeral home put the ashes in two urns.

When Joanne gave Jack Dunphy a brass urn that looked like a book and had Truman's initials on it, he thought he had all of his lover's ashes. He had no idea there was a second, simpler urn without initials that Joanne was keeping for herself. When Jack learned what Joanne had done, he never talked to her again.

In the immediate aftermath of Truman's death, there was all kinds of speculation about *Answered Prayers*. Joanne said that Truman had finished the book and hidden it away in a safety-deposit box to be discovered later. She had what she said was the key, though she had no idea where the box was located. Joanne gave the key to Truman's literary executor, Alan Schwartz, who tried unsuccessfully to locate it. It was a beautiful story to think Truman's masterpiece was lying there somewhere and would one day reappear, validating everything he had been saying all these years.

Others close to Truman did not believe Joanne. Jack had spent more time with Truman than anyone and saw how for so long he had deceived people about writing *Answered Prayers*. Jack was convinced that no manuscript existed. Truman's longtime editor, Joe Fox, speculated that there were perhaps some chapters out there, but not the finished novel Truman had been promising for so long.

Joanne turned her sprawling house above Sunset Boulevard into a shrine for Truman. At the auction of Truman's belongings, she focused on buying not just major pieces but plates, bowls, and all kinds of knickknacks that only she knew had been Truman's. She placed them all around her house. She kept his bedroom behind the kitchen the way it had been when he was alive.

Joanne said that shortly before Truman died, she taped him telling her how to do the Los Angeles eighties counterpart of his famous Black and White Ball. For Halloween in 1988, Joanne decided to give what she was convinced would be the party of the decade. With Truman's recorded guidance, she felt it was impossible to fail.

That evening, her driveway was full of about thirty wildly unhappy paparazzi and entertainment reporters. Joanne had sent her invitations out to the movie kingdom elite, but no celebrity worth his star on Hollywood Boulevard was going to attend a party hosted by Johnny Carson's ex and then risk never again being invited to appear on *The Tonight Show*. The entertainment journalists were having a miserable evening standing there with no celebrities to interview or photograph.

Inside were all these empty tables around the swimming pool, all this uneaten food and unopened wine bottles. Practically the only stars were a senile Mr. Magoo, Jim Backus, sitting propped up on the sofa, and Esther Williams, almost unrecognizable from her days as the queen of swimsuit epics. A reporter and photographer from *People* were there, but it was clear they weren't going to chronicle this disaster.

At midnight, the guests were supposed to remove their masks. Soon after that, Joanne came running out of the kitchen. "There's been a theft," she yelled. "From Truman's room they've taken jewelry, his last manuscript and his ashes, my God, they've taken Truman's ashes." If there had been such a robbery, it would have been expected Joanne would call the police, but she did not do that. Desperate to be featured in *People*, she doubtlessly made the whole thing up.

The purported theft was a *People* magazine story if there ever was one, made even more dramatic by what Joanne told the weekly happened a few days later: "Under cover of darkness, a mysterious car had screeched in and out of Carson's driveway, and when the trembling Joanne looked outside, she found Truman's mortal remains resting inside a coil of garden hose on her back steps."

Joanne felt she could not risk having Truman's ashes in her house any longer, and she had to do something. On a morning in early November 1988, she was wearing a warm-up suit and sneakers and looked positively sportif as she decided she must take dramatic action. Carrying Truman's ashes, Joanne drove down to Sunset Boulevard in her Mazda RX-7, darting in and out of the traffic as if she had an urgent destination.

"Oh, Truman, Truman, what are we going to do?" Joanne asked, looking over at the urn. "Where do you want to be?"

As Joanne carried on an animated conversation with the late Truman, she became more and more overwrought. Eventually, she decided to take the urn to the Westwood Village Memorial Park, a few miles east of her house. It did not look like a mortuary and cemetery but more like a place for a new age seminar.

As soon as Joanne entered the main building, a dark-suited representative greeted her. In LA, even morticians are obsessed with celebrity. The man was obviously impressed that he was dealing with two famous people that morning: Truman Capote and Johnny Carson's ex-wife.

The gentleman was extremely solicitous of Joanne. "Oh, Mrs. Carson, I'm so sorry about your accident," he said.

"My accident?" Joanne asked.

"Yes," he said, pointing to a piece of tape that ran down her forehead.

"Oh, that," Joanne said, "that's to prevent wrinkles."

The representative took her to what appeared to be rows of mailbox slots. Joanne could scarcely envision leaving Truman there, and she moved on. The man opened a door to what appeared to be a library. "Oh, that's so poetic, marvelous," Joanne said. "But Truman, why, he's one of the greatest writers of the age, how can he be a book between other books that aren't writers?" She had a point, and they moved on up the pathway to a grand marble wall that housed crypts.

"Oh, my goodness, there's Marilyn Monroe," Joanne said. "This is where you belong, Truman."

As Joanne stood looking up, the representative said, "Mrs. Carson, I'm afraid they're all taken."

"Oh, that's terrible, terrible."

"But you see that one there," the man said. "That's Mr. Peter Lawford."

"Oh, yes," Joanne said, looking at the crypt containing the

ashes of the actor who had been married to JFK's sister Patricia Kennedy.

"Well, the Kennedys haven't paid, and we would be willing to cut a special deal with you and remove Mr. Lawford."

Joanne knew a bargain when she saw one, but she could not bear to part with her share of Truman. Back at her house, after pouring out half the ashes into a separate urn, she added her late dog's ashes. Then she returned to Westwood Village Memorial Park to have the urn sealed in the crypt. As for Lawford's ashes, they were cast out on the ocean, a considerable savings from the price of a crypt.

For the rest of her life, Joanne kept that remaining share of the ashes in a carved Japanese box on her mantelpiece. After her death in 2015, Joanne's estate auctioned off Truman's ashes—or, more accurately, a quarter of Truman's ashes. The Julien's auction house had certain qualms about putting the ashes up for sale, but when they thought of how the highly regarded Christie's had auctioned Napoleon's penis off in 1977 for $3,000, they felt better about the idea. Perhaps using Napoleon's penis as a benchmark, they estimated the ashes would sell for between $4,000 and $6,000. Instead, they went for an astronomical $45,000. As for Joanne's ashes, they were placed in the crypt next to the other quarter of Truman's ashes, where they remain today.

What a marvelous set piece Truman would have made of this tale. Nothing in life was too bizarre for his scrutiny. If he was sitting over dinner with his swans, he would have regaled them with this business, spinning it out in all kinds of ways. Napoleon's was not the best penis he would have ever seen—*Time* described it as looking like "a maltreated strip of buckskin shoelace"—but it had once been attached to the invader of Russia and ruler of half of Europe. And a quarter of Truman's ashes had gone for fifteen times the price.

Truman understood the myriad ironies of his life better than any-one. He had written two books that will live, *In Cold Blood* and *Break-fast at Tiffany's*, but he had not finished his self-described masterpiece, *Answered Prayers*.

Brilliant of mind, merciless in ambition, shrewd in social rela-tions, Truman believed that he could enter the swans' domaine and leave with a chef d'oeuvre in his hand. But he got all tangled up in the swans' world and in his own personal demons. In the end, *Answered Prayers* proved to be as much Truman's story as it was the swans'.

People bid for Truman's presence in death, and bid royally, just as they had in life. As long as people read Truman's books, talk about him, and fight over some measure of his presence, he is still alive, be-guiling the world with his stories.

20

The Swans

BARBARA "BABE" PALEY.
July 5, 1915–July 6, 1978

Sixty-three-year-old Babe was the first of the swans to die. In her last months, she wrote her will and included pieces of porcelain for C.Z., Gloria, Slim, and Marella. She had shared so much with these women, and she wanted them to have these tokens of remembrance. She also prepared detailed instructions for her funeral, including an invitation list that did not include Truman.

GLORIA GUINNESS.
August 27, 1912–November 9, 1980

Gloria was married to a man who treated her as little more than an interloper. After years of traveling between many homes, their lives became a repetitive drama. When she died in the Guinness villa in Épalinges, Switzerland, at the age of sixty-eight, supposedly of a heart attack, there were those who thought she committed suicide, doing it the careful, judicious way she did everything.

SLIM KEITH.
July 15, 1917–April 6, 1990

Slim married her third husband largely so she would not be alone. Lord Keith was a pompous, tedious man, and the marriage ended in divorce. In the last years of her life, Slim decided to write her memoir. It took her several years and three writers before she finished *Slim*. A heavy smoker, Slim died of lung cancer at the age of seventy-two in New York City, just before the book's publication.

PAMELA HARRIMAN.
March 20, 1920–February 5, 1997

In Washington, D.C., Pamela became a leading political figure, raising millions of dollars for centrist Democratic candidates. After the death of her husband Averell Harriman, President William Clinton appointed her ambassador to France, and she returned to Paris, the city in which she had lived for many years. Seventy-six-year-old Pamela died after suffering a cerebral hemorrhage while taking her daily swim in the Paris Ritz pool.

C. Z. GUEST.
February 19, 1920–November 8, 2003

C.Z. was a defender of the old order, not so much an economic system as a set of standards and common values. She did not cook because she did not have to cook. She loved her gardens and spent much time tending them. When she developed cancer and lost her hair, C.Z. bought a blond wig and fought the dying of the light until the very end, at the age of eighty-three.

LEE RADZIWILL.
March 3, 1933–February 15, 2019

Lee wrote two text-and-picture books about herself, *Happy Times* and *Lee*. They did not deal with her life in anything like its complexity. Her third marriage was to the film director Herbert Ross, and like the other two, it did not last. She became a successful interior decorator, but when it became difficult and complicated, she gave it up. Her son, Anthony, died of cancer at the age of forty in 1999. She continued to project the image that she lived in happy times until she died at the age of eighty-five.

MARELLA AGNELLI.
May 4, 1927–February 23, 2019

In November 2000, Marella's only son, Edoardo, killed himself by jumping off a high bridge in Turin. His father, Gianni, was devastated beyond measure, in part because he had treated Edoardo so poorly. Gianni's despair likely accelerated the cancer that killed him a little over two years later. To deal with her own grief, Marella did what she always did. She built herself a splendid new home, Ain Kassimou, in Marrakech. A few years before she died at the age of ninety-one, Marella wrote a memoir titled *The Last Swan*. And so she was.

Acknowledgments

Truman Capote knew there was a great novel in the lives of the elegant women he called his swans, even if in the end, he could not write it. That failure left it open to write a nonfiction book about the same subject. So many times, I wished I could have spoken to Truman. I had so much I wanted to tell him, so much I wanted to ask. I felt the same way about the women who were his closest friends. What I would have given to have spent time with them.

I wrote most of this book during the pandemic. Those months were so much easier to take because I got up every morning to enter the lives of a group of fascinating people. Stuck with me in our home was my wife, Vesna Obradovic Leamer, who was there for me in endless ways. Raleigh Robinson read the many versions of the manuscript, and Lisa Kessler made her astute suggestions. My Hollywood agent, Matthew Snyder, introduced me to my new literary agent, David Halpern, who shepherded *Capote's Women* along brilliantly. In taking this book to Putnam executive editor Michelle Howry, he hit a home run that easily would have lifted over the Green Monster in

Fenway Park. Ashley Di Dio marched the manuscript through the production process with aplomb.

Anyone writing about Capote turns first to Gerald Clarke's prodigiously researched *Capote: A Biography*. The Library of Congress, the District of Columbia Public Library, and the Palm Beach County Library were all invaluable. So was newspaper.com and the British Newspapers Archives.

I really should thank in profuse comments most of the individuals who helped me, but I'm simply going to mention their names: Fern Mallis, Matthew Snyder, Don Spencer, Terry Lee Katy, Lawrence Grobel, Raleigh Robinson, Rene Silvin, Gerald Clarke, Lisa Kessler, Susan Braudy, Annette Tapert, Eve Pell, Nelson W. Aldrich Jr., Lewis Lapham, Michael Donald, Kristina Rebelo, David Patrick Columbia, Todd McCarthy, Cornelia Guest, Sally Quinn, Stephen Stolman, Norman Sunshine, Judy Bachrach, Alan Shayne, Susan Nernberg, Amy Fine Collins, Joanne Carson, R. Couri Hay, Dale Coudert, Richard DuPont, Anne Taylor Fleming, Beatrice Cayzer, Craig Bachove, Edwina Churchill, Paulette Cooper, Richard Cowell, Nigel Hamilton, Alvin Felzenberg, Dan Moldea, Nancy Lubin, Eric Dezenhall, Mark Perry, Mark Olshaker, Bob Bates, Peter Ross Range, Edward Leamer, Robert Leamer, Antonio Mantilla, Daniela Mantilla, Emilia Mantilla, Alejandro Mantilla, Joel Swerdlow, Gus Russo, Heath King, Mark Oberhaus, and Rich Gardella.

Notes

Chapter 1: Answered Prayers

3   **"It may be that the enduring . . .":** Truman Capote, "A Gathering of Swans," in *Portraits and Observations: The Essays of Truman Capote* (New York: Modern Library, 2008), 219.

3   **"If expenditure were all . . .":** Ibid., 218.

7   **would *not* be happy:** Gerald Clarke, email interview with author.

7   **"Naaaah, they're too dumb":** George Plimpton, *Truman Capote: In Which Various Friends, Enemies, Acquaintances, and Detractors Recall His Turbulent Career* (New York: Doubleday, 1997), 339.

Chapter 2: Babe in the Woods

9   **"*Who* is this?":** Gerald Clarke, *Capote: A Biography* (New York: Simon & Schuster Paperbacks, 2010), 281.

9   **"wonderful but bad little boy":** Ibid., 238.

10   **"a few jealous pangs . . .":** Ibid., 281.

10   **"the most beautiful woman of the twentieth century":** Ibid., 283.

10   **"When I first saw her . . .":** Ibid.

11   **talked about his first orgasm:** Ibid., 276.

11   **"Mrs. P. had only one fault":** Ibid., 280.

12   **"You know, he liked . . .":** Sally Bedell Smith, *In All His Glory* (New York: Simon & Schuster, 1990), 343.

12   **"You cannot be too rich . . .":** Fred Shapiro, "You Can Quote Them," *Yale Alumni Magazine*, January/February 2008.

13   **"There was no use in trying . . .":** Edith Wharton, *The Age of Innocence* (New York: D. Appleton, 1920), 123.

13   **"craving for the external . . .":** Edith Wharton, *The House of Mirth* (New York: Charles Scribner's Sons, 1905), 17.

15   **on the arm of the most:** "The Inaugural Ball in Washington," *New York Herald Tribune*, March 12, 1933.

15   **a holiday party:** "Boston Young Folks White House Guests," *Boston Globe*, December 30, 1933.

16   **small party that included:** AP, "Capital Hopeful as 1934 Arrives," *New York Times*, January 1, 1934.

16   **severe auto accident:** David Grafton, *The Sisters* (New York: Villard Books, 1992), 56.

16   **Betsey threw a tea dance:** Ibid., 39.

20   **up to the observation car:** Clarke, *Capote*, 13.

20   **"I pounded and pounded . . .":** Anne Taylor Fleming, "The Private World of Truman Capote," *New York Times*, July 9, 1978.

22   **"Perhaps it was strange for a . . .":** Truman Capote, *The Complete Stories of Truman Capote* (New York: Vintage, 2005), 243.

22   **he inveighed Nelle:** Plimpton, *Truman Capote*, 15.

22   **writing scenes in his little:** Ibid., 13.

22   **"He was a happy child until . . .":** Lawrence Grobel, "Truman's Aunt Remembers," *Redbook*, December 1986.

23   **"The other kids liked . . .":** Fleming, "The Private World of Truman Capote."

24   **far more excited:** Smith, *In All His Glory*, 251.

25   **"No one held it . . .":** Eve Pell, *We Used to Own the Bronx: Memoirs of a Former Debutante* (Albany: State University of New York Press, 2009), 19.

25   **"Uncle Stanley was a . . .":** Eve Pell, phone interview with author, 2020.

25   **police concluded was:** "Harriman Son-in-Law Recovering After Shooting; Stanley Mortimer Improves Following What Police Call an Attempted Suicide," *New York Times*, June 21, 1969.

25   **Stanley went the next day:** Grafton, *The Sisters*, 62.

26   **second-best-dressed woman:** UP, "Duchess is Best Dressed," *Santa Cruz Sentinel*, January 1, 1942.

26   **around 350,000 women served:** History.com Editors, "American Women in World War II," History.com, March 5, 2010, last updated February 28, 2020, https://www.history.com/topics/world-war-ii/american-women-in-world -war-ii-1.

27   **further training in Quonset:** "462 Graduated Into The Navy In Swanky Style," *New York Daily News*, April 11, 1942.

28   **Babe headed the list:** "New Yorker is Again Cited as 'Best-Dressed,'" *Fort Worth Star-Telegram*, December 26, 1945; and *New York Daily News*, January 21, 1946.

28 **"Would the outfits . . .":** Henry McLemore, "Sickening Stylishness,"
    Montgomery Advertiser, January 11, 1946.
28 **"with a navy wife's . . .":** "Best Dressed, She Has 'Few' Clothes," *Des Moines
    Tribune,* December 26, 1945.
29 **"habitually intemperate from . . .":** "Boston Beauties Seem to Meet the
    Right Men After a Couple of Tries," *New York Daily News,* August 3, 1947.

Chapter 3: Lilies of the Valley

32 **"EXIT SMILING":** "Wife Who Sought Glamour Plunges 17 Stories to
    Death," *Detroit Free Press,* March 9, 1940.
32 **"You are everything in this world":** Ibid.
33 **"I knew this was his illness":** Smith, *In All His Glory,* 231.
33 **The images he sketched:** Ibid., 225.
35 **"Being a great beauty, and *remaining* . . .":** Capote, "A Gathering of Swans,"
    in *Portraits and Observations,* 218.
38 **"the sheer restfulness . . .":** Nelson W. Aldrich, *Old Money: The Mythology of
    Wealth in America* (New York: Allworth Press, 1996), 83.
39 **"the single worse person in my life":** Clarke, *Capote,* 41.
40 **entered one of the back rows:** Ibid., 44.
40 **"kissing, fondling, and 'belly rubbing'":** Ibid., 45.
41 **When his modest time came:** Ibid., 52.
42 **"Always from the time I . . .":** Plimpton, *Truman Capote,* 29.
42 **"It wasn't just social climbing . . .":** Ibid., 48.
43 **"I once said if . . .":** Michael Donald, phone interview with author, 2020.
44 **"We had an understanding":** Clarke, *Capote,* 283.
45 **Babe and Truman locked:** Ibid., 286.
46 **"A lot of people would . . .":** Aram Saroyan, *Trio: Oona Chaplin, Carol
    Matthau, Gloria Vanderbilt: Portrait of an Intimate Friendship* (New York:
    Sidgwick & Jackson, 1986), 114.
47 **"as though, attending a . . .":** Capote, "A Gathering of Swans," in *Portraits and
    Observations,* 218.
47 **"she was afraid Bill . . .":** Clarke, *Capote,* 287.
47 **shared a manicurist:** David Patrick Columbia, phone interview with author,
    2020.
48 **Babe tried to kill:** Clarke, *Capote,* 287.
48 **"Bill bought you":** Ibid.

Chapter 4: Slim Pickings

49 **"some extraordinary parrot . . .":** Amanda Mackenzie Stuart, *Diana
    Vreeland: Empress of Fashion* (New York: Harper, 2013), 3.

49   "a garden in hell": Ibid., 153.

50   "I was enchanted by him": Slim Keith with Annette Tapert, *Slim: Memories of a Rich and Imperfect Life* (New York: Simon & Schuster, 1990), 219.

51   "as the roughest lumberjack...": "'Big Boy' Bray Beats Androff," *Los Angeles Times*, August 31, 1938.

51   *Caliente* and the *Tango*: "Goddess of Chance," *New York Daily News*, May 22, 1938.

52   evening won $5,700: Ibid.

53   "Do you want to be...": Keith with Tapert, *Slim*, 57.

54   "Hawks liked it when...": Todd McCarthy, phone interview with author, 2020.

54   "Sex was simply...": Keith with Tapert, *Slim*, 90.

55   "exactly the package...": Ibid., 60–61.

56   Slim went out to the cemetery: Ibid., 25.

56   "If you also leave...": Ibid., 31.

57   One of her editors later speculated that Slim: Annette Tapert, phone interview with author, 2020.

58   "Why are you here...": Keith with Tapert, *Slim*, 37.

59   contributed poetry to the *Red & Blue*: Plimpton, *Truman Capote*, 35.

60   "No, you don't ever need...": Saroyan, *Trio*, 18–19; and Plimpton, *Truman Capote*, 33–34.

62   "There I was, bent...": Clarke, *Capote*, 76; and Plimpton, *Truman Capote*, 40.

63   "The Greatest Show on Earth": David Nasaw, *The Chief: The Life of William Randolph Hearst* (New York: Houghton Mifflin, 2000), loc. 10472–79, Kindle.

64   choir stalls from a cathedral: Wikipedia, s.v. "Hearst Castle," last modified January 17, 2021, 19:57, https://en.wikipedia.org/wiki/Hearst_Castle.

65   home in Mexico: Ancestry.com, passenger master list from plane from Ensenada, Mexico, to San Diego, December 3, 1937.

65   Ernest Hemingway's home: "Hawks Visitor in Miami Beach," *Miami Herald*, December 18, 1939.

66   shot their full share: Todd McCarthy, *Howard Hawks: The Grey Fox of Hollywood* (New York: Grove Press, 2000), 290.

66   staying close to Slim: Ibid., 329.

67   Barbara Stanwyck and her husband: Ibid., 328.

67   "Of course, you can...": Keith with Tapert, *Slim*, 72.

67   Gary Cooper to give her away: "Hollywood Notables at Howard Hawks, Nancy Gross Wedding," *Boston Globe*, December 11, 1941.

68   "Well, you have to do it now": Keith with Tapert, *Slim*, 76.

69   had more shoes, dresses: Lauren Bacall, *Lauren Bacall by Myself* (New York: Knopf, 1978), 66.

69   forty-seven dresses: McCarthy, *Howard Hawks*, 430.

70   **naming her Slim:** Joseph McBride, *Hawks on Hawks* (Berkeley: University of California Press, 1982), Kindle.

71   **She entered Good Samaritan Hospital:** Keith with Tapert, *Slim*, 106; and McCarthy, *Howard Hawks*, 336.

CHAPTER 5: THE MARITAL GAME

73   **than an affair:** Name withheld, phone interview with author, 2020.

74   **"He was funny. He laughed a lot . . .":** Smith, *In All His Glory*, 233.

75   **breaking the grasp:** Keith Munroe, "Leland Howard," *Life*, September 20, 1948.

76   **"Why don't you quit?":** Keith with Tapert, *Slim*, 116.

77   **"Is he going to be all right?":** Ibid., 130.

77   **"Yes, I think so":** McCarthy, *Howard Hawks*, 130.

82   **Newton loved it and left feeling renewed:** Plimpton, *Truman Capote*, 64.

82   **"Truman behaved in the most . . .":** Ibid., 63.

82   **throwing a glass:** Keith with Tapert, *Slim*, 156.

83   **Slim would do hers Sundays:** Ibid., 166.

84   **"You never confide . . .":** Ibid., 157.

84   **"Oh, he wouldn't do that to me":** Ibid., 156.

85   **not squandering his presence:** Munroe, "Leland Howard."

86   **"had become a companionate one":** Sally Bedell Smith, *Reflected Glory: The Life of Pamela Churchill Harriman* (New York: Simon & Schuster, 1996), 203.

87   **lasted for six months:** Ibid.

87   **"Slim was naturally very bright":** Annette Tapert, phone interview with author.

87   **be better in February 1958:** INS, "Reds Can Duck; Capote is There," *Cincinnati Enquirer*, February 18, 1958.

88   **"But inside that ball . . .":** Clarke, *Capote*, 277.

88   **"No one loves me":** Keith with Tapert, *Slim*, 225–26.

89   **"She was so vain . . .":** Smith, *Reflected Glory*, 203.

90   **Sterling Silver hybrid roses:** Christopher Ogden, *Life of the Party: The Biography of Pamela Digby Churchill Hayward Harriman* (Boston: Little, Brown, 1994), 268.

91   **"As a matter of fact . . .":** Clarke, *Capote*, 315.

91   **"I think we should have a talk . . .":** Keith with Tapert, *Slim*, 250.

92   **managed a short affair:** Smith, *Reflected Glory*, 210.

92   **placing red stickers:** Keith with Tapert, *Slim*, 254.

CHAPTER 6: THE NOTORIOUS MRS. C

93   **"that bitch":** Gerald Clarke, ed., *Too Brief a Treat: The Letters of Truman Capote* (New York: Vintage Books, 2004), 268.

94   **"We spent a lot of time ..."**: Clarke, *Capote*, 486.

95   **"When I am grown up ..."**: *CBS Morning News*, 1983, quoted in Ogden, *Life of the Party*, 44.

96   **the finest ponies:** Ibid., 59.

96   **One of her few friends was:** Ibid.

96   **Pamela breaking down in tears after one party:** Smith, *Reflected Glory*, 45.

97   **"the dairy maid":** Ogden, *Life of the Party*, 69.

98   **"red-headed tart":** Ibid., 74.

98   **"Red-headed and rather fat ...":** Anita Leslie, *Cousin Randolph* (London: Hutchinson, 1985), 47.

99   **leave a male heir:** Brian Roberts, *Randolph: A Study of Churchill's Son* (London: Hamish Hamilton, 1984), 189.

100   **off in the arms:** Ogden, *Life of the Party*, 100.

101   **"the most exciting time ..."**: Smith, *Reflected Glory*, 78.

101   **now wore wool socks:** Laurence Leamer, *The Kennedy Women: The Saga of an American Family* (New York: Villard, 1994), 146.

102   **"was the most important ..."**: Rudy Abramson, *Spanning the Century: The Life of W. Averell Harriman, 1891–1986* (New York: William Morrow, 1992), 312.

103   **"could have gone the other way":** Lynne Olson, *Citizens of London: The Americans Who Stood with Britain in Its Darkest, Finest Hour* (New York: Random House Trade Paperbacks, 2011), 103.

105   **$178,000 today:** "Computing 'Real Value' Over Time with a Conversion between U.K. Pounds and U.S. Dollars, 1791 to Present," MeasuringWorth, accessed August 18, 2020, https://www.measuringworth.com/calculators/exchange.

106   **"Let's just say if she ..."**: Nelson W. Aldrich Jr., phone interview with author, 2020.

106   **Truman appropriated the line:** Truman Capote, *Answered Prayers* (New York: Random House, 1987), 19.

106   **"like living inside an electric bulb":** Clarke, *Capote*, 206.

106   **room so full of flowers:** Clarke, *Too Brief a Treat*, 55.

106   **He learned to ride a scooter:** Ibid., 56.

106   **dinner with the gay French writer André Gide:** Ibid., 55.

107   **"precocious, self-confident ..."**: Orville Prescott, "Book of the Times," *New York Times*, January 21, 1948.

107   **"Come":** Clarke, *Capote*, 164.

108   **never would have slept:** Ibid., 193.

108   **Success had turned Jack's wife:** Plimpton, *Truman Capote*, 99.

109   **sending her regular stipends:** Smith, *Reflected Glory*, 114.

109   **wrote Pamela love letters:** Olson, *Citizens of London*, 153.

110   **"a big, big blow":** Pamela Digby Churchill Hayward Harriman Papers, 1909–1997, at the Library of Congress, quoted in Olson, *Citizens of London*, 244.

111   **"You're spoiled":** Olson, *Citizens of London*, 340.

111   **didn't particularly like sex:** Ogden, *Life of the Party*, 238.

CHAPTER 7: A TUB OF BUTTER

116   **Her choice was Gloria:** Ogden, *Life of the Party*, 207.

117   **"You fall in love . . .":** *L'Avvocato*, "Famous Phrases of Gianni Agnelli," https://www.l-avvocato.com/en/gianni-agnelli-quotes

117   **"Pamela's a geisha girl who made every . . .":** Clarke, *Capote*, 486.

118   **hookers into her bedroom:** Ogden, *Life of the Party*, 222.

118   **shot a spate of bullets through her bedroom:** Ibid., 227.

119   **if she agreed to it:** Ibid., 226–27; and Smith, *Reflected Glory*, 157.

119   **Gianni bragged about the beautiful:** Ogden, *Life of the Party*, 227.

120   **"grande nuits blanche":** *Agnelli*, directed by Nick Hooker, aired on December 18, 2017, on HBO.

121   **having an affair with the Greek:** Smith, *Reflected Glory*, 159.

122   **"one of the most . . .":** Clarke, *Capote*, 486.

124   **unseen musicians played the Arab music:** Ibid., 201.

124   **screaming out, "Goodbye! Goodbye!":** Plimpton, *Truman Capote*, 105.

124   **In the torrid afternoons he napped:** Clarke, *Too Brief a Treat*, 93.

125   **Truman wrote his high school:** Ibid., 95.

126   **"nothing but a hillbilly . . .":** Clarke, *Capote*, 215.

127   **Truman called out, "Jack . . . ! Jack . . . !":** Jack Dunphy, *"Dear Genius . . .": A Memoir of My Life with Truman Capote* (New York: McGraw-Hill, 1987), 14.

127   **"sinister and rather sickening excursion into a hot-house . . .":** Orville Prescott, "Books of The Times," *New York Times*, October 2, 1951.

128   **"a horse and a saber":** Smith, *Reflected Glory*, 166.

128   **"old toad":** Ibid., 167.

129   **she wanted to drive straight:** Ibid., 171.

129   **Rupp arrived in St. Moritz:** Ibid., 194.

130   **he left angry:** Ibid., 210.

130   **king's ransom of $500,000:** Ibid., 211.

131   **"was noteworthy because . . .":** Cholly Knickerbocker, "Game of Solitaire Has a Romantic Ring," *San Francisco Examiner*, March 16, 1961.

132   **Ethel Merman got up:** Elsa Maxwell, "Stars Warm up Hayward Home," *Philadelphia Daily News*, March 21, 1961.

132   **"I can see that Leland . . .":** Marie Brenner, "The Prime of Pamela Harriman," *Vanity Fair*, July 1988.

134   **May 1967, she felt:** Leonard Lyons, "Lyons Den," *Post-Standard* (Syracuse, NY), May 29, 1967.

136   **"Truman claimed that she . . .":** Ogden, *Life of the Party*, 329.

136   **all evening long poor Averell:** Peter Duchin with Charles Michener, *Ghost of a Chance: A Memoir* (New York: Random House, 1996), 322; and Ogden, *Life of the Party*, 329.

137   **"Jesus wept!":** Duchin with Michener, *Ghost of a Chance*, 323.

137   **"It wasn't the lamp . . .":** Ibid., 325.

137   **the Digby family's convoluted crest:** Ogden, *Life of the Party*, 343.

Chapter 8: Gloria in Excelsis

139   **swimmer after swimmer doing the same:** Clarke, *Capote*, 277.

140   **"the King of the Beasts":** Tommy Fitzgerald, "Sonny Liston: The Champion," *Miami News*, February 23, 1964.

140   **they focused their cameras:** Eleanor Lambert, "Fashion Champ Provides Fights Only Knockout," *Miami Herald*, February 28, 1964.

140   **"There are certain women . . .":** Clarke, *Capote*, 486.

141   **"I am very disappointed with you":** Robin Green, "Sic transit Gloria's yogurt," *Globe and Mail*, March 15, 1978.

142   **little guest house:** Clarke, *Capote*, 271.

142   **Loel did not listen:** Plimpton, *Truman Capote*, 150.

143   **"last impulsive and adventurous dresser . . .":** Gloria Guinness, "Elan Is," *Harper's Bazaar*, December 1968.

143   **They were not invited:** Cholly Knickerbocker, "The Smart Set," *News-Dispatch* (Shamokin, PA), March 16 and April 20, 1960.

143   **giant tin of iced caviar:** Florence Pritchett Smith, "Supper dance in Florida," *Philadelphia Inquirer*, June 9, 1960.

144   **"Early in life, I knew only . . .":** Gloria Guinness, "Gloria Guinness on Influence," *Harper's Bazaar*, February 1965.

145   **she cut the cloth and stitched:** Ibid.

145   **"Gloria, you are the most beautiful . . .":** Aline, Countess of Romanones, *The Spy Wore Red* (New York: Random House, 1987), 258.

146   **"I knew how to sing and to dance":** Gloria Guinness, "To Be a Mexican," *Harper's Bazaar*, July 1968.

146   **"Do all Mexican women look like you?":** Ibid.

147   **"A woman's best friend . . .":** Gloria Guinness, "A Woman's Best Friend is Not a Diamond," *Harper's Bazaar*, October 1963.

148   **Champagne arrived from France:** Roger Moorhouse, *Berlin at War* (New York: Basic Books, 2010), 95.

148   **four hundred thousand *Zwangsarbeiter*, or forced laborers:** Ibid., 118, 121.

148   **Berliners were profoundly suspicious:** Ibid., 134–35.

148   **1,800-kilogram bombs:** Ibid., 308.

149   **"I heard from my husband . . .":** Aline, Countess of Romanones, *The Spy Wore Red*, 259.

149   **"dashing and elegant":** Walter Schellenberg, *Walter Schellenberg: The Memoirs of Hitler's Spymaster*, trans. and ed. Louis Hagan (London: André Deutsch, 2006), loc. 619 of 9436, Kindle.

149   **"the better type of people":** Ibid.

150   **"Well, he gawked like a baby":** Aline, Countess of Romanones, *The Spy Wore Red*, 292.

150   **"exaggerated":** Schellenberg, *Walter Schellenberg*, loc. 942.

150   **he had an affair:** Joshua M. Zeitz, "The Nazis and Coco," *New York Times*, May 8, 2005; and Judith Warner, "Was Coco Chanel a Nazi Spy?" *New York Times*, September 2, 2011.

150   **an upscale Berlin brothel:** Schellenberg, *Walter Schellenberg*, loc. 880.

151   **seventy to one hundred Germans:** Ibid., loc. 2669.

151   **Next to him sat Gloria:** Aline, Countess of Romanones, *The Spy Wore Red*, 193.

151   **capsule of cyanide:** Schellenberg, *Walter Schellenberg*, loc. 400.

152   **"One night after the opera . . .":** Aline, Countess of Romanones, *The Spy Wore Red*, 291.

152   **"become a messenger . . .":** *The Observer*, June 14, 1997.

153   **"a very convenient medium . . .":** Gloria Guinness, "Money Matters!" *Harper's Bazaar*, August 1970.

153   **"For the first time . . .":** John Julius Norwich, ed., *The Duff Cooper Diaries* (London: Phoenix, 2006), 406.

154   **"I never heard nightingales . . .":** Ibid., 408.

154   **"She said I was . . .":** Ibid., 416.

154   **"I suppose it is all . . .":** Ibid., 424.

155   **a trip to Australia:** "The Muslim Faithful," *New York Daily News*, July 19, 1935.

156   **in April 1951:** *New York Times*, April 8, 1951.

Chapter 9: "She Is"

158   **eclectic mix of antiques:** Wendy Moonan, "Bidding on a Chapter of History," *New York Times*, March 13, 2003.

158   **a baked potato as big:** Elsa Maxwell, "The News of International Society," *Philadelphia Daily News*, September 26, 1961.

158   **Duke and Duchess of Windsor:** *New York Daily News*, May 25, 1955.

159   **"completely idiotic":** Graham Payn and Sheridan Morley, eds., *The Noël Coward Diaries* (New York: Little, Brown, 1982).

159   **invited them to stay:** Helen Van Hoy Smith, "Palm Beach Gets Ready for the Windsors Visit," *Miami Herald*, February 23, 1958.

160 **"a beautiful play"**: Brooks Atkinson, "Truman Capote's First Drama, 'The Grass Harp,' Is Acted at the Martin Beck," *New York Times*, March 28, 1952.

160 **"I don't know what it's about"**: John Chapman, "Capote's 'Grass Harp' Screwiest Play in Town, but Excellently Staged," *New York Daily News*, March 29, 1952.

160 **he had hung out**: Clarke, *Capote*, 260.

160 **"lovely light color(ed)"**: Capote, *The Complete Stories of Truman Capote*, 197.

162 **"I can't tell you what . . ."**: Clarke, *Too Brief a Treat*, 224.

163 **spend a little over a year**: Clarke, *Capote*, 257.

164 **In October 1955**: "Weds Titled Step-Sis in Tangled Family Tree," *New York Daily News*, October 23, 1955.

164 **started around noon**: Cholly Knickerbocker, "How to Relax on The Riviera," *San Francisco Examiner*, August 14, 1955.

165 **"An inspiration to fashion . . ."**: *Women's Wear Daily*, November 15, 1962.

165 **"You come out of Mexico . . ."**: Nancy Rudolph, "Chic Fur Flies In Fashion Debate," *New York Daily News*, March 13, 1964.

166 **"You look terrible . . ."**: Robert Colacello, "Suzy Had the Scoop!," *Vanity Fair*, February 2017.

166 **black mink coats**: Eugenia Sheppard, "Pedigreed Sable Coats High Fashion," *St. Louis Post-Dispatch*, October 7, 1962.

166 **same with turbans**: Eugenia Sheppard, "The Look That's In—'Ears' Out," *Honolulu Advertiser*, December 21, 1962.

166 **"Chanel suits are for . . ."**: Eugenia Sheppard, "Nothing But Chanel," *Post-Standard* (Syracuse, NY), November 2, 1961.

167 **on the Guinness plane**: Eleanor Lambert, "Private Clients Order Their Paris Fashions," *Honolulu Advertiser*, August 26, 1964.

168 **"What the fuck are you . . ."**: Plimpton, *Truman Capote*, 97.

168 **"I did a play once . . ."**: AP, "Mrs. Gloria Guinness Wins Prize for Magazine Journalism," *The Mercury* (Pottsdam, PA), November 3, 1967.

169 **"desperately wanted to have . . ."**: James Reginato, "Mary's Big Life," *W*, May 2002.

170 **"They are original . . ."**: Gloria Guinness, "Who's Chic, Who's with It," *Harper's Bazaar*, July 1965.

170 **"God created Eve . . ."**: Gloria Guinness, "Eve and the First Dress," *Harper's Bazaar*, March 1964.

171 **"Damn Those Young Girls!"**: Gloria Guinness, "Damn Those Young Girls!," *Harper's Bazaar*, December 1971.

171 **"the slightest little bit . . ."**: Gloria Guinness, "The Short, Short, Short Life of the Short, Short, Short Skirt," *Harper's Bazaar*, June 1966.

171 **"I can't help but . . ."**: Gloria Guinness, "The Young and Crazy Years," *Harper's Bazaar*, December 1969.

172   **a beige hat from Balenciaga:** Eugenia Sheppard, "Gloria Guinness: The Woman Who Has Everything," *The Gazette* (Montreal, Canada), November 6, 1967.

172   **"the saddest woman I ever met":** *W*, May 2002.

CHAPTER 10: A GUEST IN THE HOUSE

174   **"shimmering in the blue smoky . . .":** C. Z. Guest, *First Garden: An Illustrated Garden Primer* (New York: Rizzoli, 2003).

174   **"ice cream reserve":** Ibid.

174   **"that lurking inside this . . .":** Ibid.

177   **"by the strictest Boston society . . .":** Cleveland Amory, *The Proper Bostonians* (New York: Dutton, 1948), 276.

177   **"home was entirely transformed . . .":** Ibid.

178   **As C.Z. and her sister:** Arthur Siegel, "When Yanks Bear Down They Are 'Nonchalanting,'" *Boston Globe*, July 19, 1962.

178   **One evening in December 1936:** "Distinguished Audience Sees 'Jane Eyre' at the Colonial," *Boston Globe*, December 29, 1936.

180   **Sergeant Gene Autry to Greer Garson:** Elizabeth Watts, "Minked Coats Top Fashion Parade at 'Winged Victory' Premiere," *Boston Globe*, November 3, 1943.

181   **North Atlantic guarding:** "Captain Marquis Lauds WACS Sharing African Hardships," *Boston Globe*, December 8, 1943.

181   **"Victor Mature to wed Lucy . . .":** Walter Winchell, "On Broadway," *Tampa Bay Times*, June 23, 1943.

181   **The actor was already divorced:** AP, "Mrs. Victor Mature Wins Nevada Divorce," *Boston Globe*, February 10, 1943.

182   **suite at the Ritz:** Alice Hughes, "A Woman's New York," *Star Press* (Muncie, IN), April 6, 1944.

182   **understudy the ingenue:** Ibid.

182   **"It is too bad, and possibly . . .":** John Chapman, "'House of Flowers' Rich in Music and Exotically Set and Costumed," *New York Daily News*, December 31, 1954.

182   **"he [Truman] lacks the flair . . .":** Brooks Atkinson, "Theatre: Truman Capote's Musical," *New York Times*, December 31, 1954.

182   **Jack called "the peacocks":** Clarke, *Capote*, 267.

182   **Truman went off to Jamaica:** Clarke, *Too Brief a Treat*, 236.

183   **"Was *this* the Portrait . . .":** Ibid., 238.

183   **"I have done nothing . . .":** Ibid.

183   **"sleek collection of dark green cars":** Capote, "A Gathering of Swans," *Portraits and Observations*, 91.

184   **"If the Russians were . . .":** Ibid., 171–72.

185   **"It was quite apparent . . .":** Plimpton, *Truman Capote*, 142.

185 **"I have to go over to Fishers . . .":** Ibid., 143.

185 **That fall, Truman and Jack:** Clarke, *Too Brief a Treat*, 242.

185 **Truman showed guests the whole:** Plimpton, *Truman Capote*, 132.

186 **"a little gabardine cape . . .":** Ibid., 134.

186 **"die of adrenaline overflow":** Ibid.

186 **Hollywood producer Darryl Zanuck met:** Mayne Ober Peak, "Boston's Lucy Cochrane Kept Under Wraps for Film Debut," *Boston Globe*, December 27, 1944.

188 **"You can have . . .":** Sally Quinn, "C.Z. Guest: The Rich Fight Back," *Washington Post*, May 1, 1977.

188 **club titles in tennis and golf:** *Palm Beach Post*, February 24, 1940.

188 **pigeon-shooting championship:** *Pensacola News Journal*, February 6, 1942.

189 **part of his trigger finger:** Hugh Fullerston Jr., "Sports Roundup," *Appeal-Democrat* (Marysville, CA), May 27, 1944.

189 **rushed back into:** "Mrs. Amy Phipps Risks Life for Babies, but Rescues Them Both," *Pittsburgh Daily Post*, August 7, 1908.

189 **the first woman pilot:** Franklin G. Smith, "Resorts, Hotels, Travel," *Miami News*, July 20, 1952; and Susan Ware, *Still Missing: Amelia Earhart and the Search for Modern Feminism* (New York: Norton, 1993), 44.

190 **purchased it for 15,000 pesos:** *Time*, July 20, 1962.

CHAPTER 11: A TIME OF RECKONING

192 **gossip columnists started writing:** Walter Winchell, "Gossip of the Nation," *Philadelphia Inquirer*, June 7, 1948; Danton Walker, "Broadway," *New York Daily News*, April 13, 1949; and Dorothy Kilgallen, "The Voice of Broadway," *The Mercury* (Pottstown, PA), September 19, 1950.

192 **"The Winston Guests are . . .":** Earl Wilson, "It Happened Last Night," *Honolulu Star-Bulletin*, June 11, 1952.

192 **"Manners have been . . .":** Quinn, "C.Z. Guest."

192 **"Style is about surviving . . .":** https://www.pinterest.com/pin /330522060154608775/.

193 **on the island in 1916:** Stacey Bewkes, "Palm Beach Chic," *Quintessence: Living Well with Style and Substance*, October 1, 2015, https:// quintessenceblog.com/palm-beach-chic.

193 **"Ah, good boy":** Guest, *First Garden*, 18.

194 **"I remember seeing C.Z. . . .":** Annette Tapert and Diana Edkins, *The Power of Style: The Women Who Defined the Art of Living Well* (New York: Aurum Press, 1995), 182.

195 **Best-Dressed List in 1952:** INS, "Mamie Makes Best Dressed List," *The Gazette* (Cedar Rapids, IA), December 17, 1952.

195 **"Fashion is appalling . . .":** Aldrich, *Old Money*, 78.

195   **The three-hundred-acre estate:** Susanna Salk, *C.Z. Guest: American Style Icon: Celebrating Her Timeless World at Home, in Her Garden & Around Town* (New York: Rizzoli, 2013), 106.

196   **"You must be either . . .":** Clarke, *Capote*, 273.

196   **"At Babe Paley's table, or C.Z.'s . . .":** Guest, *First Garden*, 21.

196   **"I'd rather have one . . .":** Salk, *C.Z. Guest*, 114.

197   **rode into the grand:** Nancy Randolph, "Horses, Others at Waldorf for Paris April Ball," *New York Daily News*, April 16, 1955.

197   **"a home and a husband and dogs . . .":** Guest, *First Garden*, 17.

198   **"a large novel, my magnum opus . . .":** Clarke, *Too Brief a Treat*, 257–58.

199   **"a whole breed of . . .":** Eric Norden, "Playboy Interview: Truman Capote," *Playboy*, March 1968.

199   **"The main reason I wrote . . .":** Ibid.

200   **"For over fifteen years . . .":** "Excerpt from *The Feminine Mystique*," *New York Times*, February 5, 2006.

201   **C.Z.'s daughter, Cornelia:** Cornelia Guest, phone interview with author, 2020.

201   **followed Mr. Buffett:** Salk, *C.Z. Guest*, 228.

202   **"That doesn't mean . . .":** Quinn, "C.Z. Guest."

202   **Winston felt even worse:** Tapert and Edkins, *The Power of Style*, 186.

203   **"Cold. Soignée. The Ice Cream Lady . . .":** Guest, *First Garden*, 18.

203   **"Perhaps more is expected of those . . .":** Quinn, "C.Z. Guest."

203   **"Look at the jobs . . .":** Ibid.

204   **"What's wrong with women . . .":** WWD Staff, "Obituary: C.Z. Guest, Social Star and Style Icon," *Women's Wear Daily*, November 10, 2003.

204   **"All those dirty, filthy people . . .":** Quinn, "C.Z. Guest."

204   **"All young people want . . .":** WWD Staff, "Obituary: C.Z. Guest, Social Star and Style Icon."

205   **"Oh, C.Z., how great you look . . .":** Jessica Kerwin, "Great Dame: With Wit, Style and a No-Nonsense Approach to the Good Life," *W*, January 2004.

205   **may have had to ask permission:** Steven Stolman, phone interview with author, 2020.

206   **Winston received $600,000:** *Time*, December 8, 1967.

206   **took out $265,000:** Ibid.

208   **"he has several different . . .":** Theo Wilson, "Guest Odds and Ends Bring $815,275," *New York Daily News*, December 3, 1967.

208   **"were said to have been . . .":** Ibid.

208   **fifteen-and-a-half-acre estate:** Salk, *C.Z. Guest*, 106.

CHAPTER 12: ONLY MAIDS FALL IN LOVE

209   **agreed with his assessment:** Marella Agnelli and Marella Caracciolo Chia, *Marella Agnelli: The Last Swan* (New York: Rizzoli, 2014), 134.

209   **"closest friends . . .":** Ibid.

210   **"Is the blue room empty?":** Ibid.

211   **"It was kinda fun . . .":** Clarke, *Too Brief a Treat*, 419.

211   **sell off much of the family:** Judy Bachrach, "La Vita Agnelli," *Vanity Fair*, May 2003.

212   **could have been executed:** Agnelli and Chia, *Marella Agnelli*, 14.

212   **sought to delay the wedding:** Marella Caracciolo, "Marella and Me," *New York Times*, September 23, 2014.

213   **When she arrived at the Turin station:** Agnelli and Chia, *Marella Agnelli*, 70.

213   **"this sense of being . . .":** Marella Caracciolo Chia, "Marella Agnelli's Enchanting Estate in Northern Italy," *Architectural Digest*, September 1, 2014.

213   **"its association with important royal figures . . .":** Marella Agnelli, Marella Caracciolo, and Paolo Peirone, *The Agnelli Gardens at Villar Perosa: Two Centuries of a Family Retreat* (New York: Harry N. Abrams, 1998), 48.

213   **born in Villar Perosa:** Ibid, 50.

214   **there for the birth of the Fascist dictatorship:** *The Observer*, November 19, 2000.

214   **a submachine gun named:** Wikipedia, "Villar Perosa Aircraft Submachine Gun," last modified January 21, 2021, 04:11, https://en.wikipedia.org/wiki /Villar_Perosa_aircraft_submachine_gun.

214   **"You need quite a lot . . .":** Alan Friedman, *Agnelli: Fiat and the Network of Italian Power* (New York: New American Library, 1989), 31.

214   **trouser-less chauffeur:** Ibid.

215   **The Agnellis were no different:** Susanna Agnelli, *We Always Wore Sailor Suits* (New York: Bantam, 1976), 164–65.

215   **Around forty thousand Italians:** Stephen Gundle, *Death and the Dolce Vita: The Dark Side of Rome in the 1950s* (Edinburgh: Canongate, 2011), 94.

216   **"For someone who is . . .":** Friedman, *Agnelli*, 45.

216   **"The Italians have always . . .":** Luigi Barzini, *The Italians* (New York: Simon & Schuster, 1964), 90.

217   **"Some are indeed irresistible . . ."** Ibid., 7.

217   **"How cocky he looks,":** Ibid., 199–200.

217   **"He has never said . . .":** Friedman, *Agnelli*, 53.

217   **"I spent the first months . . .":** Chia, "Marella and Me."

218   **"To catch a man . . .":** Ibid.

218   **"Many women have chosen . . .":** Ibid.

218   **"Paternal attention is not . . .":** Sally Bedell Smith, "Agnelli: The Rules of the Game," *Vanity Fair*, July 1991.

219   **"My central preoccupation . . .":** Chia, "Marella and Me."

219   **"The garden was relatively small . . .":** Russell Page, *The Education of a Gardener* (London: William Collins, 1962), 285.

220   **"Oh, but Villar is different . . .":** Agnelli, Caracciolo, and Peirone, *The Agnelli Gardens*, 89.

220   **"No detail within the boundaries . . .":** Ibid., 40.

220   **"One must learn . . .":** Agnelli and Chia, *Marella Agnelli*, 49.

CHAPTER 13: DIVIDED LIVES

222   **he spent that day and a portion:** Plimpton, *Truman Capote*, 199.

222   **"assistant researchist":** Casey Cep, *Furious Hours: Murder, Fraud, and the Last Trial of Harper Lee* (New York: Alfred A. Knopf, 2019), 181.

223   **him a tin of black caviar:** Clarke, *Capote*, 323.

223   **They began at a lesbian bar:** Plimpton, *Truman Capote*, 171.

223   **"was like someone . . .":** Clarke, *Capote*, 321.

224   **pillbox-style hat:** Plimpton, *Truman Capote*, 169.

224   **"a pink negligee, silk with lace . . .":** Ibid., 170.

224   **Much of the furniture had been taken:** Ibid., 168.

226   **"his chunky, dwarfish legs . . .":** Truman Capote, *In Cold Blood: A True Account of a Multiple Murder and Its Consequences* (New York: Modern Library, 2013), 31.

227   **thick folder of typed notes:** Cep, *Furious Hours*, 189.

227   **two maids, a cook, and a gardener:** Clarke, *Capote*, 332–33.

227   **"All they ask is . . .":** Ibid., 333.

227   **selling half a million copies:** Cep, *Furious Hours*, 193.

228   **rich load of porn from Greece:** Clarke, *Too Brief a Treat*, 252.

228   **charged him with being:** UPI, "Profs Held in Obscenity Raid," *Chicago Tribune*, September 4, 1960.

228   **"a gentle, charming gifted boy . . .":** Clarke, *Too Brief a Treat*, 291–92.

228   **The Massachusetts Supreme Court:** "Smith Professor Wins Obscenity Case Appeal," *Boston Globe*, March 1, 1962.

228   **Docking was going to commute:** Clarke, *Too Brief a Treat*, 290.

228   **"I saw myself being . . .":** Smith, "Agnelli: The Rules of the Game."

229   **Ekberg for several years:** Gundle, *Death and the Dolce Vita*, 286.

229   **his purported relationship with Marella's:** Bachrach, "La Vita Agnelli."

229   **Marella throwing a tantrum:** Friedman, *Agnelli*, 52.

229   **"I didn't like especially . . .":** Smith, "Agnelli: The Rules of the Game."

230   **Avedon had perfected:** Osman Ahmed, "The 1950s Richard Avedon Portrait Which Helped Define Modern Beauty," *AnOther*, September 7, 2018, https://www.anothermag.com/art-photography/11117/the-1950s-richard -avedon-portrait-which-helped-define-modern-beauty.

230   **Dior was so taken:** Ibid.

231   **stunning green velvet gown:** Betty Beale, "Kennedy Party Gala Affair," *Cincinnati Enquirer*, November 19, 1961.

231   **shepherd her around:** "A Cruise," *Miami Herald,* August 14, 1962.

231   **A photo of him moving to apply:** Sam Kashner and Nancy Schoenberger, *The Fabulous Bouvier Sisters: The Tragic and Glamorous Lives of Jackie and Lee* (New York: Harper Perennial, 2019), 110.

231   **"I wouldn't be surprised":** *Agnelli,* HBO.

231   **"monastery life":** Clarke, *Capote,* 339.

231   **"would not have been executed . . .":** Clarke, *Too Brief a Treat,* 361.

232   **"a trick to make . . .":** Ibid., 375.

232   **"Alvin, when the real time . . .":** Ibid., 367.

232   **"should be good and nuts":** Ibid., 340.

233   **"perhaps even surrogate lover":** Clarke, *Capote,* 344.

233   **"They had become . . .":** Plimpton, *Truman Capote,* 188.

234   **"of this place—or one small area of it":** Clarke, *Too Brief a Treat,* 392.

234   **Rose and Jackie Kennedy had come:** Ibid., 394.

234   **"I've been told that . . .":** Clarke, *Capote,* 346.

234   **"Just got the cable . . .":** Clarke, *Too Brief a Treat,* 412.

234   **"I've only heard about the . . .":** Ibid.

235   **Truman cabled back:** Clarke, *Capote,* 354.

235   **ran out of the building:** Plimpton, *Truman Capote,* 188.

236   **"When he came back . . .":** *The Capote Tapes,* directed by Ebs Burnough, 2019.

Chapter 14: Princess from an Ancient Realm

237   **"Oh, forget it . . .":** Agnelli and Chia, *Marella Agnelli,* 124.

239   **"Truman and I were good . . .":** Katharine Graham, *Personal History* (New York: Alfred A. Knopf, 1997), 393.

239   **"I think he was tired . . .":** Ibid., 391.

239   **"I often thought that his famous . . .":** Agnelli and Chia, *Marella Agnelli,* 136.

240   **"They say that intelligent boys . . .":** *Agnelli,* HBO.

241   **"the harsh and stony Montenegrin . . .":** Capote, "A Gathering of Swans," in *Portraits and Observations,* 265.

242   **Her appearance that evening was:** Kashner and Schoenberger, *The Fabulous Bouvier Sisters,* 147.

243   **"as spectacular a group . . .":** Ruth La Ferla, "Unearthing the Notebook that Unnerved Society," *New York Times,* November 25, 2001.

243   **Mailer in a rumpled trench coat:** Deborah Davis, *Party of the Century: The Fabulous Story of Truman Capote and His Black and White Ball* (New York: Wiley, 2007), 223.

243   **"I remember thinking . . .":** Lee Radziwill, as quoted in *The Capote Tapes.*

243   **to play poker at Elaine's:** Davis, *Party of the Century,* 234.

244 **Gondoliers ferried the formally:** *The Observer*, August 13, 1967.

244 **"It's a sort of *roman à clef*...":** C. Robert Jennings, "Truman Capote: Hot Shorty with Tall Cool," *Los Angeles Times*, April 28, 1968.

245 **20th Century Fox sewed up the film rights:** Clarke, *Capote*, 406.

245 **"Truman, I really don't understand...":** Ibid., 413.

245 **drove out to Palm Springs:** Guest, *First Garden*, 21.

246 **Randy McKuen was his name:** In his biography of Truman Capote, Gerald Clarke referred to the then living McKuen as "Danny" to protect his privacy. Clarke, email interview with author.

246 **"the nearest thing to nothing...":** Keith with Tapert, *Slim*, 232.

247 **"No, except for that time...":** Clarke, *Capote*, 424.

247 **"I never understood it...":** Plimpton, *Truman Capote*, 316–17.

248 **the fashion daily ran:** "Ladies Man," *Women's Wear Daily*, December 4, 1970.

248 **"Oh, well, darling...":** Agnelli and Chia, *Marella Agnelli*, 135.

250 **"Oh, Truman, this is a gossip column...":** Ibid.

250 **"He would tell you about...":** Plimpton, *Truman Capote*, 338.

250 **"For him I remained Mrs. Agnelli...":** Ibid., 148.

251 **to tell her the most vicious tales:** Ibid., 158.

251 **"Why don't you want to see me?":** Ibid.

Chapter 15: Fairy Tales

253 **"Had lunch one day...":** Clarke, *Too Brief a Treat*, 337.

253 **drove with her mother and her older sister, Jackie:** Diana DuBois, *In Her Sister's Shadow: An Intimate Biography of Lee Radziwill* (New York: St. Martin's Paperbacks, 1997), 13.

255 **an ironmonger and his wife a servant:** Ibid., 9.

256 **"From that moment on...":** Kashner and Schoenberger, *The Fabulous Bouvier Sisters*, 16.

257 **Their names were Shahday:** DuBois, *In Her Sister's Shadow*, 2.

258 **"To arrive there, as a child...":** Kashner and Schoenberger, *The Fabulous Bouvier Sisters*, 20.

258 **one day a pony rolled:** DuBois, *In Her Sister's Shadow*, 20.

258 **"All I ever heard was how...":** J. Randy Taraborrelli, *Jackie, Janet & Lee: The Secret Lives of Janet Auchincloss and Her Daughters Jacqueline Kennedy Onassis and Lee Radziwill* (New York: St. Martin's Press, 2019), 23.

259 **The infirmary was worried enough:** DuBois, *In Her Sister's Shadow*, 33.

259 **a stunning strapless pink gown:** Kashner and Schoenberger, *The Fabulous Bouvier Sisters*, 24.

260 **Lee ended up:** DuBois, *In Her Sister's Shadow*, 37.

261 **"in a cross-fire of flame belching anti-tank guns"**: Jacqueline and Lee Bouvier, *One Special Summer* (New York: Rizzoli, 2006).

261 **"He set a spark burning . . ."**: Ibid.

261 **"I wish you would someday . . ."**: Kashner and Schoenberger, *The Fabulous Bouvier Sisters*, 53.

261 **"the little people"**: Vera Glaser, "Mystery Cloaks Lee Radziwill," *Charlotte Observer*, March 26, 1964.

263 **"He will never be able to afford . . ."**: DuBois, *In Her Sister's Shadow*, 68.

265 **"In those days I never knew . . ."**: Ibid., 93.

265 **terraced house in Victoria**: Mitchell Owens, "Lee Radziwill's Iconic Entrance Hall," *Architectural Digest*, January 23, 2018, https://www .architecturaldigest.com/story/lee-radziwill-turville-grange-iconic -entrance-hall.

Chapter 16: Everything

266 **"Princess Lee Radziwill Adds Charm . . ."**: Charlotte Curtis, "Princess Lee Radziwill Adds Charm to Any Setting," *New York Times*, November 27, 1961.

267 **"You're just like me—you have . . ."**: Lee Radziwill, *Lee* (New York: Assouline, 2015), 67.

267 **"when she and Jackie are talking . . ."**: Betty Beale, "A Few Try the New Dance Craze at the White House Dance," *News and Observer* (Raleigh), November 19, 1961.

268 **"Never do that again"**: Kashner and Schoenberger, *The Fabulous Bouvier Sisters*, 95.

268 **"tour has turned into an . . ."**: Marjorie Hunter, "First Ladies Visit to Asia a Project," *New York Times*, February 26, 1962.

269 **"She's a real looker, that one"**: Taraborrelli, *Jackie, Janet & Lee*, 172.

270 **Lee took the large bedroom**: DuBois, *In Her Sister's Shadow*, 200.

271 **"Somebody has to tell Truman . . ."**: Suzy Knickerbocker, "And They All Wore Long Dresses," *San Francisco Examiner*, April 28, 1967.

272 **"She has none of the feelings . . ."**: Jane Howard, "Girls Who Have Everything Are Not Supposed to Do Anything," *Life*, July 14, 1967.

272 **"Miss Bouvier had her clothes designed . . ."**: J. R. Bruckner, "A Dazzling Debut for Princess Radziwill," *Los Angeles Times*, June 22, 1967.

272 **"at least laid a golden egg"**: "Lee Radziwill Fails to Impress Critics," *Miami Herald*, June 22, 1967.

272 **Susskind announced that Lee**: Matt Messina, "Lee Bouvier Signed for a Special," *New York Daily News*, June 29, 1967.

273 **"*Laura*, you know the movie . . ."**: Alan Shayne and Norman Sunshine, *Double Life: A Love Story from Broadway to Hollywood* (New York: Magnus Books, 2011), 125.

273 **"Truman didn't write any . . .":** Alan Shayne, in-person interview with author, 2020.

273 **"Lee thought she was a great . . .":** Ibid.

274 **to bring in Elizabeth Taylor:** Shayne and Sunshine, *Double Life*, 134.

274 **In one scene, the phone rings:** Shayne, in-person interview with author.

274 **"There was no question of who murdered . . .":** Gary Gowren, "Supporting Stars Tops in TV Show," *Chicago Tribune*, January 25, 1968.

274 **finished in a year:** Jennings, "Truman Capote."

275 **and tore the coat into chewable pieces:** Plimpton, *Truman Capote*, 313.

275 **crashed into another vehicle:** DuBois, *In Her Sister's Shadow*, 206.

275 **"How could she do this to me!":** Ibid., 209.

276 **Twentieth Century Fox insisted he repay:** Clarke, *Capote*, 440.

277 **reporting in Kansas City:** "Damage Suit," *Des Moines Register*, June 25, 1972.

277 **"Come out, you old queen":** Keith Richards with James Fox, *Life* (New York: Little, Brown, 2010), 330–31.

278 **"They'll be nothing when mine appears . . .":** Plimpton, *Truman Capote*, 412.

279 **"My deep regret is that . . .":** *Interview*, February 2, 1975.

280 **"It was the first time . . .":** DuBois, *In Her Sister's Shadow*, 267.

280 **Lee was infuriated:** Ibid., 268.

280 **Tina packed up:** Ibid., 251.

280 **"first-class intelligence . . .":** Truman Capote, "Lee: A Fan Letter from Truman Capote," *Vogue*, June 1976.

281 **"She's a remarkable girl . . .":** Lee Wohlfert, "Lee Radziwill Slams 'Ludicrous Talk' of Rivalry with Jackie Kennedy," *People*, November 1, 1976.

Chapter 17: "Naaaah, They're Too Dumb"

283 **"That's gossip! That's bullshit!":** Clarke, *Capote*, 466.

284 **"I adore them, I always have . . .":** Capote, *Answered Prayers*, 148.

285 **"Why would an educated, dynamic . . .":** Ibid., 141.

285 **"Whether he confesses to it . . .":** Ibid., 142.

287 **"I've got a double dose . . .":** Ibid., 140.

287 **"looked like a baby . . .":** Anne Taylor Fleming, "The Descent from the Heights," *New York Times*, July 16, 1978.

288 **read scarcely a page:** Keith with Tapert, *Slim*, 238.

288 **"unrefined, exaggerated . . .":** Capote, *Answered Prayers*, 127.

289 **"It could be anyone":** Keith with Tapert, *Slim*, 237; and Plimpton, *Truman Capote*, 347.

290 **"My wife is very ill":** Clarke, *Capote*, 471.

290 **May 1975, surgeons removed:** Smith, *In All His Glory*, 489–90.

291 **Truman laughed:** Gerald Clarke, email interview with author.

292 **"Here's a dumpy little guy":** Capote, *Answered Prayers*, 51.

Chapter 18: The Good Pocket

294   **dirty little cubicles, puddles of water:** Plimpton, *Truman Capote*, 385–89.

294   **"Truman always got it out of the good pocket":** R. Couri Hay, phone interview with author, 2020.

295   **"You're nothing but a tired old queen":** Richard DuPont, phone interview with author, 2020.

295   **"He was a mass of confusion at that point":** Anne Taylor Fleming, phone interview with author, 2020.

295   **"I will be all in white . . .":** Fleming, "The Descent from the Heights."

296   **they drove him to the airport:** Clarke, *Capote*, 514.

296   ***Women's Wear Daily* put a picture:** "Stepping Out," *Women's Wear Daily*, September 14, 1978.

297   **purchased the movie rights for $300,000:** Clarke, *Capote*, 526.

298   **"Annnnnd . . . he insulted Jackie's mother . . .":** Richard Zoerink, "Truman Capote Talks About His Crowd," *Playgirl*, September 1975.

298   **Gore sued Truman for $1 million:** Donald Flynn, "Vidal Sues Capote for $1M in 'Libel,'" *New York Daily News*, February 19, 1976.

298   **"Capote has spent most of his . . .":** Sally Quinn, "Hot Blood—and Gore, Chapter Two," *Washington Post*, June 7, 1979.

298   **Truman said that originally Lee:** Ibid.

298   **"not recall ever discussing . . .":** DuBois, *In Her Sister's Shadow*, 299.

298   **Lee did not tell her closest friend:** Liz Smith, "Feuds or How Close Friends Fall Out," *New York Daily News*, June 4, 1979; and Liz Smith, "Carps, Candor and Critiques," *New York Daily News*, June 10, 1979.

299   **"I am tired of Truman riding on my coattails to fame . . .":** Liz Smith, "Truman's True Love," *New York Daily News*, September 23, 1984.

299   **Andy Warhol thought she might:** Andy Warhol and Pat Hackett, ed., *The Andy Warhol Diaries* (New York: Warner Books, 1989), 228.

300   **"I'll tell you something about fags . . .":** Sally Quinn, "In Hot Blood," *Washington Post*, June 6, 1979.

300   **"From that day until he died . . .":** Smith, "Truman's True Love."

301   **"He seemed to be . . .":** David Patrick Columbia, "On Becoming a Writer and Having Met Mr. Capote," *New York Social Diary*, 2007.

301   **did a few lines of cocaine:** David Patrick Columbia, phone interview with author.

301   **"Don't you realize you have . . .":** Ibid.

302   **John was a nondescript:** Clarke, *Capote*, 444.

302   **sent associates out to break:** Ibid., 496–97.

303   **He pummeled Truman:** Ibid., 529.

303   **vowing to rejoin AA:** Ibid., 532.

304   **"I only remember that we flew . . .":** DuBois, *In Her Sister's Shadow*, 2.

305   **"that when talking about . . ."**: Kashner and Schoenberger, *The Fabulous Bouvier Sisters*, 7.

305   **sitting with Truman a half hour**: Clarke, *Capote*, 540.

306   **"I dream about it, and . . ."**: Ibid., 544.

306   **large assortment of votive candles**: Plimpton, *Truman Capote*, 419.

306   **began work on**: David Remnick, "The Original Truman Capote," *Washington Post*, August 27, 1984.

307   **"What do you mean, let you go?"**: Plimpton, *Truman Capote*, 426–27.

CHAPTER 19: AFTERWORD

308   **never talked to her again**: Plimpton, *Truman Capote*, 434; and Joanne Carson. The author was friendly with Mrs. Carson in the eighties and had many discussions with her about Mr. Capote and other matters.

308   **hidden it away in a safety-deposit box**: Plimpton, *Truman Capote*, 449.

309   **Truman's longtime editor, Joe Fox, speculated**: Capote, *Answered Prayers*, xxi.

309   **Inside were all these empty**: The author was present at the party that evening, and several days later accompanied Mrs. Carson when she took Mr. Capote's ashes to the Westwood Village Memorial Park.

310   **"Under cover of darkness . . ."**: "Even in an Urn, Truman Capote Remains the Talk of the Party," *People*, November 28, 1988.

311   **"That's Mr. Peter Lawford"**: Some news reports suggest Mr. Lawford's ashes were removed earlier, but his name was on the crypt that day, and the representative said his ashes were there.

312   **penis off in 1977 for $3,000**: Independent.co.uk, April 3, 2014.

312   **an astronomical $45,000**: Julie Miller, "The Man Auctioning Off Truman Capote's Ashes Explains Himself," *Vanity Fair*, August 17, 2016.

312   **"a maltreated strip of buckskin shoelace"**: "Art: Napoleon's Things," *Time*, February 14, 1927.

CHAPTER 20: THE SWANS

314   **pieces of porcelain**: Smith, *In All His Glory*, 618, 620.

Bibliography

Abramson, Rudy. *Spanning the Century: The Life of W. Averell Harriman, 1891–1986.*
New York: William Morrow, 1992.

Adams, Samuel, Sarah Adams, Ann Haly, and Pamela Horn. *The Complete Servant.*
East Sussex: Southover, 2004.

Agnelli, Marella, and Marella Caracciolo Chia. *Marella Agnelli: The Last Swan.* New
York: Rizzoli, 2014.

Agnelli, Marella, Marella Caracciolo, and Paolo Peirone. *The Agnelli Gardens at Villar
Perosa: Two Centuries of a Family Retreat.* New York: Harry N. Abrams, 1998.

Agnelli, Susanna. *We Always Wore Sailor Suits.* New York: Bantam, 1976.

Aldrich, Nelson W. *Old Money: The Mythology of Wealth in America.* New York:
Allworth Press, 1996.

Aline, Countess of Romanones. *The Spy Wore Red.* New York: Random House, 1987.

Amory, Cleveland. *The Proper Bostonians.* New York: Dutton, 1948.

———. *Who Killed Society?* New York: Harper, 1960.

Bacall, Lauren. *Lauren Bacall by Myself.* New York: Alfred A.Knopf, 1978.

Baldwin, Billy. *Billy Baldwin: An Autobiography.* Boston: Little, Brown, 1985.

Barzini, Luigi. *The Italians.* New York: Simon & Schuster, 1964.

Beaton, Cecil. *The Parting Years, Diaries 1963–1974.* London: Weidenfeld and
Nicolson, 1978.

Benjamin, Melanie. *The Swans of Fifth Avenue: A Novel.* New York: Bantam Books,
2016.

Blanch, Lesley. *The Wilder Shores of Love.* New York: Simon & Schuster, 2010.

Bouvier, Jacqueline and Lee. *One Special Summer.* New York: Rizzoli, 2006.

Braudy, Susan. *This Crazy Thing Called Love: The Golden World and Fatal Marriage of Ann and Billy Woodward*. New York: Alfred A. Knopf, 1992.

Brinnin, John Malcolm. *Truman Capote: Dear Heart, Old Buddy*. New York: Delacorte Press/Seymour Lawrence, 1986.

Capote, Truman. *Answered Prayers*. New York: Random House, 1987.

———. *Breakfast at Tiffany's & Other Voices, Other Rooms*. New York: Modern Library, 2013.

———. *The Complete Stories of Truman Capote*. New York: Vintage, 2005.

———. *The Grass Harp*. New York: Penguin, 1966.

———. *In Cold Blood: A True Account of a Multiple Murder and Its Consequences*. New York: Modern Library, 2013.

———. *Portraits and Observations: The Essays of Truman Capote*. New York: Modern Library, 2008.

Castle, Charles. *La Belle Otero: The Last Great Courtesan*. London: Michael Joseph, 1981.

Cep, Casey. *Furious Hours: Murder, Fraud, and the Last Trial of Harper Lee*. New York: Alfred A. Knopf, 2019.

Churcher, Sharon. *New York Confidential*. New York: Crown, 1986.

Clark, Jennifer. *Mondo Agnelli: Fiat, Chrysler, and the Power of a Dynasty*. New York: Wiley, 2012.

Clarke, Gerald. *Capote: A Biography*. New York: Simon & Schuster Paperbacks, 2010.

———, ed. *Too Brief a Treat: The Letters of Truman Capote*. New York: Vintage Books, 2004.

Davis, Deborah. *Party of the Century: The Fabulous Story of Truman Capote and His Black and White Ball*. New York: Wiley, 2007.

D'Emilio, John, and Estelle Freedman. *Intimate Matters: A History of Sexuality in America*. Chicago: University of Chicago Press, 2013.

de Courcy, Anne. *1939: The Last Season*. London: Phoenix, 2003.

DuBois, Diana. *In Her Sister's Shadow: An Intimate Biography of Lee Radziwill*. New York: St. Martin's Paperbacks, 1997.

Duchin, Peter, with Charles Michener. *Ghost of a Chance: A Memoir*. New York: Random House, 1996.

Dunphy, Jack. *"Dear Genius . . .": A Memoir of My Life with Truman Capote*. New York: McGraw-Hill, 1987.

———. *John Fury: A Play in Four Parts*. New York: Harper & Row, 1946.

Foulkes, Nick. *High Society: The History of America's Upper Class*. New York: Assouline, 2008.

Friedan, Betty: *The Feminine Mystique*. New York: Norton, 1963.

Friedman, Alan. *Agnelli: Fiat and the Network of Italian Power*. New York: New American Library, 1989.

Grafton, David. *The Sisters: Babe Mortimer Paley, Betsey Roosevelt Whitney, Minnie Astor Fosburgh: The Life and Times of the Fabulous Cushing Sisters.* New York: Villard Books, 1992.

Graham, Katharine. *Personal History.* New York: Alfred A. Knopf, 1997.

Grobel, Lawrence. *Conversations with Capote.* New York: HMH Press, 1985.

Guest, C. Z. *First Garden: An Illustrated Garden Primer.* New York: Rizzoli, 2003.

Gundle, Stephen. *Death and the Dolce Vita: The Dark Side of Rome in the 1950s.* Edinburgh: Canongate, 2011.

Harris, Warren G. *Clark Gable: A Biography.* New York: Three Rivers Press, 2005.

Hayward, Brooke. *Haywire.* New York: Knopf, 1977.

Hood, Clifton. *In Pursuit of Privilege: A History of New York City's Upper Class and the Making of a Metropolis.* New York: Columbia University Press, 2019.

Howard, Jean, and James Watters. *Jean Howard's Hollywood: A Photo Memoir.* New York: Harry N. Abrams, 1989.

Inge, M. Thomas, ed. *Truman Capote: Conversations.* Oxford: University Press of Mississippi, 1989.

Kahn Jr., E. J. *Jock: The Life and Times of John Hay Whitney.* New York: Doubleday, 1981.

Kaplan, Justin. *When the Astors Owned New York: Blue Bloods and Grand Hotels in a Gilded Age.* New York: Penguin Books, 2017.

Kashner, Sam, and Nancy Schoenberger. *The Fabulous Bouvier Sisters: The Tragic and Glamorous Lives of Jackie and Lee.* New York: Harper Perennial, 2019.

Keith, Slim, with Annette Tapert. *Slim: Memories of a Rich and Imperfect Life.* New York: Simon & Schuster, 1990.

Lahr, John. *Tennessee Williams: Mad Pilgrimage of the Flesh.* New York: W. W. Norton, 2015.

Lambert, Angela. *1939: The Last Season of Peace.* London: Bloomsbury, 2012.

Lapham, Lewis H. *Money and Class in America: Notes and Observations on the Civil Religion.* New York: Pan Books, 1989.

Larson, Erik. *The Splendid and the Vile: A Saga of Churchill, Family, and Defiance during the Bombing of London.* New York: Crown, 2020.

Leamer, Laurence. *The Kennedy Women: The Saga of an American Family.* New York: Villard, 1994.

Lee, Harper. *To Kill a Mockingbird.* New York: Vintage Classics, 2020.

Leslie, Anita. *Cousin Randolph.* London: Hutchinson, 1985.

Masson, Georgina. *Courtesans of the Italian Renaissance.* London: Secker & Warburg, 1975.

McBride, Joseph. *Hawks on Hawks.* Berkeley: University of California Press, 1982. Kindle.

McCarthy, Todd. *Howard Hawks: The Grey Fox of Hollywood.* New York: Grove Press, 2000.

Metz, Robert. *CBS: Reflections in a Bloodshot Eye*. New York: New American Library, 1976.

Moorhouse, Roger. *Berlin at War*. New York: Basic Books, 2010.

Nasaw, David. *The Chief: The Life of William Randolph Hearst*. New York: Houghton Mifflin, 2000. Kindle.

Norwich, John Julius, ed. *The Duff Cooper Diaries*. London: Phoenix, 2006.

Oddie, E. M. *The Odyssey of a Loving Woman: Being a Study of Jane Digby, Lady Ellenborough*. New York: Harper & Brothers, 1936.

Ogden, Christopher. *Life of the Party: The Biography of Pamela Digby Churchill Hayward Harriman*. New York: Little, Brown, 1994.

Olson, Lynne. *Citizens of London: The Americans Who Stood with Britain in Its Darkest, Finest Hour*. New York: Random House Trade Paperbacks, 2011.

Page, Russell. *The Education of a Gardener*. London: William Collins, 1962.

Paley, William S. *As It Happened: A Memoir*. New York: Doubleday, 1979.

Payn, Graham, and Sheridan Morley, eds. *The Noël Coward Diaries*. New York: Little, Brown, 1982.

Pell, Eve. *We Used to Own the Bronx: Memoirs of a Former Debutante*. Albany: State University of New York Press, 2009.

Pinkus, Karen. *The Montesi Scandal: The Death of Wilma Montesi and the Birth of the Paparazzi in Fellini's Rome*. Chicago: University of Chicago Press, 2003.

Plimpton, George. *Truman Capote: In Which Various Friends, Enemies, Acquaintances, and Detractors Recall His Turbulent Career*. New York: Doubleday, 1997.

Radziwill, Lee. *Lee*. New York: Assouline, 2015.

Richards, Keith, with James Fox. *Life*. New York: Little, Brown, 2010.

Roberts, Brian. *Randolph: A Study of Churchill's Son*. London: Hamish Hamilton, 1984.

Salk, Susanna. *C.Z. Guest: American Style Icon: Celebrating Her Timeless World at Home, in Her Garden & Around Town*. New York: Rizzoli, 2013.

Saroyan, Aram. *Trio: Oona Chaplin, Carol Matthau, Gloria Vanderbilt: Portrait of an Intimate Friendship*. New York: Sidgwick & Jackson, 1986.

Schellenberg, Walter. *Walter Schellenberg: The Memoirs of Hitler's Spymaster*. Edited and translated by Louis Hagan. London: Andre Deutsch, 2006. Kindle.

Schultz, William Todd. *Tiny Terror: Why Truman Capote (Almost) Wrote* Answered Prayers. Oxford: Oxford University Press, 2011.

Sewall, Gilbert. *The Eighties: A Reader*. New York: Addison-Wesley, 1997.

Shayne, Alan, and Norman Sunshine. *Double Life: A Love Story from Broadway to Hollywood*. New York: Magnus Books, 2011.

Smith, Sally Bedell. *In All His Glory: The Life & Times of William S. Paley and the Birth of Modern Broadcasting*. New York: Simon & Schuster, 1990.

———. *Reflected Glory: The Life of Pamela Churchill Harriman*. New York: Simon & Schuster, 1996.

Staggs, Sam. *Inventing Elsa Maxwell: How an Irrepressible Nobody Conquered High Society, Hollywood, the Press, and the World*. New York: St. Martin's Griffin, 2013.

Stuart, Amanda Mackenzie. *Diana Vreeland: Empress of Fashion*. New York: Harper, 2013.

Talley, André Leon. *Chiffon Trenches*. New York: Fourth Estate Ltd., 2020.

Tapert, Annette, and Diana Edkins. *The Power of Style: The Women Who Defined the Art of Living Well*. New York: Aurum Press, 1995.

Taraborrelli, J. Randy. *Jackie, Janet & Lee: The Secret Lives of Janet Auchincloss and Her Daughters Jacqueline Kennedy Onassis and Lee Radziwill*. New York: St. Martin's Press, 2019.

Ware, Susan. *Still Missing: Amelia Earhart and the Search for Modern Feminism*. New York: Norton, 1993.

Warhol, Andy, and Pat Hackett, ed. *The Andy Warhol Diaries*. New York: Warner Books, 1989.

Wasson, Sam. *The Big Goodbye: Chinatown and the Last Years of Hollywood*. New York: Faber and Faber, 2020.

———. *Fifth Avenue, 5 A.M.: Audrey Hepburn and the Making of Breakfast at Tiffany's*. New York: Aurum, 2013.

Waugh, Evelyn. *The Diaries of Evelyn Waugh*. Edited by Michael Davie. Boston: Little, Brown, 1976.

Wharton, Edith. *The Age of Innocence*. New York: D. Appleton, 1920.

———. *The House of Mirth*. New York: Charles Scribner's Sons, 1905.

Photo Credits

Index

Caroyan, William, 45
Carson, Joanne, 286–87, 306–7, 308–12
Cavendish, Charles, Lord, 101
Cerf, Bennett, 198, 246–47
Chanel, Coco, 150
Chaplin, Charlie, 61, 162
Chaplin, Oona, 60, 61, 162
Chapman, John, 160, 182
Chia, Marella Caracciolo, 218
Chicago Daily News, 272
Chicago Tribune, 274
Christie's auction house, 312
Churchill, Pamela. *See* Harriman,
    Pamela Churchill
Churchill, Randolph, 33, 89–90,
    98–105, 106, 122, 129
Churchill, Winston (prime minister),
    98, 99, 100, 102–3, 110
Churchill, Winston (Randolph's son),
    116, 119, 135
Clarke, Gerald, 6–7, 233, 282, 287–88,
    290–91
Clift, Montgomery, 161
Clover Club, 51–52, 53, 65
Clutter family murders, 224–25. *See
    also In Cold Blood*
Cochrane, Alexander Lynde, 176
Cochrane, Lucy Douglas. *See* Guest,
    Lucy Douglas "C. Z."
Columbia, David Patrick, 300–301
Cooper, Duff, 153–55
Cooper, Gary, 66–67
Cope, Newton, 299
Courrèges, André, 171–72
Coward, Noël, 159, 195
Cushing, Harvey, 14
Cushing, Katharine Stone, 14–15, 17–19
Cushing, Minnie. *See* Astor, Minnie
Cushing, William, 14–15

Dalí, Salvador, 195
Davenport, Dorothy, 70
Davies, Marion, 63, 64–65
Dempsey, Jack, 20–21
Dewey, Alvin, 231–32
Dewey, Marie, 231
DiCicco, Pat, 61
Dietrich, Marlene, 52
Dior, Christian, 230
Docking, George, 228, 231–32
Doisneau, Robert, 122

Donald, Michael, 43
Dorius, Joel, 228
Duchin, Cheray, 136
Duchin, Eddy, 105
Duchin, Peter, 136–37, 243
Dunn, Mary, 98
Dunphy, Jack: background, 108; and
    Capote's death and remains, 308–9;
    and Capote's writing struggles, 244;
    opinion of Capote's friends, 162,
    167–68, 182, 227; relationship with
    Capote, 108–9, 167–68, 246, 293,
    299; summer in Connecticut, 184–85;
    travels in Europe, 123–27, 160–62,
    197, 226–27, 231–33, 234, 246
DuPont, Richard, 295

Education of a Gardener, The (Page), 219
Ekberg, Anita, 229
Elizabeth II, Queen of England, 267
Embiricos, André, 121
End of the Game, The (Beard), 275–76
Esquire, 6, 282–83, 286–87, 287–89,
    289–92
Estainville, Anne-Marie d', 120

Fabbrica Italiana di Automobili Torino
    (Fiat), 5, 115–17, 122, 195, 209,
    213, 214–16, 220–21, 239–40
Fairchild, John, 194
Fakhry, Ahmed, 152, 153
Farrow, Mia, 243
Faulk, Joey, 245
Faulk, Sook, 21–22, 78
Feminine Mystique, The (Friedan), 200
Ferrer, Mel, 182
First Garden (Guest), 296
Flaubert, Gustave, 13
Fleming, Anne Taylor, 295
Flynn, Errol, 187, 204
Fonda, Henry, 78, 132
Fonda, Jane, 132
For Whom the Bell Tolls (Hemingway), 67
Fouts, Denham, 107
Fox, Joe, 235, 309
Francis, Arlene, 273
Friedan, Betty, 200
Friedman, Alan, 216
Frost, Robert, 62–63
Frost, Winston, 63
Furnace Creek Inn, 57–58